D1443060

Beyond the Beat

Beyond the Beat

MUSICIANS BUILDING
COMMUNITY IN NASHVILLE

Daniel B. Cornfield

PRINCETON UNIVERSITY PRESS
Princeton and Oxford

Copyright © 2015 by Princeton University Press
Published by Princeton University Press, 41 William Street, Princeton, New Jersey 08540
In the United Kingdom: Princeton University Press, 6 Oxford Street, Woodstock, Oxfordshire
  OX20 1TW

press.princeton.edu

ISBN 978-0-691-16073-3
Library of Congress Control Number: 2015941945

British Library Cataloging-in-Publication Data is available

This book has been composed in Sabon Next LT Std and Adobe Caslon Pro

Printed on acid-free paper ∞

Printed in the United States of America

10 9 8 7 6 5 4 3 2 1

To my parents Edith and Melvin Cornfield, who illuminate pathways to a new humanity

Contents

Preface and Acknowledgments

As champions of artistic freedom, artist activists promote artistic and intellectual expression and cultural pluralism in a democratic society. Expressive occupations, such as musicians, writers, visual artists, actors, critics, journalists, dancers, poets, filmmakers, academics, curators, and bloggers, constitute a creative and critical force that encourages societal self-reflection and inspires humanistic social transformation. Peer occupational communities provide the requisite social spaces for promoting individual artistry, peer mentoring, professional development, networking, solidarity, and advocacy for the whole occupation. In large-scale democratic societies, where bureaucratic economic and political institutions may compel conformity, activist members of expressive occupations serve as a countervailing force by sustaining their peer communities and artistic and intellectual expression.

Beyond the Beat focuses on the artist activists themselves. Oriented toward promoting their peers' artistry and livelihoods, artist activists enact multiple roles to strengthen their peer communities, including the roles of artist-producer, social entrepreneur, and arts trade union reformer. Sociologically, the set of artist activist roles is a repertoire of individual and collective action for building and sustaining inclusive, peer communities of expressive occupations. This book is a sociological examination of how artist activists fashion their activist roles to strengthen their peer communities.

In Nashville, musicians are actively building an inclusive peer community in several genres of popular music. This new community of independent artists has emerged in the decades-long musician migration to Nashville alongside of and from the ranks of the established musician community in country music. Throughout the migration, as the level of musician concentration in Nashville increased to the highest levels of U.S. music-recording cities by the mid-2000s, local artist-producers, social entrepreneurs, and arts trade union reformers have continuously arisen to create a diverse peer community of independent artists. These artist activists, as visionary artist peers, are creating the requisite social spaces for new generations of their peers to express their diverse social identities in a widening range of musical genres. The array of Nashville-produced musical genres now includes country, gospel, Americana, urban, neo-soul, jazz, Latin jazz, pop, punk, and rock.

Sustaining inclusive peer communities is not a foregone conclusion, and the emergent Nashville musician community has yet to fully crystallize with an overarching organization. Rather, it is sustained by a loosely coupled set of micro-organizational initiatives undertaken by artist activists and closely aligned impresarios. Beyond the inherent instability of these initiatives, the new Nashville musician community emerges as the music scene enters a local and national, risky era of non-union, entrepreneurial music production in which intellectual property is contested terrain; and an era of artist self-promotion in dynamic, but evasive, niche markets of music-downloading consumers.

Artist activism also occurs in a local and national context of identity politics. Heightened awareness of one's social identity has accompanied the social movements for civil, women's, and LGBT rights of the late twentieth and early twenty-first centuries, and the movement for immigrant rights stimulated by the large post-1990 wave of immigration to the United States. In Nashville, a cumulating sequence of the women's, LGBT, and immigrant rights movements has unfolded with the initial momentum generated by Nashville's pioneering, non-violent civil rights movement of the early 1960s. The cumulating sequence of social movements, global immigration, and the musician migration to Nashville has afforded artist activists the opportunity to build an inclusive peer community that expresses a range of social identities in an expanding selection of musical genres.

In *Beyond the Beat*, I develop a new sociological theory of artist activism that addresses how artists of any expressive occupation envision, assume, and enact their activist roles in strengthening their peer communities. The evidence for the theory is based on seventy-five in-depth interviews my research team and I conducted with diverse Nashville music professionals of varying career stages and "hyphenated" occupations. The empirical focus of the book is on sixteen detailed profiles of artist activists enacting an array of activist roles. They are presented in ascending order of the extent of collective action embodied in their roles, and in the approximate historical sequence of their appearance in the post-1980 musician migration to Nashville. The presentation of artist activist profiles begins with the pioneering transformative generation of enterprising artists who broke from corporate commercial music production in the 1980s and went on to mentor and produce new generations of diverse self-promoting, indie artists. Next are the social entrepreneurs who arose subsequently to create social spaces for artist development in clubs, schools, and artist development enterprises. The book culminates in the contested election of 2008 for the presidency of Nashville Local 257 of the American Federation of Musicians among two generations of arts trade union reformers. The theory of artist activism attributes variations in the blend of individual and collective action envisioned and taken by artist activists to their subjective orientations toward success, audience, risk, and career inspiration, and to their career-biographical pathways to becoming artist activists.

Beyond the Beat presents an artist-centered approach to building an inclusive artist peer community. As Nashville musicians respond to the beat of their migration history, they take an approach for building a peer community for a new era. It is for an entrepreneurial era of art-making and artist self-promotion in which the artist increasingly assumes the risks of making and distributing art; and for an era of identity politics and musical genre diversity. It is an approach for re-creating artist peer communities, re-socializing and minimizing the risks of making art, and for encouraging cultural pluralism in a democratic society.

* * *

I am greatly indebted to my extraordinary colleagues Bill Ivey and Steven Tepper, director and associate director of the Curb Center for Art, Enterprise, and Public Policy at Vanderbilt University when I started the research for *Beyond the Beat*. Bill and Steven inspired and helped shape and launch this project by sharing with me their vast storehouse of knowledge about arts policy, artist communities, and the Nashville music scene, their networks, and their tremendous enthusiasm for the project. At the Curb Center, they cultivated a community of affiliated campus colleagues whose regular meetings in the Creativity Workshop provided the constructively critical forum for vetting our research projects and honing our research skills. I am also very grateful to Bill and Steven for the generous financial support of the Curb Center for my research.

The venerable Labor and Employment Relations Association has encouraged social scientific research on innovations in collective representation in workplaces for more than six decades and generously awarded me its Susan C. Eaton Scholar-Practitioner Grant in support of this research project.

Musicians are extraordinarily insightful, prophetic, and expressive individuals. I am deeply indebted to the seventy-five Nashville music professionals whose probing and inspiring interviews generated the 2,500 pages of interview transcripts for *Beyond the Beat*. On the condition of anonymity, they generously shared with me their dreams and aspirations, personal challenges and achievements, career biographies, perspectives on Nashville and artistic freedom, and their pathways to artist activism, and referred me to their colleagues for interviews. I am indebted to the interviewees for the lessons I learned about visioning, self-determination, peer community, and artistic expression in a democratic society.

Transcriptionist Cathy Kaiser expertly and efficiently produced high-quality transcripts of the interviews.

From the music scene, several artists and artist advocates generously shared their expertise by providing me with background materials about artist peer communities in Nashville and elsewhere. Erika Wollam-Nichols, C.O.O./President of Bluebird Café, "A-team" musician Mark Casstevens, and songwriter Sam Lorber provided me with invaluable insights and approaches to designing the interview schedule. Archivist John Rumble of the Country Music Hall of Fame helped me to identify documents signifying pivotal moments in Nashville music history. Garth Fundis shared with me an illuminating depiction of the role of the music producer. Manuel Delgado explained to me the role of the luthier in a guided tour of his East Nashville shop. Roger Nichols provided me with a prescient tour of contemporary studio spaces in Berry Hill. Will Kimbrough described for me the life of the independent artist in a guided tour of his backyard home studio. Harold Bradley and Dave Pomeroy, former and current presidents of Nashville Local 257 of the American Federation of Musicians, respectively, provided me with important archival information about innovations in arts trade unionism and collective bargaining. David Cohen of the AFL-CIO Department for Professional Employees and Stephen Yokich of the Cornfield and Feldman law firm advised me on trends in labor law in the arts. Kristin Thomson and Jean Cook of the Future of Music Coalition, and their innovative work on the Artist Revenue Streams project, have educated me on the careers and intellectual property challenges artists face in our contemporary enterprising era. Kristen Etzler of United Record Pressing provided me with an historical overview of vinyl record production in a guided tour of the record-pressing facility. Ken Paulson, author and narrator of Nashville's annual "Freedom Sings" event at the Bluebird Café, continues to demonstrate for me the vital relationship among peer community, artistic expression, the First Amendment, and democracy.

I work in a vibrant and inspiring academic community that has encouraged my research for many years. My colleagues in the Department of Sociology at Vanderbilt University continue to bring much humor, depth, and insight about humanity to our daily disciplinary discussions in Garland Hall and local eateries. For constructive criticism and collegial support of *Beyond the Beat*, I am especially grateful to Larry Isaac, Shaul Kelner, Richard Lloyd, Holly McCammon, and, not least of all, to Steven Tepper, who advised me every step of the way in writing the whole manuscript. Over the course of his career, the late Richard A. Peterson re-invented the field of cultural sociology by extending and applying his initial expertise in industrial sociology to the music production that was taking place on Music Row in his own backyard. A giant in the field, Pete influenced my sociological imagination, and his work on cycles of cultural production and consumption, bureaucracy and democracy, and entrepreneurship and audiences contribute explicitly to the framing of this book.

Teaching is a two-way street, and I am grateful to many Vanderbilt graduate and undergraduate students for their insights about their generation that informed my writing *Beyond the Beat*. A team of Vanderbilt sociology graduate students participated in all phases of the research process—from problem formulation, critical engagement of literature, research design, sampling and recruitment, interviewing, transcription, text and archival analysis, to co-authoring conference papers. The team met regularly at the Vanderbilt Center for Nashville Studies, administered efficiently and graciously by Nashville poet Stephanie Pruitt to whom we are grateful for the Center's hospitality, logistical support, and generative work environment.

For their extraordinary research assistance and collegiality, I am very grateful to Sandra Arch, Jon Cochran, Jonathan Coley, Becky Conway, Katherine

Everhart, Sarah Glynn, Harmony Newman, Carly Rush, Sammy Shaw, Rachel Skaggs, and Damian Williams.

The classroom discussions in my undergraduate, first-year sociology seminar "Artistic Dreams, Communities, and Pathways" have been an inspiring venue of criticism and insight for the writing of *Beyond the Beat*. Beginning in the fall 2010 semester, I seized the opportunity to create and offer a seminar organized around the theme and table of contents of a manuscript that would become the present volume. Throughout the four semesters I have now offered this seminar, the students have enlightened me about contemporary patterns of music consumption and production, offered fresh insights on classical scholarly sociological work in this field, and helped me hone my ideas by criticizing the conference papers I co-authored with my research team of graduate students.

My academic community also encompasses an engaging and visionary group of faculty, Vandy alumni, and community members of the greater Vanderbilt-Nashville area who convene on tennis courts, in cafes, at political functions, over dinner and, occasionally, in our offices. I am grateful, for their wisdom, joviality, and encouragement of *Beyond the Beat*, to Debby Alexander, George Barrett, Bruce Barry, John Beck, Frank Bloch, Gilbert and Noreen Cornfield, Dennis Dickerson, Robert Early, Ted Fischer, Volney Gay, Gary Gerstle, Matt Grimes, Doug Knight, Cliff Knowles, Irwin Kuhn, Geoff Macdonald, Mark Miller, Oscar Miller, Michael Schoenfeld, and Jon Shayne.

In the realm of social science, several colleagues have generously provided me with sage scholarly insight, constructive criticism of drafts, and their enthusiasm for this research project. Timothy Dowd and William Roy commented on the entire manuscript, broadening, deepening, and focusing the scholarly contributions of *Beyond the Beat*. I am also gratefully indebted to Howard Aldrich, Stephen Barley, Paul Dimaggio, Lois Gray, Randy Hodson, Arne Kalleberg, Thomas Kochan, Gina Neff, and Vicki Smith for their insightful comments on drafts and about the social organization of arts occupations and labor markets in the context of our discipline, history, and society.

I am grateful to Eric Schwartz, my editor at Princeton University Press, who believed in the book from the start, gave me strategic guidance, and brought *Beyond the Beat* to publication. Ryan Mulligan and Seth Ditchik of the Princeton University Press editorial team guided me sagaciously through the final book production stages.

I hail from an artistically and politically expressive family who inspired my writing *Beyond the Beat*. I was raised in a household filled with music, history, social theory, and social criticism, themes that we pursued throughout the year and revisited at the Seder table. My mother Edith, a pianist, and my father Melvin, a lawyer, lovingly launched me on an expressive pathway of envisioning just and inclusive communities, the pathway that led to the writing of this book. My wife Hedy Weinberg and our daughter Hannah are a constant source of inspiration and encouragement. Their support and humor kept me ahead of the beat to complete this book.

CHAPTER I

Creating Community in an Individualistic Age

Artist activists are re-creating a musician community in Nashville. These visionary peers of a musician community are transforming their community as they enter a risky era of entrepreneurial music production and artist self-promotion. As their careers increasingly unfold outside of the unionized corporate confines of major-label artist rosters, new generations of enterprising artists themselves bear the risks of production and distribution, an instance of Ulrich Beck's "individualization of risk."[1] In this post-bureaucratic moment, artist activism in re-creating peer community is an act of occupational self-determination for new generations of enterprising artists. Their activism is directed at minimizing risk by creating social spaces—such as production companies, studios, and performance venues—and a new arts trade unionism that promote their own and their peers' artistry and livelihoods.

Nashville artist activists have been initiating a wide range of individual and collective actions in re-creating a peer community over the last few decades. For example,

- In a 2011 interview with *Rolling Stone* magazine contributing editor Josh Eells, recording artist Jack White explained how he conceived of the new building for his label Third Man Records, whose Nashville presence had been established two years earlier:[2] "When I found this place ... I was just looking for a place to store my gear. But then I started designing the whole building from scratch." Eells reported in the *New York Times* that the building "[n]ow ... holds a record store, [Jack White's] label offices, a concert venue, a recording booth, a lounge for parties and even a darkroom. 'The whole shebang,' White said. It's a one-stop creativity shop."[3] At Third Man Records, the guitarist-singer-songwriter produces his own and others' music, and has many of the label's vinyl records pressed just a few blocks away at Nashville's legendary United Record Pressing, the nation's largest vinyl record plant located in the emerging Wedgewood-Houston arts district.[4]

- In 1987, recording engineer Mervin Louque partnered with businessman Rick Martin to establish Douglas Corner, "a music venue aimed at showcasing new singers and songwriters in Nashville. It soon grew to become a well-known 'Home Away From Home' for Nashville's top songwriters and future music stars," including the likes of Alan Jackson, Trisha Yearwood,

1

Marc Collie, The Kentucky Headhunters, Billy Dean, John Berry, Blake Shelton, and Garth Brooks.[5]

- In 2008, insurgent candidate Dave Pomeroy defeated eighteen-year incumbent and iconic Music Row co-founder Harold Bradley in an unusual and hotly contested election for the presidency of Nashville Local 257 of the American Federation of Musicians. Labeling it a "power shift," *Nashville Scene* writer Brantley Hargrove wrote that "To onlookers on the coasts, Local 257 had become a battleground far larger than Nashville's city limits, in a sort of proxy grudge match for control. At stake was leadership of the fourth largest local in the world's largest trade organization for professional musicians. That's in a town where music, according to a Belmont University study, is a $6.4 billion industry."[6] Union leadership change also signaled a new approach for revitalizing Local 257, whose sagging membership, like that of many unions in all economic sectors, had declined over the previous decade.[7]

Artist activists have arisen throughout the post-1980 musician migration to Nashville. By the mid-2000s, Nashville had become the U.S. city with the third highest concentration of musicians and, by 2011, it was proclaimed the nation's "Best Music Scene" by *Rolling Stone* magazine.[8] Artist activists have arisen as the steady stream of musicians created an increasingly genre-diverse pool of "indie" enterprising artists of diverse social backgrounds in Nashville. Over the last half-century, Nashville's established musician community had crystallized around a group of "A-team" recording musicians, songwriters, producers, arts trade unions, and recording artists on the rosters of a few corporate major labels that distributed commercial country music through mass broadcasting. The established community, according to music historian Robert Oermann, "was insulated from the pop-music world as well as from mainstream Nashville. As the booking agencies, publishers, and record labels clustered on Music Row in the 1960s, the personalities who populated them became friends as well as competitors."[9] Contemporary artist activists are reconstituting the musician community as the genre-diversifying musician migration moves Nashville into a post-bureaucratic, entrepreneurial era of music production and artist self-promotion in risky niche consumer markets.

Beyond the Beat is about the artist activists themselves. How do individualistic, entrepreneurial artistic peers sustain their occupational community during a competitive phase of what sociologists Richard Peterson and David Berger called the "concentration-competition cycle"[10] of popular-music production? This book, and the new sociological theory of artist activism derived from the Nashville case, address this question of re-socializing risk by re-creating occupational community for an individualistic, diversifying, and entrepreneurial art-making era. I define *artist activism* as an act of occupational self-determination that is directed at minimizing risk by creating social spaces and a new arts trade unionism for promoting artist activists' and their peers' artistry and livelihoods.

The changing Nashville music scene has spawned three types of artist activists. I refer to these ideal-typical, artist activist roles as "enterprising artists," "artistic social entrepreneurs," and "artist advocates." The sociological theory of artist activism addresses how artist activists fashion their roles as artist activists. Together, the three artist activist roles constitute a repertoire of individual and collective action for re-creating a peer artist community. The theory attributes variations among artist activists in their assumption and enactment of individualistic and collective roles to the artist activist's subjective orientations toward success, audience, risk, and career inspiration.

Jack White, Douglas Corner, and the power struggle within Local 257 illustrate the emergent ensemble of artist activist roles—"enterprising artists," "artistic social entrepreneurs," and "artist advocates," respectively. I define *artist activists* as those visionary artistic peers and closely aligned impresarios who create inclusive, place-based artist communities in an increasingly entrepreneurial art-making era. John Van Maanen and Stephen Barley define an occupational community as a "group of people who consider themselves to be engaged in the same sort of work; who identify (more or less positively) with their work; who share a set of values, norms, and perspectives that apply to, but extend beyond, work related matters; and whose social relationships meld the realms of work and leisure."[11] In an otherwise vertically organized rational-bureaucratic economy, occupational communities, for Van Maanen and Barley, are the horizontal communal organization by which workers achieve self-control, collective autonomy, and social solidarity and form their identities.[12]

In Nashville, artist activists are building an inclusive, place-based expressive occupational community among indie musicians in a widening range of popular-music genres. This emerging community consists of a spatial ecology and "loosely coupled"[13] set of local micro-organizational initiatives undertaken by diverse artist activists who are advancing the well-being of their peer community. The community is "expressive" in its focus on the artistic occupation of musician; "place-based" in being co-extensive and thematically linked to the Nashville music scene; and "inclusive" in the diversifying set of artist social identities—race, ethnicity, gender, sexual orientation, religion—and corresponding widening array of musical genres that are expressed by its members.

Artist activists arise to sustain individual artists and the whole occupation. Their local organizational initiatives constitute a repertoire of individual and collective actions that address the artist-communal functions of artist professional development; networking and job referrals; and the economic interests of the whole occupation.[14] The *typology of artist activist roles* that I derived from my interviews with seventy-five Nashville music professionals consists of *enterprising artists* who produce and distribute their own and others' work and mentor early-career artists; *artistic social entrepreneurs* whose social enterprises, such as schools, live performance venues, and artist development companies, have the explicit social mission of maintaining social spaces and networks for promoting professional development opportunities and job referrals; and *artist advocates* who, as arts trade union reformers, are creating new guild-like unions by revamping collective bargaining, contract language, and union organizational functions in order to resonate with a new generation of enterprising artists whose individualism exceeds that of earlier generations of their peers.

The purpose of this book is to develop a sociological theory of artist activism. The theory concerns how artist activists' subjective orientations toward success, audience, risk, and career inspiration shape the array of roles they create, assume, and enact to reconstitute artist community in a post-bureaucratic, entrepreneurial art-making era. In the words of the late sociologist Richard A. Peterson, the advent of an entrepreneurial art-making era was a stage of "competition and creativity" in the "concentration-competition cycle" of cultural production. In this cycle, an artistically competitive, innovative, and genre-diverse era succeeds an era of mounting economic concentration in a bureaucratic culture-producing industry whose increasingly homogeneous content had run its course in the market.[15] Readers who are interested more in the detailed, career-biographical profiles of the artist activists than in the sociological and policy mission of this book may wish to proceed to chapters 3 through 6.

In the terms of ancestral sociologist Emile Durkheim, reconstituting a community of enterprising artists in Nashville is driven by a shift in the occupational division of labor of music professionals. The shift is from vertically organized, occupational specialization toward a horizontal occupational generalism, a shift that has accompanied the advent of independent art-making throughout the arts and entertainment sector in the United States during the last several decades.[16] Over the last quarter-century, the unionized, corporate Nashville music scene based in mass broadcast distribution and an emphasis on country music has been transforming into an entrepreneurial, genre-diverse, de-unionized music scene. In the corporate era, music production is organized around large major labels and publishing companies, large studios, elite producers, and artist advocacy organizations. The complex, occupational division of labor of music specialists includes songwriters, pluggers, A & R reps, producers, engineers, an "A-team" of unionized session musicians, top-charting artists, and music agents, administrators, and executives, all geographically situated in the Music Row neighborhood. In the post-bureaucratic indie era, in contrast, the simple occupational division of labor of music generalists comprises entrepreneurial artists—self-promoting and self-contained bands who perform a wide range of their own artistic, art-production, and art-support functions, often conducted in their homes or small studios throughout multiple neighborhoods of greater Nashville, and directly engage their niche markets of fans and consumers in live venues and over the Internet.

In Durkheimian terms, reconstituting a post-bureaucratic community of artists entails the development of a new "social solidarity" or sense of togetherness based in a simplifying occupational division of labor. In a community built around a complex division of labor of occupational specialists, "organic social solidarity" was achieved from the interdependence among specialists.

In contrast, "mechanical social solidarity" was achieved in a community based on an occupational sameness that prevailed in a simple occupational division of labor.[17]

In Nashville, artist activists are creating a "mechanically solidary" community of entrepreneurial artists alongside and partly from the ranks of an older, organically solidary corporate-era artist community. Nashville entrepreneurial musicians constitute themselves as a community by producing and performing for one another, showing up to each others' showcases, and extending mutual aid during trying moments in their lives. According to Ken Paulson, an astute participant-observer of the Nashville musician community, Nashville entrepreneurial artists "cross-promote. And they cross-promote in an unselfconscious way.... [T]he community is largely very supportive of each other's art."[18]

From a Durkheimian perspective, however, reconstituting community and achieving a new social solidarity are not a foregone conclusion. Social change is punctuated and interrupted by moments of "anomie," Durkheim's term for the destabilizing normlessness that arises with a shift in the inspirational and organizational norms of an occupational community. Anomic historical moments are often accompanied by the marginalization of minority groups and intergenerational group conflict in a changing community,[19] as in the epochal, contested election in Local 257. These anomic moments nonetheless can constitute a "wellspring of innovation," as Richard Peterson put it in his masterful treatment of the institutionalization of Nashville country music through the 1990s. In a "dialectic of generations," Peterson contended, "[i]nnovative young artists, that is, those who fabricate a contemporary way of expressing authenticity, commonly feel that they are doing so in opposition to the music they have grown up with."[20]

As community builders, artist activists are also challenged by anomic historical moments beyond those inherent in their occupational community. In our contemporary neoliberal era of "risk individualization"[21] and "identity politics,"[22] occupational communities are embedded in a societal web of increasingly precarious employment relations and polarized status-group relations.[23] Beyond meeting the Durkheimian challenge of achieving a new social solidarity among occupational generalists, artist activists must also solidify an occupational community composed of "free agents"[24] who hail from diverse social backgrounds.

As community builders, artist activists express an occupational self-determination for managing and minimizing risk in a precarious era of risk individualization. Employment precarity is symptomatic of a regime of casual employment relations. Risk individualization is manifested in declining labor movements, shrinking public commitments to social welfare and social insurance, and the shift from cradle-to-grave organizational careers in large bureaucracies toward casual, post-bureaucratic careers as, in Vicki Smith's words, "free agents."[25] Arne Kalleberg shows that the trend toward risk individualization, as indicated by the advent of flexible, nonstandard employment arrangements such as contingent labor and temporary employment and labor union decline, is linked to the trend of increasing income inequality in the United States throughout the last several decades.[26]

In an era of identity politics, art worlds are imbued with and expressive of artist and consumer social identities.[27] The large post-1990 wave of immigration to the United States is the largest since the great immigration wave of the 1880–1924 era. Steven Tepper argues that, in a democracy, public controversies over artistic expression effectively constitute a public deliberation over community identity, especially during anomic times of rapid social change. The findings of his seventy-city study of cultural conflict in the United States during the 1990s indicate that the level of community conflict over public displays of art and literature in a city was directly associated with the rate of immigrant settlement in a city: the higher the rate of immigrant settlement in a city, the higher was the level of cultural conflict in the city. As a "new-destination" city for a rapidly growing number of immigrants from Africa, Asia, Latin America, and the Middle East,[28] Nashville, according to Tepper, was a "relatively contentious city."[29] By sustaining and diffusing their artistic traditions in their co-ethnic communities and throughout the city, immigrant artists are playing an important countervailing role in smoothing immigrant incorporation in Nashville.[30]

As community builders in an era of identity politics, artist activists are challenged to build inclusive occupational communities of socially diverse artists. In doing so, they build genre-diverse occupational communities that are artistically expressive of their diverse social identities in niche markets of fickle, "omnivorish" music consumers.[31] In Nashville, the growing indie music scene, as well as the major-label scene, expresses a widening range of social identities defined by race, ethnicity, gender, sexual orientation, and religion.[32] A major-label A & R vice president I interviewed put it this way:

> Today I think the biggest competition is everything. Is it possible to have mass success? I don't know. But it is possible to have huge success. So I think the world that we're in right now, it's really about target marketing, about reaching out to your niche and your audience, and how you can speak to a specific group of people. There are the resources to do that. There's the bloggers, there's iTunes, MSN, AOL, there's MySpace and Facebook and live touring, making records and selling them on the road, selling them online, ma and pa stores and maybe traditional retailers, and maybe you'll get on satellite radio and that will only get you so far, maybe if you're lucky you'll get on pop radio because it still actually has some impact. But there's just so many different ways to connect the dots these days, it's not a linear world, and if you can embrace the notion that it's a niche culture and you can find the ways in which to reach, and use all of the resources to reach kids, and hope that the music at the end of the day is good enough that word of mouth is ultimately going to fuel it.

Artist activists envision and build expressive, peer occupational communities in an individualistic age. The communities comprise diverse entrepreneurial artists who thrive in an era of risk individualization and identity politics. The sociological theory of artist activism developed in this book addresses how artistic occupational peers envision, create, assume, and enact their roles as artist activists in an individualistic age. The theory also appears in a corresponding era of the intellectual history of sociology that increasingly privileges strategic human agency as a driving force of social change.[33]

TOWARD A SOCIOLOGY OF ARTIST ACTIVISM

Beyond the Beat treats the enduring theme of building community in an increasingly individualistic society. It also treats the theme of structure and agency in reconstituting occupational community in a post-bureaucratic society that is increasingly inhabited by free agents. Contemporary employment relations are frequently labeled "precarious" and "flexible" and risk is "individualized" in market relations rather than socialized in protective social-welfare institutions. Entrepreneurship now competes with corporate career ladders and trade unionism as a source of community and as a pathway toward upward social mobility.[34] New artist activists emerge to reconstitute peer occupational community and "safety cultures" for enterprising workers who operate in the interstices of bureaucratic institutions.[35]

This book is situated at the nexus of the "new" sociology of work and sociological studies of culture and social movements. The book extends the concept of "worker agency" in the "new" sociology of work by examining the subjective, strategic orientations of artist activists that shape how they create, assume, and enact an array of individual and collective, artist activist roles. It also elaborates on how art worlds change by incorporating the regime of artist activist roles into an analysis of how artist activists usher in an emerging art world. The changing Nashville music scene is a case in point for examining the role of artist activists in ushering in an increasingly entrepreneurial, Internet-driven, and genre-diversifying art world.[36] It is an art world emerging out of and alongside of a predominantly corporate, mass-broadcast-driven, single-genre art world.[37]

Changing Art Worlds

This book partly extends Howard Becker's sociology of art worlds.[38] An art world is a socio-spatial arena of vertical and horizontal social networks that coordinate the activities of artists and organizations in the creation, production, distribution, and legitimation of art works. Art worlds can change gradually—"drift"—and abruptly—"revolution"—in response to technological and conceptual changes and changes in the social and demographic characteristics of audiences. For Becker, the "maverick," in contrast to the "integrated professional," innovates in the content of art by defying art-world conventions and establishing new techniques, institutions, and audiences for producing and distributing new art.[39] Less attention has been given to the subjective orientations that underlie, animate, and shape the actions and the diverse types of roles and individual- and collective-action mavericks undertake in transforming an art world. Robert Faulkner has described the stable, corporate art worlds of Hollywood musicians, composers, and film-industry independent contractors who feverishly network for project work in a competitive reputational market.[40] Faulkner and Becker have recently examined the sources of occupational community—a phenomenological process of maintaining and gradually expanding "repertoire"—among stable communities of working musicians.[41]

Recent work in cultural sociology has extended Bourdieu's field theory by examining the impact of cultural entrepreneurs on field transitions.[42] This body of research has addressed the agency of cultural entrepreneurs in instituting new fields of cultural production and cultural content. For example, Andy Bennett's study of rock heritage shows how a wide range of cultural entrepreneurs—magazine editors and writers, documentary film and television producers, museum curators, webmasters, tribute bands, and the music industry itself—have produced conservative and alternative discourses for preserving and canonizing, as well as re-releasing, both classic live performances and do-it-yourself innovations in the history of rock.[43]

Related work in urban sociology and the sociology of social movements has examined the actions of cultural agents in creating new art worlds and new genres and mobilizing social movements. Richard Lloyd's pioneering work on the transformation of Chicago industrial neighborhood Wicker Park into a vibrant art scene examines how a "neo-bohemian" regime of entrepreneurs, design companies and media corporations, artists, aesthetes, and "yuppy" art consumers generated the new art scene.[44] The "cultural turn" in sociological research on social movements has systematically brought cultural agents into examinations of what Larry Isaac refers to as "aesthetic activism" in processes of social change. Building on Paul Dimaggio's concept of "cultural entrepreneurs," Isaac develops the concept of a "literary activist," a novelist whose literary works reflect and facilitate the mobilization and countermobilization of social movements.[45] Similarly, in his sociological study of the link between American folk music and the U.S. labor and civil rights movements of the twentieth century, William Roy characterized the Lomax and Seeger families as cultural entrepreneurs who "bridged institutions, playing an entrepreneurial role in the Schumpeterian sense—cobbling programs, building organizations, recombining various elements into new forms, and using a broad range of social and professional contacts to mold American folk music as ... a musical world that itself bridged institutions."[46]

Beyond the Beat extends previous research on cultural agents and art-world change in three ways. First, less attention has been given in previous research to the subjective orientations of artist activists in the process of art-world change.[47] Rather, research on mavericks, cultural entrepreneurs, and aesthetic agents has emphasized the strategic actions and techniques that are used by these cultural agents. *Beyond the Beat* extends art-world research in its emphasis on the subjective meanings and orientations artist activists apply in creating, assuming, and enacting their roles as artist activists on behalf of their peer communities. Art-world research itself extended the sociology of Everett Hughes on individual and group mobility in occupational social worlds to artistic-occupational social worlds. In the Hughesian occupational social world, the work and status mobility of occupation members were oriented toward and contextualized by the occupational "license" and "mandate."[48] Previous art-world research has emphasized the patterning and techniques of dynamic networking action and resource mobilization by entrepreneurs, but has given less attention to the subjective meanings and orientations that inspire, guide, shape, and channel these actions. Therefore, the emphasis of *Beyond the Beat* is less on networking technique, structure, and actions, and is primarily on the artist activists' self-configuration of orientations toward success, audience, and risk, the self-proclaimed sources of their original inspirations for embarking on a musical career, and their visions of new institutional models for advancing artistic expression in the emerging art world.

Second, *Beyond the Beat* extends previous art-world research by shifting the object of inquiry from cultural projects, such as the development of new art genres, to occupational community-building projects. Art-world change entails not only changes in art-making conventions and the production of new cultural products, but also may entail and presume a reorganization of the occupational division of labor, artist professional development, and artist advocacy among the artists and support personnel of an art world. In accounting for art-world change, previous research has tended to focus directly on the art-making process and has underemphasized the influence of the reorganization of the artist peer community. What is more, research on cultural agents has underemphasized the diverse occupational, professional-development, and advocacy roles artist activists create, assume, and enact as they reorganize an artist peer community. Therefore, the emphasis of *Beyond the Beat* is on how the subjective orientations of artist activists shape the diverse roles they assume and play in reconstituting artist community in a changing art world.

Third, *Beyond the Beat* extends previous art-world research by developing a new historically grounded typology of artist activist roles. The typology consists of a set of individual and collective, artist activist roles of the historical-institutional moment from which they were inductively derived. The historical moment is one of a music scene whose corporate-oligopolistic system of production and distribution is increasingly assuming an entrepreneurial-competitive form.[49] The threefold typology of artist activists—enterprising artist, artistic social entrepreneur, and artist advocate—is a set of roles played by artist activists who initiate individual and collective actions to reconstitute their artist community under these specific historical-institutional conditions. *Beyond the Beat*, then, examines the patterns of subjective orientations and array of roles artist activists play in reconstituting their artist community as they enter an entrepreneurial art-making era.

The Nashville case, as will be described in greater detail, is a case of a transforming art world, one whose logic of production and distribution is changing from a corporate organizational logic to an entrepreneurial organizational logic. This book extends art-world research by deriving empirically and inductively a threefold typology of artist activists from the original interviews with seventy-five Nashville music professionals. Artist activists respond to and facilitate drift and revolution in the conventions and organization of an art world. In the increasingly entrepreneurial Nashville music scene, artist activists pursue individual and collective strategies for creating an expressive and supportive artist community that promotes professional development, economic well-being, and, ultimately, individual artistic expression in the emerging art world.

The "New" Sociology of Work

This book also extends research in the "new" sociology of work. The newness of the new sociology of work refers to the contemporary scholarly treatment of post-bureaucratic and increasingly precarious and polarized social relations within workplaces and between service sector workers and their customers and clients. As the older sociology of work matured in the post–World War II manufacturing era of long-term steady jobs held by "organization men and women" in bureaucratic internal labor markets, and in the wake of the civil rights and women's movements, it came to analyze social inequality and disparities in career mobility outcomes in socially embedded, stable corporate workplaces. As Arne Kalleberg argues, since the 1970s, globalization, deregulation, the decline of the labor movement, and the advent of an individualistic ethos led to the casualization of corporate employment relationships, outsourcing, the rise of self-employment and "non-standard" freelance employment relations, and increasing disparities in both job quality and income.[50] The new sociology of work has emerged since the 1980s to analyze casual employment relations in all economic sectors, and especially in freelance occupational labor markets in personal and business services, arts, new media, communications, and the knowledge economy.

According to Menger, no labor force sector is more emblematic of enterprising and precarious, freelance employment than artistic labor markets.[51] As Bourdieu put it, the arts field consists of "positions that are relatively uninstitutionalized, never legally guaranteed, therefore open to symbolic challenge, and non-hereditary ..., it is the arena *par excellence* of struggles over job definition."[52]

Compared to the older sociology of work, the new sociology of work puts more emphasis on "worker agency" in the shaping of the post-bureaucratic workplace and in determining livelihoods and life chances. According to Randy Hodson, worker agency is "the active and creative performance of assigned roles in ways that give meaning and content to those roles beyond what is institutionally scripted."[53]

Two contemporary versions of the new sociology work—the occupational and institutional versions—address the relative importance of structure and agency in the determination of worker life chances.[54] In the Hughesian, occupational version of the new sociology of work, worker agency tends to be conceived as individual networking action by freelance, independent-contracting workers, such as Barley and Kunda's "itinerant professionals"; Smith's post-bureaucratic "free agents" who grapple with risk, uncertainty, and opportunity; Osnowitz's "freelancers"; and Neff's "venture labor," who attempt to secure and retain project work, often with corporate clients.[55] In the "labor market-segmentation" institutional version, worker agency tends to be conceived as the collective action of unionization and collective bargaining.[56]

This book extends and integrates both versions of the new sociology of work by treating an array of individual *and* collective expressions of worker agency as a regime of artist activist roles that are created, assumed, and enacted by artist activists who are reconstituting their peer occupational community. The threefold typology of artist activists presented in this book constitutes a regime of individual and collective roles for creating artist community and promoting individual artistic expression in the emerging entrepreneurial art world. This diverse regime derives empirically from the co-existence in the U.S. entertainment and arts sector and, specifically, the Nashville music scene, of the individual strategies of entrepreneurship and freelancing, on the one hand, and the collective strategy of a new arts trade unionism, on the other hand.[57] What is more, these strategies co-exist within an emerging art world and, as artist activist roles they can be created, assumed, and enacted simultaneously by the same artist activist. Nationally, for example, between 2003 and 2013, the percentage unionized in the U.S. "arts, entertainment, and recreation" industry decreased slightly from 7.0 percent to 6.6 percent.[58] "*Independent* artists, writers, and performers," in contrast, are projected by the U.S. Bureau of Labor Statistics to increase by 12.4 percent between 2012 and 2022, roughly two to four times the projected growth rate of all—independent and wage and salaried—actors, artists, dancers, musicians, photographers, producers and directors, and writers.[59]

Nashville as Case and Context

A national center of popular music recording, the Nashville music scene is representative of a changing art world, one that is transitioning from a corporate logic toward an entrepreneurial logic of production and distribution. The Nashville music scene employs some 8,000 workers who write, publish, perform, produce, record, and distribute music in a range of popular music genres, including country music. In recent decades, the Nashville music recording industry has become increasingly competitive with a growing, non-union sector of independent (indie) small businesses and solo practitioners rivaling the unionized, increasingly consolidated sector of major-label recording corporations.[60]

The present work examines the subjective orientations of the artist activists who are ushering in an entrepreneurial Nashville art world of country, urban, gospel, jazz, rock, and Americana music.[61] A "contemporary generation" of enterprising artists who produce music in a wide range of genres has emerged in Nashville. They launched their careers during the 1990s and 2000s, carving out an expanding range of niche consumer markets and engaging diverse audiences. For example, Nashville's alternative weekly the *Nashville Scene* recently hailed Nashville-based jazz composer and saxophonist Rahsaan Barber as:

> [a] twenty-first century jazz player unwilling to let others decide his fate. Barber is also a label executive, promoter, producer and broadcaster. He started Jazz Music City Records a year ago, because he felt "it doesn't make a lot of sense to complain about there not being labels in town willing to record jazz musicians if you're not going to do something about it."[62]

Throughout the 1980s and 1990s, Nashville attracted musicians whose careers unfolded in this growing and diversifying music scene. By 2004, Nashville had the third highest concentration of musicians, after New York and Los Angeles, and it had come to assume the status of the U.S. city with the highest concentration of music business establishments, such as record labels, distributors, recording studios, and music publishers.[63] The increasing concentration of musicians in Nashville has been attributed to the 1990-era migration of Los Angeles musicians to Nashville during the country music boom, partly compelled by the increasing automation of LA recording session work; increasing coastal major-label interest and investment in Nashville's technological infrastructure and artist development; the rise of a vital sector of independent music labels and artists; and, not least of all, the presence of a talent pool of world-class songwriters and studio musicians. Nashville has also been promoted as an affordable place to reside and work.[64]

An earlier "transformative generation" of enterprising artists embarked on their careers in the 1960s and 1970s in association with the major labels and musician unions and participated in the rise of self-contained bands and artistic production independent of the major labels. Some members of the transformative generation originated in the LA music industry and migrated to Nashville during the 1990-era boom in country music, compelled by the increasing automation of LA recording session work, while others emerged from the Nashville music industry.

The contemporary generation of enterprising artists, often mentored by the earlier transformative generation, launched their careers during the 1990s and 2000s independent of the major labels and musician unions in niche consumer markets that are demographically segmented especially by race, ethnicity, age, and gender, and by genre. A proliferation of area college music-business degree programs since the 1970s encouraged the growth of the contemporary generation of enterprising artists who are equipped with individual portfolios of artistic and music-business skills.[65]

Furthermore, the rise of the contemporary generation of enterprising artists in Nashville accompanied an increasingly diverse and socially inclusive urban context that was conducive to the production and consumption of an expanding range of demographically segmented musical genres. These contextual changes include the 1960-era Nashville civil rights movement in which Nashville desegregated by 1962, two years before the enactment of the Civil Rights Act of 1964;[66] post-1990 global immigration to Nashville from Africa, Asia, Latin America, and the Middle East, making Nashville one of the most ethnically diverse and rapidly growing "new destination" cities;[67] the subsequent transformation in 2012 of Nashville city council's "Black Caucus" into a broader "Minority Caucus" that includes Latinos;[68] and the enactment in 2009 of a Nashville non-discrimination ordinance that banned discrimination on the basis of sexual orientation and gender identity by city government, placing Nashville in the tiny minority of units of local government in the United States that have enacted such legislation.[69]

The restructuring of the Nashville recording industry is partly depicted in the growing proportion of top country recordings that were distributed on indie labels between 1964 and 2009. My compilation of top-charting music reports in *Billboard* magazine shows that the percentage of top-30 country music albums on indie labels increased from 0.0 percent to 23.3 percent and that the total number of labels with at least one top-30 album increased from seven to nineteen between 1964 and 2009. All in all, the total number of labels distributing top-charted country music, and the percentage of top-charted, indie-label country albums and singles, increased during this forty-five-year period. What is more, the increases in labels and indie-label top-charted music accelerated after the mid-1990s, presumably with the diffusion of home-based production and new-media technology and major-label consolidation.[70]

The socio-spatial decentralization of the Nashville music scene is depicted in the growing number of small and independent music-production and artistic enterprises in Davidson County, Tennessee, aka Nashville, and neighboring, suburban Williamson County, where small-scale music production has diffused for lower real-estate expenses in recent years. According to my compilation of the U.S. Census Bureau's County Business Patterns[71] data for Davidson-Williamson Counties in the 1998–2009 time period, the number of establishments and the percentage located in Williamson County in "integrated record production/distribution" increased during this time period. Consistent with the *Billboard* trends previously cited in the growing presence of indie labels, the number of integrated record production/distribution establishments—roughly half of which have fewer than five employees—increased from nineteen to thirty-six and the percentage located in Williamson County increased from 0 to 16.7 percent. Consistent with the U.S. Bureau of Labor Statistics' national forecast, the number of "independent artists, writers and performers"—some 80 percent of which are establishments with fewer than five employees—increased from 116 to 206, but the percentage in Williamson County remained stable during this period. The numbers of establishments in "record production" and "sound recording studios" remained stable, but the percentage located in Williamson County increased between 1998 and 2009. The percentages of establishments in record production and sound recording studios located in Williamson County increased, respectively, from 19.2 percent to 33.3 percent and from 12.7 percent to 24.1 percent. The number and location of "musical groups and artists" and "music publishers" remained stable throughout this period.

* * *

The empirical basis of this book rests on the 2,500 pages of transcripts of interviews that my research team and I conducted with an original semi-structured interview schedule with seventy-five Nashville music professionals. Half of the interviewees were employed in artistic occupations—musicians and songwriters, and half work in music-industry occupations, including producers, audio engineers, publishers, artist managers, club managers, trade union officers, and A & R reps. In light of the trend toward entrepreneurship, occupational generalism, and "hyphenated" occupations like singer-songwriter, the occupations of many of the interviewees defied conventional occupational classifications. The median age of the interviewees is forty-five. Twenty-one percent of the interviewees are women and 17.1 percent are people of color. The snowball sample was generated through referrals from a purposive, occupationally and demographically diverse, root sample.

Interviews addressed individual career and personal biographies, orientations toward inspiration, aspiration, success, risk, audience, advocacy, professionalism, and entrepreneurship, employment and work attitudes, and changes in the artistic, social, organizational, and technological characteristics of the Nashville music scene. Interviews were granted on the condition of anonymity, and were conducted privately in the office of the researcher or the respondent between September 2006 and September 2013. Ninety-five percent of the interviews were conducted by January 2008. They were voice-recorded and ranged in length from 2 hours to 4.5 hours. The full interview schedule is presented in the appendix.

* * *

In the chapters that follow, I develop a new sociological theory of artist activism and derive a research agenda for a new sociology of artist activism, as well as assess community-building policy implications for artist activists. The theory, which I present in chapter 2, addresses how individual subjective orientations shape the repertoire of individual and collective, community-building actions among a group of artistic occupational peers. Specifically, the theory addresses individual variations in how visionary artist peers configure their orientations toward success, audience, risk, and career inspiration to fashion their roles as artist activists and the new initiatives they undertake to strengthen their peer community. The chapter presents new, inductively derived typologies of an artist activist's orientations toward success, audience, risk, and career inspiration, as well as propositions linking these orientations to her creation, assumption, and enactment of any part or all of the regime of individual and collective artist activist roles.

In chapters 3 through 6, the theory is evidenced with a cascading examination of the three artist activist roles during the post-1980 musician migration to Nashville. Each of these chapters presents in-depth profiles of representatives of one of the three artist activist roles. They proceed in ascending order of the extent of collective action embodied in each artist activist role. The chapters also proceed in the approximate historical sequence of the appearance of the artist activist roles in Nashville, culminating with the new arts trade unionism of the mid-2000s in chapter 6. Two generations of the most individualistic "enterprising artists"—the early transformative and the contemporary generations—are covered in chapters 3 and 4, respectively. "Artistic social entrepreneurs" have appeared throughout the period and are discussed in chapter 5. "Artist advocates," the artist activist role most engaged in collective action, is treated in chapter 6.

A total of sixteen artist activists—four per chapter—are profiled pseudonymously in terms of their visions, strategic orientations, risk orientations, and career-biographical pathways to becoming an artist activist. I refer to a *vision* as the artist activist's concept of a local organizational initiative he envisions for building an artist community; a *strategic orientation* as an individual orientation toward success and audience; and a *risk orientation* as one's attribution of the sources of risk to impersonal market and institutional forces, interpersonal relations and networks, or to oneself, defined and typologized in chapter 2. Following Kathleen Blee's work on grassroots activism, I adopt her definition of a *pathway* as "human actions ... that move through social institutions or *projects*. As people travel through society, they are continually confronted with new influences, information, and feelings that lead them toward certain actions ... They still make choices, but these are constrained by the earlier decisions."[72]

In chapter 7, the concluding chapter, I present a new, post-bureaucratic research agenda in the new sociology of work derived from the sociological theory of artist activism. The agenda consists of three themes for future research. First is the generalizability of the Nashville model of artist activism across cities that differ in terms of their mix of art-production and-consumption activity and their levels and history of arts trade unionism. The second theme pertains to the influence of biographical pathways, risk orientations, and occupational socialization through intergenerational peer mentoring on the formation of the next generation of artist activists. The third theme is an assessment of the effectiveness of the several prevailing models of guild-like labor organizations for freelancers and artists on advancing individual and occupational professional and economic interests. I conclude with policy implications for building and strengthening inclusive and expressive, urban occupational communities in an era of risk individualization and identity politics.

CHAPTER 2

Artist Activism

Building Occupational Communities in Risky Times

At the heart of Nashville's diversifying and decentralizing music scene is an emerging community of artists. Alongside of Nashville's major-label, country music art world, this emergent, racially diverse, and multi-genre artist community is being driven by visionary musician peers and impresarios, independent owners of new labels, venues, and music schools, independent artist-producers, self-contained bands, professional associations, and self-reinventing musician unions. I refer to these *artist activists* as visionary musician peers who are re-creating their musician community as Nashville transitions into an entrepreneurial era of music production in dynamic but risky niche markets. Associated Press writer Chris Talbott captured part of this community in his interview with Black Keys guitarist Dan Auerbach: "When Dan Auerbach moved from Ohio to Music City, he found a local rock 'n' roll scene populated with bands that not only like each other, but also work toward a greater good. The Black Keys guitarist sees it as an uncommon harmony.... 'It's really pretty cool and it's very much its own thing,' Auerbach said. 'There doesn't seem to be too much ego.'"[1]

Similarly, *Nashville Scene* writer Sean Maloney referenced Lovenoise, an urban music promotion company co-founded by Eric Holt, as the primary catalyst of Nashville's growing urban music scene: "Lovenoise is the nexus in Nashville's widening urban music network ... consistently putting local up-and-comers on bills with national artists.... In an era when polarization is the norm, Lovenoise has marked out a social center—a middle path that allows artists and audiences to flourish."[2]

Throughout the post-1980 musician migration to Nashville, artist activists have arisen to reconstitute a musician community that resonates with risky entrepreneurial music production. Nashville's transition into an entrepreneurial era of music production compels musicians to engage in acts of occupational self-determination that socialize and minimize the risk of joblessness. In the emerging place-based, peer community of enterprising artists, risk is increasingly borne by the artists themselves, rather than by large organizations such as major labels, studios, publishers, and arts trade unions. This instance of Ulrich Beck's "individualization of risk" compels artists to re-create the requisite peer community for furthering professional development, employment and careers, and artist advocacy.[3] Artist activists—enterprising artists, artistic social entrepreneurs, and artist advocates—are the agents of this

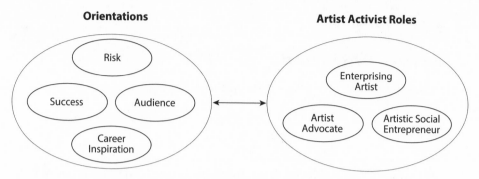

FIGURE 2.1. Artist Orientations toward Artist Activist Roles

emerging peer community. Through their individual and collective actions, they create new social spaces and micro-organizational initiatives for the emerging peer community of enterprising artists.

How do artist activists fashion their roles as artist activists? In this chapter, I present a new sociological theory of artist activism that addresses this question. I refer to *artist activism* as acts of occupational self-determination taken by artist peers in organizing and reorganizing their peer community. Specifically, the theory addresses how individual subjective orientations shape the repertoire of individual and collective actions and roles assumed and enacted by artist activists. The theory attributes individual variations in role assumption and enactment to artist orientations toward success, audience, risk, and career inspiration, as shown in figure 2.1. This is a theory-building project of the new sociology of work. Research in the new sociology of work has addressed individual risk-management strategies for advancing individual careers and social mobility of free agents. In contrast, the sociological theory of artist activism presented here addresses how artist activists build a peer community for sustaining the livelihoods of individuals and the whole occupation.

At its core, the new sociology of work is, to use Everett Hughes's terms, a sociology of "individual and collective occupational mobility" and the "social drama of work."[4] It addresses the enduring issue of occupational mobility, not in the post–World War II context of rigid bureaucracy and organizational careers, but in the freelance context of our enterprising era. Comparing careers in "rigidly structured" and "freer" societies, Hughes wrote:

In a highly and rigidly structured society, a career consists, objectively, of a series of status and clearly defined offices. In a freer one, the individual has more latitude for creating his own position or choosing from a number of existing ones; he has also less certainty of achieving any given position. There are more adventurers and more failures; but unless complete disorder reigns, there will be typical sequences of position, achievement, responsibility, and even of adventure. The social order will set limits upon the individual's orientation of his life, both as to direction of effort and as to interpretation of its meaning.[5]

In the remainder of this chapter, I present and typologize the chief subjective orientations of artist activists that influence their assumption and enactment of artist activist roles. The typology of artist activist roles, defined in chapter 1, comprises roles that range between the most individualistic—"enterprising artist," through "artistic social entrepreneur," to "artist advocate," the most collective role. The assumption and enactment of these roles by artist activists is the chief object of explanation ("categorical dependent variables") of the theory. Each of the typologized artist subjective orientations—what I refer to specifically as "strategic orientations," "risk orientations," and "orientations toward career inspiration," is an explanatory variable ("categorical independent or intervening variable") of the theory. All of these typologies consist of ideal types of roles and orientations. In practice, an artist activist assumes and enacts a blended activist role with blended orientations toward strategy, risk, and career inspiration. I conclude the chapter with a full typology of artist activists and theoretical propositions, derived inductively from my interviews with Nashville music professionals. The propositions link the subjective orientations to artist activists' assumption and enactment of their roles—namely, their roles as enterprising artists, artistic social entrepreneurs, and artist advocates.

STRATEGIC ORIENTATIONS

Artist activists harbor a strategic orientation that, in a Hughesian sense, orients them toward both the individual and group mobility of their occupation and peers, and toward re-shaping the emerging "mandate" and "license" of their occupation. In the present epoch of risk individualization, increasing "indie" entrepreneurship, and occupational generalism, artist activists are oriented strategically toward developing a community of interdependent artists that promotes their own and peers' freedom of expression in a direct engagement with the fans and music consumers. The Nashville artist activists profiled in chapters 3 through 6 represent two generations of artist activists who are envisioning and building an emergent community of artists. This emergent artistic community, in the present moment, constitutes a spatial ecology of loosely coupled artist activists who are addressing the expression, professional development, and economic well-being of their occupational peers of enterprising artists.

I refer to a *strategic orientation* as the artist activist's orientation toward success and audience. Much sociological research has examined the social, political and biographical antecedents of individual activism or participation in socially transformative initiatives and movements.[6] The argument here is that, regardless of these antecedents of individual activism and movement participation, an artist activist's strategic orientation toward the mandate and license of his changing occupation and peers is a necessary if insufficient subjective factor in an artist's or arts professional's assumption of any or all of the artist activist roles. I now unpack the two component orientations of a strategic orientation by presenting inductively derived typologies of an artist activist's orientations toward success and audience.

Success Orientations

In his original formulation, James Truslow Adams depicted an American Dream that extolled both a consumerist ideal of materialist acquisition and an unhampered individual freedom to pursue one's career and realize one's dreams:

> that dream of a land in which life should be better and richer and fuller for every man, with opportunity for each according to his ability or achievement.... It is not a dream of motor cars and high wages merely, but a dream of a social order in which each man and each woman shall be able to attain the fullest stature of which they are innately capable, and be recognized by others for what they are, regardless of the fortuitous circumstances of birth or position.... It has been a dream of being able to grow to fullest development as man and woman, unhampered by the barriers which had slowly been erected in older civilizations, unrepressed by social orders which had developed for the benefit of classes rather than for the simple human being of any and every class.[7]

Previous research on career success in the arts, and in other economic sectors, has imputed success, and the American Dream, as commercial or economic success and status attainment. A few studies have inductively derived concepts of success and the American Dream but have not typologized meanings of success.[8]

I refer to a *success orientation* as a subjective benchmark by which workers pursue career mobility and gauge their career success. In my interviews with Nashville music professionals, I discerned their success orientations by asking them open-ended questions about their meanings of "success" and the "American Dream." A *threefold typology of success orientations* emerged from the dominant responses during my interviews (see figure 2.2).

In a reputational labor market, such as those in which freelance artists work, having *fame*, as in topping the musical charts, is, for many artists, an important market-based validation of their individual artistry.[9] For this songwriter, for example, having a number one song is an important indicator of success, professional reputation, and self-worth:

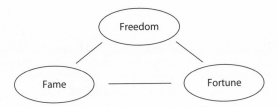

FIGURE 2.2. Typology of Success Orientations

That's what gets us up every day, honestly. It might sound like a vain goal, completely out of pride, but it's not. Whatever I do, whether it be an engineer, whether it be a songwriter, whether it be anything, I want to be the best at what I do, because if I'm not, that means I'm not working hard. It's my own, it's internal. It's not that I want people to think I'm the best, it's that I want to be as good as I can be. If I'm working my hardest and I'm still not good, I'm happy with that. I'll change professions. That number one song, that's the goal. That's success in my business. I want that, because if I don't get that, I kind of consider myself a failure, and I don't want to be a failure.

Success as *fortune* was typically linked to sustaining a comfortable material lifestyle. This musician envisions a pastoral getaway home in which he and his spouse are sufficiently financially secure to pursue their artistic interests:

My American dream would be to have about 100 vintage instruments that I'd be able to pick myself, to have them paid for, to have no bills and have a house paid for, have a really nice studio, have my wife not be able to work part-time, to have her just be able to focus on her art all the time, and to have a house in Maine that we can go to.... With a studio in it, of course.

Having the *freedom* to pursue one's own artistry was the most commonly expressed meaning of success by my interviewees. This senior saxophonist distinguished success as freedom from financial success:

I've been able to basically do what I wanted to do. There were times I did things I definitely didn't want to do because I was trying to bring the money in, pay the bills, but in a sense I've been able to make a living doing what I wanted to do and not have to really want ... I've retained what I think is a love and a passion for what I still love, I still enjoy doing it, still want to keep doing it. So in that sense yeah, that's been pretty successful. But I've known lots of people that made a lot more money and are miserable.

Audience Orientations

Pearl Jam vocalist Eddie Vedder's death-defying leaps into the audience during the 1990s affirmed the new, interactive artist-audience relationship. They also differed from the conventional and remote, institutional engagement of the audience by the artist, and from Howard Becker's characterization of the musician's attitude about the "square" audience as "hostile."[10] A sea change in the artist-audience relationship—the new mutually interactive one consisting of "co-authorship" and even "personal practice"—has accompanied and is a component of the emerging, self-promoting entrepreneurial indie art world.[11] For Becker, the audience is one of several external forces that compel changes in art-world conventions.[12] The new, mutually engaged artist-audience relationship compels a reconceptualization of an emerging entrepreneurial art world of popular music as one that increasingly internalizes the consumer as a co-authoring participant in the art-making process.

Research on artistic audiences rests on a distinction between the production and consumption of symbolic goods and tends to take an organization-centered and consumer-centered approach to the examination of audiences. Much of this research has examined the corporate fabrication of cultural markets and audiences, meaning and interpretation of art by art consumers, the impact of the socio-demographic characteristics of art consumers on their tastes and patterns of art consumption, and the development of consumptive social identities.[13]

In contrast, Bourdieu's fourfold typology of audiences aims to link producer and market and is based on a three-dimensional classification and comparison of late nineteenth-century French literary genres. The four audience types are: intellectual audience, bourgeois audience, mass audience, and no audience. These are based on a simultaneous classification of the genres by the consecration level (age) of the writer, the degree of economic autonomy of the genre, and the social hierarchy of consumers of the genre (intellectual, bourgeois, mass).[14]

I refer to an artist's *audience orientation* as the chief actor whom the artist intends to engage with her artistry. Indeed, artists enter a field with a mission to engage different audiences. For example, Lena and Cornfield found that immigrant artists strategically serve as co-ethnic community agents, either to preserve the traditional culture among assimilating, young co-ethnic consumers, to educate a hostile native community and prospective native consumers about their cultural traditions, or both.[15]

I discerned artist audience orientations from interviewee responses to open-ended questions about the importance the artist designated to having her music please any or all of several hypothetical music consumers, including the artist him- or herself, "fans," "other music professionals," "music executives," "family and friends," and whose recognition of the artist's artistry means the most to the interviewee. Almost all of the interviewees mentioned "other

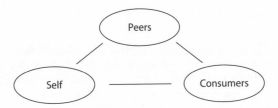

FIGURE 2.3. Typology of Audience Orientations

music professionals," and large majorities mentioned "fans" and "self." Only a minority mentioned "music executives" and "family and friends." The *threefold typology of audience orientations* derived from the Nashville music professionals consists of self, peers, and consumers (see figure 2.3).

This songwriter's response to the audience question illustrates a *self*-engagement with one's artistry: "If I don't like it, nobody else will. That is the number one rule. Because as soon as you start compromising what you think is good to try to please someone else, you write crap … it's all about satisfying yourself first. Everything else is secondary. Especially in a creative business." In contrast, this singer-songwriter expressed a strong engagement with the music *consumer*: "Well I guess that's the most important thing to me, is having people be able to connect with it.… My goal in making a piece of music [is] making a piece of music that can immediately grab people and make them want to keep listening to it, make them feel something basically from the minute that they hear it. That's kind of my goal in making songs and music."

For this senior recording artist-producer, *peer* recognition provides him with deep meaning, community, and gratification: "the peer group thing is just really strong. If you really like something that somebody else creates and you think they're really great at it, and if they turn around and tell you that they really like what you do, it really does make a difference. It makes you feel a part of a community, it makes you feel accepted, it makes you feel like you didn't make a bad move somewhere along the way."

The changing artist-audience relationship, especially from the artist's perspective, is an important distinguishing feature of the strategic orientations of two generations of artist activists. The two generations of enterprising artists—the transformative and contemporary generations—are profiled in chapters 3 and 4, respectively, and the two generations of arts trade union activists—the corporate and entrepreneurial generations, are profiled in chapter 6. The contemporary generations of enterprising artists and arts union activists harbor a more mutually engaged orientation toward fans and music consumers than that of the earlier and more senior generations, *with both generations of artist activists also sustaining a peer-centered strategic orientation including success as artistic freedom.*

RISK ORIENTATIONS AND ROLE ASSUMPTION

In reconstituting a community of artists in an increasingly individualistic music scene, an artist activist envisions a new community or institution that manages and minimizes the risk of joblessness inherent in the music scene. The artist activist's vision, in turn, reflects the artist activist's perception of the source of the risk of joblessness, or what I refer to as the artist activist's "risk orientation." Sources of risk range from the artist himself, to peers and gatekeepers, to technological and political-legal change and market forces in the music industry. The type of artist activist role assumed by the artist activist— enterprising artist, artistic social entrepreneur, and artist advocate—reflects the artist activist's risk orientation.

A sociology of worker risk-management action has emerged with the advent of "risky" post-bureaucratic employment relations and, more generally, the individualization of risk. Pioneering studies on worker risk-management action have addressed the career-mobility strategies and actions taken by post-bureaucratic, enterprising workers—"free agents" as Vicki Smith refers to them—who strive to minimize the risk of joblessness as they strategize and act to balance work and family and pursue upward career mobility.[16] Smith, for example, details the range of individual risk-management strategies that vary in their degree of proactivity, depending on the economic viability and opportunities for career mobility in the site of one's employment.[17]

The wide repertoire of individual *and* collective risk-management actions— acts of occupational self-determination—workers have taken as they build occupational communities have received less attention.[18] A robust repertoire of individual and collective risk-management actions is especially pronounced in self-determining, freelance occupations. These occupations include artistic occupations, many self-employed professionals, building trades, and other organized occupations whose members harbor a strong occupational peer-centered identity, may belong to occupational trade unions or professional associations, and who do project work.

Risk orientations are linked to the repertoire of individual and collective actions of artist activists. I refer to a *risk orientation* as a cognitive frame by which a worker comprehends and identifies the *source* of the risk of joblessness, whether in himself, in his interpersonal interactions with peers and gatekeepers, or in impersonal market and industry conditions.

Pioneering research on the unemployed during the Great Depression of the 1930s suggested that a range of individual and collective worker risk-management actions—such as accumulating personal savings, entrepreneurship, unionization, political action—were linked to their risk orientations. For Warner and Low, the 1933 shoe factory workers' strike in Yankee City constituted a collective effort taken by ordinarily inert, individualistic workers, aimed at the forces to which they attributed the decline in their livelihoods, in order to regain control over their social mobility chances.[19] Similarly, in his field research on 200 New Haven families who were unemployed in 1933, Bakke

FIGURE 2.4. Typology of Risk Orientations

uncovered a set of personal forces, such as employers, and impersonal "hazards for earners," such as mechanization, to which workers attributed joblessness and economic insecurity and that they therefore endeavored to control.[20]

From my interviews with Nashville music professionals, I discerned a *threefold typology of artist risk orientations* that surfaced during my open-ended discussions about the interviewee's career-biography and her or his assessment of trends in employment opportunities in the Nashville music industry. Each of the three types of risk orientation emphasizes the chief *risk factor*—that is, a source of risk—to which an arts professional attributes the risk of joblessness, as shown in figure 2.4. First, *personal risk factors* constitute a "personal risk orientation" in which an artist locates the risk of joblessness in herself. The artist attributes the risk of joblessness to factors that originate in the individual's personal life and individual actions, such as aging and poor health, family stressors, and erring in one's strategy toward networking, that influence a worker's availability to participate in the labor market. For example, this songwriter regrets not having deployed a more aggressive co-writing strategy earlier in his career:

Respondent: I wasn't really making use of making contacts and really being out there and doing that kind of stuff.

Interviewer: [Y]ou mean pushing the next song, or pushing the song to say there's more where this came from type of thing?

R: Yes. Using my success to get in with the bigger writers here who are really getting the cuts. That's the regret, that had I been around more I probably could have done a lot more of that. So that opportunity kind of faded away a little bit, and then just because the nature of who I am I lost confidence and didn't really pursue it.

Second, interpersonal risk factors pertain to the openness and social closure of an artist's relationships and networks with peers and gatekeepers. Risks of inclusion and exclusion in artistic projects arise in the course of networking and working among peers and employment gatekeepers. *Interpersonal risk factors* originate in these interpersonal social interactions and constitute an *interpersonal risk orientation*. Interpersonal risk factors include entry barriers, such as nepotism and discrimination, and precarious employment relations and contractual instability arising from adverse social relationships among collaborators and uncertainty in decision making by music companies. Interviewees often referred to social closure in peer networks by the artist's region of origin, race, gender, age, college music program, and musical genre.

Interpersonal risk factors play an important role in artist discovery at music showcases. The following story illustrates the influence of interpersonal risk factors in the discovery of an artist who would go on to have a multi-platinum career. A senior, award-winning record producer shared with me the story of how elite major-label executives, the producer, an artist, and an audience of peers led to the artist's signing a record deal with one major label and not with the other major label represented at a Nashville music showcase:

> I had gotten [music executive A] to commit to coming over and ... some friends of ours, and other A&R people at the label, and then to hedge my bets I also invited [music executive B] who was at [another major label] at the time and he brought a couple of his folks with him. We did our show, our 10 songs, and the place was packed because [the artist] knew so many songwriters from doing demos and everybody loved [the artist]. We packed the place out and we both just got all of our friends to come and it was great, and people just went wild. So there's [music executive B] and [music executive A] sitting there kind of looking around and going there's something going on here. And [music executive A] was reserved, he was kind of holding back, he was like yeah, maybe a demo deal, the musical direction I'm not so sure about yet. On the other side of that talking to [music executive B] after it he's like where'd you get those songs, those are amazing. He said [the artist] sounds like radio, [the artist] is ready. So he couldn't have been more excited. Ultimately we signed with [music executive B]'s company and the rest is history.

Third, *impersonal risk factors* attribute the risk of joblessness to market, technological, and industry structural factors that influence the volume of employment opportunity, such as the business cycle, technological change, and industry restructuring. An *impersonal risk orientation* is comprised of impersonal risk factors. For example, this enterprising audio engineer described a long-term cyclical pattern of market fluctuations that influence self-employment opportunities:

> [T]he music business is like any other business, so ... it's a supply and demand that you ... kind of have to fit within. And, there is the opportunity. The only thing I would say about it is when I moved here [Nashville] in the 80s there was this big growth and even into the late 90s. It was as if anything goes.... Over the last 10 years that's tapered off and it has been just like every other aspect of the economy and it just has sort of filtered down to the point where you have to really have a plan.

Illegal downloading of music over the Internet was frequently mentioned as a source of economic and employment insecurity in the music industry. For this songwriter, Internet-based illegal downloading is reflected in the music property real estate signs along the main avenues of Nashville's fabled "Music Row":

> The Internet is the main reason why you see so many "For Sale" signs and "Vacancy" signs up and down 16th and 17th Avenues. The whole downloading killed us. It's a lot more under control now, but we're still recovering. I forget the statistics, but six or seven years ago I think the music industry as a whole lost ... like 30 to 40% of their income. That's millions and millions of dollars. It was free downloading. So many people lost their jobs because of it.

In sum, the type of artist activist role assumed by the artist activist—enterprising artist, artistic social entrepreneur, and artist advocate—ranges between individual and collective risk-management strategies, respectively. The three artist activist roles also reflect the range of artistic risk orientations. Enterprising artists harbor a personal risk orientation for encouraging individual artistic expression in micro-communities. The artistic social entrepreneur harbors an interpersonal risk orientation for devising stable and inclusive social enterprises and creative social spaces. The artist advocate harbors an impersonal risk orientation for advancing the collective economic interests of the whole occupation. *An artist activist, then, assumes an artist activist role, and envisions a new community or institution, that addresses the risk factors that make up her risk orientation.*

SOURCES OF CAREER INSPIRATION AND ROLE ENACTMENT

In enacting a role as artist activist, each Nashville music professional I interviewed performed an array of artistic and art-support functions. In Becker's art world, participants specialize in performing a wide range of what he calls "artistic" and "support" functions. Artistic functions, performed by artists themselves, pertain to conceiving and making the art object and performance. Support functions, performed by art-support workers, include displaying and distributing the art, producing art-making tools and providing studio space, providing critiques of performances, legitimizing and promoting the genre, and protecting freedom of expression.[21]

In this enterprising era of occupational generalism, however, each Nashville artist activist performed both artistic and support functions. Artistic functions advanced individual artistic expression of self and peers, while support functions advanced the art-making capacity and well-being of the occupation of Nashville musicians and songwriters.

Table 1. Types of Artist Activists by Role and Role Enactment

	ARTIST ACTIVIST ROLE		
TYPE OF ENACTMENT	ENTERPRISING ARTIST	SOCIAL ENTREPRENEUR	ARTIST ADVOCATE
Artistic	Artist leader of self-contained band	Portfolio entrepreneur	Union leader obtains contracts for musicians
Supportive	Artist-producer of other artists	Organizational entrepreneur	Union leader promotes labor solidarity within union

Nonetheless, regardless of which of the three roles an artist activist assumed, the artist activist enacted her or his role with a blend of artistic and support functions, as shown in table 1. Occupational examples of artist activists whose role enactment emphasized artistic functions over support functions—what I refer to as *artistic enactment*—are shown in the top row of table 1. Occupational examples of artist activists who emphasized support functions over artistic functions—*supportive enactment*—are shown in the bottom row of table 1.

From my interviews with Nashville music professionals, I discerned a patterned relationship between an individual's self-proclaimed source of original career inspiration and how an artist activist enacted—artistic or supportive enactment—his role as an artist activist. Generally, musicians are inspired to embark on a musical career in their childhood and adolescence by multiple social and cultural factors, such as family, school, teachers, religion, peers, and the popular culture of their adolescence.[22] From a "family-embeddedness" theoretical perspective, the family and other social factors inspire and empower creative individuals to embark on enterprising artistic careers by providing them with personal resources, knowledge, and capital.[23]

The Nashville music professionals I interviewed tended to highlight two sources of their original inspiration for embarking on a musical career—either family or the cultural movement of their adolescence. In response to my open-ended question, "Who and what inspired you to embark on a career in music?" almost all of the interviewees unhesitatingly identified their family or the popular-cultural movement of their adolescence as the primary original source of their career inspiration. I refer to a *family-inspired* musician as one who claims his family as the primary source of the musician's career inspiration, and a *movement-inspired* musician as one whose primary career inspiration is the cultural movement of the musician's adolescence.

For family-inspired musicians, listening to and playing music with family members during childhood and adolescence often unified and strengthened the bonds among family members. Jerome,[24] a family-inspired musician-producer-label owner, recounted the profound influence of multiple generations of his family on his becoming a musician:

I think my grandmother is kind of the fountain from which we all flow. She played organ and piano at our church for 15 years, as well as taught in the public school system for 34 years ... And I can remember as a kid going to sleep and hearing her playing Debussy at the piano, and waking up in the morning for school and she would be finishing practicing, just a really beautiful work ethic that didn't seem so much like work for her as just a labor of love. My other early memory is of Bob ... he was ... a cousin of ours and he played organ ... Bob ... I do remember in that role as the organ player at the church. Just an amazing musician. He taught jazz over at [a university] and then played gospel organ every Sunday, and his musicianship, I've yet to meet a piano player that I really think was as profound a musician in a lot of ways. So those two early on.

Also, Jerome's father infused a politicized social meaning of music in his childhood household:

My dad is really a kid from [Southern city] and loves the blues, loves his dashikis, and at the point where there was a real mission to reconnect with the African sense of heritage, my dad was very much a part of that ... I think, where in the house that my mom grew up in, my grandmother's jazz tastes were Duke Ellington and Count Basie, and then my dad's musical tastes, which are always kind of political in certain ways.... And I think jazz in a lot of ways kind of allowed them to meet in the middle because my mom had a respect for the musicianship and for the craft, and my dad has a respect for the creativity of the genre and the possibilities.

Having a musical career enables Jerome to express his family legacy. Jerome told me that during his "freshman year [in college], both of my dad's parents passed away and Bob ... was 54 at the time, which seemed very young, passed away. All in the same 3½ months. I think I found a purpose in music."

In contrast, movement-inspired musicians are often whisked away from their families by the cultural and political movements of their adolescence into music careers, often over their parents' objections to their career choice. In the biography of a new musician, playing music in a band is collaboration in the cultural and political expression of the historical moment that coincides with the musician's adolescence and young adulthood.

Barry,[25] a movement-inspired musician-producer, for example, was originally swept up by the racially integrationist music and political movement of the 1960s:

Well, being of the age and coming out of music in the '60s from when I was a teenager, it's hard to pinpoint one particular thing. So many of us back then that are doing what we do now started as musicians and were inspired by the music that we loved back then. For me a lot of it was black music, Motown music, James Brown and then obviously the Beatles when they came along. It was just such an exciting time for music that it was very invigorating and there was a lot of satisfaction in just playing music, and playing that kind of music.... My own personal story, after I'd gone away to college and then I started a job as an actuary, and then left town, I quit that job and left town with my band. Of course my parents were devastated because even as I was playing in bands and supporting myself and putting myself through college I didn't think that I'd really necessarily have a music career ... The inspiration just came out of the love of music.

Barry's immersion in music was intertwined with integrationist race politics of the 1960s:

I did not participate in any of the organized school bands. In high school I played in a few bands, and then my primary thing that really launched, got me going, was just out of high school when I got into this band that was like a soul review, and this was [Midwestern City] in 1966, 1967, and then we got our first black guy in the band, the first black singer. We became this mixed band, the first of its kind in the Midwest.... A lot of stories about that, being a black/white band, it was really interesting.

The Midwestern City of Barry's adolescence struggled with racial integration. Barry's racially mixed band was on the vanguard of advancing racial integration in his hometown, but interracial fights in the audience were known to break out at the live venues where Barry's band performed:

Well, our band ... brought together the black and white youth that had never been together.... There was [sic] a lot of interracial mixtures that happened, specially with white girls and black guys that the white guys resented just terribly, and it led to some rather drastic results. There were a few fights I remember, the worst of which, we used to play at this one teen club.... One night it was just packed, it probably held about 200 or 300 kids. We were playing and all of a sudden I see everybody falling over ... well there was a big race fight and somebody got stabbed, nobody got killed, somebody got shot at later, and unfortunately it closed down this club and we lost our main place to play.... So it was big growing pains for the interracial community in [Midwestern City] at the time and we really played a part of it. It was a big part of it, and a lot of memories, that even people I still talk to in [Midwestern City], it goes back to that time.

A *twofold typology of inspired career pathways* that artists would take in becoming artist activists emerged from my interviews. These pathways are consistent with Aldrich and Cliff's "family embeddedness perspective"[26] of entrepreneurship and ethnomusicologist Paul Berliner's description of the complex of family, cultural, and early-career influences on the professional formation of jazz musicians.[27] Following Kathleen Blee's concept of grassroots activism as a path-dependent sequence, I conceive of a *pathway* toward becoming an artist activist as "human actions ... that move through social institutions or *projects*. As people travel through society, they are continually confronted with new influences, information, and feelings that lead them toward certain actions.... They still make choices, but these are constrained by the earlier decisions."[28] Family-inspired artists embarked on what I refer to as "family-inspired pathways," and movement-inspired artists embarked on "movement-inspired pathways."

How an artist activist enacts her artist activist role is linked to the social meaning of music they internalized during their childhood and adolescence. According to Blee, culture as meaning-making "is central to activism because activist groups are more than vehicles through which people assert political claims in public life and gain political advantage. They also are venues in which people work collectively to understand their world, decide what is just or unjust, and express their values."[29]

As the retrospective cases of Jerome and Barry suggest, an individual's source of original career inspiration instills a social meaning of music in the artist that partly orients him along a career pathway. For family-inspired Jerome, music was a source of family togetherness, continuity, and community; for movement-inspired Barry, music was a medium for personal growth and cultural expression for his age generation, independent of his family. The sixteen cases of artist activists profiled in chapters 3 through 6 suggest that those whose careers unfolded along family-inspired pathways tended to engage in supportive role enactment; whereas those on movement-inspired career pathways tended to engage in artistic role enactment. This patterned relationship between source of original career inspiration and type of role enactment suggests that artist activists develop a social meaning of music that informs how they interact with their peer community: *those on family-inspired career pathways develop a communal meaning of music that informs a supportive enactment of their artist activist roles; those on movement-inspired pathways develop a culturally expressive meaning of music that informs an artistic enactment of their artist activist roles.*

TOWARD A SOCIOLOGICAL THEORY OF ARTIST ACTIVISM

In our era of "indie" music-making and risk individualization, artist activists in the Nashville music scene are reconstituting an occupational peer community for themselves and their peers. The artist activists have arrayed themselves across the local scene in three roles that range between individual and collective strategies for change, respectively: enterprising artist, artistic social entrepreneur, and artist advocate. A sociological theory of artist activism deepens our understanding of how a group of artistic peers re-socialize risk by reconstituting

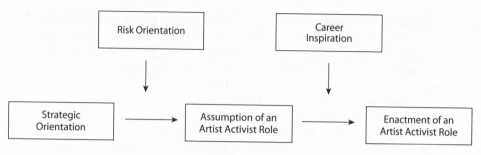

FIGURE 2.5. A Sociological Theory of Artist Activism

themselves as a solidified, occupational peer community. The sociological theory of artist activism developed here addresses how an artist activist's subjective orientation toward success, audience, risk, and career inspiration shapes one's assumption and enactment of the three artist activist roles. Note that these roles are ideal types—in daily life, an artist activist may simultaneously assume and enact any or all of the artist activist roles. The theory is summarized in figure 2.5.

The *sociological theory of artist activism* seeks to explain variations in an individual's assumption and enactment of any or all of the three artist activist roles. Each role is a vehicle for implementing the artist activist's envisioned, community-building initiative. The initiative, in turn, is the artist activist's project for re-socializing and minimizing the risk of joblessness for himself and his peers.

The theory consists of the typology of artist activists in table 1 and three propositions that attribute the artist activist's assumption and enactment of her role to the artist's strategic orientation, risk orientation, and original source of career inspiration. An artist's strategic orientation distinguishes the artist activist from her peers in the artist community. *The first proposition is that members of an artist peer community whose strategic orientations conceive of success as artistic freedom, and audience as their peers, are most likely to become artist activists in their peer community.*

Artist activists distinguish themselves from one another by the artist activist role each assumes. Role assumption is the artist activist's selection of an approach to re-socializing and minimizing risk that counteracts a specific set of personal, interpersonal, or impersonal risk factors that he believes may threaten livelihoods in the peer community. Therefore, role assumption is shaped by the artist activist's risk orientation. *The second proposition is that artist activists of a peer community who harbor*

1. *personal risk orientations are most likely to become enterprising artists;*
2. *interpersonal risk orientations are most likely to become artistic social entrepreneurs; and*
3. *impersonal risk orientations are most likely to become artist advocates.*

Artist activists enact their roles by encouraging artistic expression or by sustaining social relationships for mutual support in professional development and advocacy among peers. How an artist activist enacts her role—artistic or supportive enactment—depends on the social meaning the artist activist gives to music. The social meaning given to music, in turn, is linked to the artist activist's original source of career inspiration. Family-inspired artist activists internalized a communal social meaning of music; movement-inspired artist activists internalized a culturally expressive social meaning of music. *Therefore, the third proposition is that family-inspired artist activists are most likely to engage in supportive role enactment and movement-inspired artist activists are most likely to engage in artistic role enactment.*

We turn now to the sixteen cases of artist activists whose actions are reconstituting peer community among Nashville musicians. They illustrate how variations in their orientations toward success, audience, risk, and career inspiration influence their assumption and enactment of roles as artist activists and the community-building initiatives they envision. Two generations of enterprising artists—the transformative and contemporary generations—are profiled in chapters 3 and 4, respectively; artistic social entrepreneurs in chapter 5; and artist advocates in chapter 6.

CHAPTER 3

Self-contained, Self-expression

The Transformative Generation of Enterprising Artists

Michael Hann, music editor for the *Guardian*, recently observed that many of Nashville's contemporary, indie rock bands have emerged with the encouragement of an earlier generation of enterprising Nashville artists who had shaken up the major-label paradigm of music production. Robert Ellis Orrall, for example, the Nashville-based, major-label rock artist, producer, and award-winning songwriter, founded the influential indie label Infinity Cat[1] and has recorded many of Nashville's contemporary underground bands, including Jeff the Brotherhood, formed in 2001 by his sons Jake and Jamin.[2] Chris Talbott of the Associated Press concurs, noting in the *Huffington Post* that "the Orralls run Infinity Cat Records with their dad, Bob, who also was an early Taylor Swift producer and songwriting partner. Like Swift, he's helped nurture the local scene—almost literally. The label has put out 74 releases in its 10 years and many on the roster are childhood friends of his sons."[3]

This chapter examines the subjective orientations and pathways of an earlier generation of Nashville artists who helped shape the community of Nashville's increasingly entrepreneurial, popular-music musicians. Sociologically, this chapter depicts the subjective orientations toward success, audience, and risk and the career pathways taken by four individual representatives of what I refer to as the *transformative generation of enterprising artists* of the changing Nashville music scene. They are "transformative" in their roles as artist activists in an intergenerational process of re-creating musician community in the Nashville music scene.

An enterprising artist is the most "individualistic" artist activist in the threefold typology of artist activists who are theorized in chapter 2. The enterprising artist is individualistic in that his community-building action expresses his own artistry and is directed at enhancing the artistry of individual fellow artists. In contrast to the specialized recording musician and solo artist, an *enterprising artist* is an occupational generalist who performs both artistic and support tasks in making art. In the era of the self-contained band, the enterprising artist may be a band member who also leads, manages, records, produces, promotes, writes, composes, and/or arranges for his band or for other artists and bands independent of a major label.

As an artist activist engaged primarily in individual action, the enterprising artist thrives on self-expression, continuous self-instruction in a widening skill

34

portfolio of artistic and support functions, self-promotion, and on maintaining mutually beneficial relations with colleagues. Enterprising artists sustain their ongoing relations with colleagues, as the profiles in this chapter show, by maintaining trusting and equitable, collegial relations, relations that may succumb to interpersonal animosity, rivalry, jealousy, and betrayal.

Throughout the 1980s and 1990s, Nashville attracted musicians whose careers unfolded in this growing and diversifying music scene. By 2004, Nashville had the third highest concentration of musicians, after New York and Los Angeles, and it had come to assume the status of the U.S. city with the highest concentration of music business establishments, such as record labels, distributors, recording studios, and music publishers.[4] The increasing concentration of musicians in Nashville has been attributed to the growing popularity of country music; periodic recessionary slumps in the Los Angeles recording industry that generated musician exodus to other national music scenes; Nashville's affordable cost of living; increasing coastal major-label interest and investment in Nashville's technological infrastructure and artist development; increasing musician wage scales; the rise of a vital sector of independent music labels and artists; and, not least of all, the presence of a talent pool of world-class songwriters and studio musicians. Award-winning songwriter Michael Kosser, in his astute analysis of the Nashville music industry, partly attributes Music City's rise to national music prominence to the work of music executive Jimmy Bowen who, during his 1977–95 stint in Nashville, encouraged the digitalization of music-production technology, raised the wages of recording musicians, and developed artists whose crossover music appealed to an expanding range of music consumers. So great was Bowen's impact on Nashville's transformation, according to Kosser, that "[t]he history of modern country music is now divided into two separate eras, B.B. and A.B.: *Before Bowen* and *After Bowen*."[5]

Nashville's genre diversification was accompanied by a restructuring of music production and distribution. Increasingly, enterprising artists themselves assumed the risk of music production and distribution and seized opportunities for their own artistic self-expression with the reduction of major-label artist rosters accompanying the consolidation of the major labels, radio airplay, and mass retail; the deterioration of the music economy from illegal downloading and economic recessions; and the differentiation of music consumers into niche genre markets. Enterprising artists implemented the restructuring by incorporating a rock model of self-contained bands into the Nashville music recording industry. The incorporation of the self-contained band into Nashville was facilitated by the advent of home-production music technology and social media for music distribution. These technological changes, however, succeeded the changes in consumer tastes and the "anti-establishment" political and cultural attitudes of the enterprising artists who drove the restructuring of Nashville music production during the 1980s and 1990s.

Inspired by the folk/blues revival, R & B, and rock cultural movements of the 1960s and 1970s, the four artists profiled in this chapter are white, male self-trained professionals who launched their careers during this time period of their late adolescence and early adulthood, and subsequently created, enacted, and incorporated the role of enterprising artist into the Nashville music scene. They took one of two career pathways. They either launched their careers in Nashville in the commercial country music industry, or they arrived mid-career in Nashville from Los Angeles and other music scenes as enterprising artists already associated and experienced with self-contained pop and rock bands. They created, assumed, and enacted the role of enterprising artist with their own bands or by working with others' bands and other artists.

Notwithstanding the different pathways and roles these enterprising artists took on, the four profiled members of the transformative generation share three features of their orientation toward making music and musician community-building. First, in strategic terms, they conceive of success as achieving the creative capacity for self-satisfying, artistic self-expression that sustains themselves and their families economically through a direct engagement with their fans, the music consumer. Second, they harbor an individualistic risk orientation grounded in personal risk factors such as individual creative competence based in self-instruction and motivation and in interpersonal risk factors such as loyalty and friendship with immediate collaborators. Third, they took movement-inspired career pathways in that they attributed their original inspiration for embarking on their musical careers to the anti-establishment musical movements of their adolescence.

Each profile consists of the artist's vision of an enterprising artist, his strategic orientation, and his career pathway.[6] I first profile Martin and Jerry, whose careers began in Nashville commercial country music, and then turn to James and Doug, who imported the role of enterprising artist from LA with their mid-career arrival in Nashville around 1990.

STARTING OFF IN NASHVILLE

Martin

An enterprising artist of the transformative generation, Martin is a "partner" and musician in an award-winning, self-contained, commercial country band. Martin arrived in Nashville at the start of his career in the 1970s; his subsequent market and entrepreneurial success in developing the band helped to transform a Nashville country music scene based in major labels and individual artists into an organizationally diverse scene of corporate and independent recording artists. Although the band achieved market success in the context of major-label recording, its image as a group exuded an awkwardness at music industry award ceremonies that emphasized images of solo, corporate-sponsored recording artists, as Martin described:

As a recording act we constantly were up against the obstacle of being a band and there was a bias against bands because when it comes to performances on award shows, when it comes to performances on TV, when it comes to interviews and stuff like that, whether it's print or TV, it's [several] people ..., photos, any of that type of stuff, stacking this to make it visually look well on camera.... An awards show will only have performance by one, maybe two bands, and everything else will be male vocalists and female vocalists. So if you're not the one or two bands, well you're not getting a performance on the show, which speaks directly to sales.

In order to overcome the awkwardness of being recognized in what was a public display of mainly solo artists, the band was compelled to select one band member to represent the band.

Vision of an Enterprising Artist

When I asked him about his current line of work, Martin mentioned that he wore "lots of hats": musician, business partner, recording artist, songwriter, publisher, producer, engineer, swag marketer, and teacher. He performs most of these roles for his band, which, in recent years, has been recording in a band member's home, and for himself.

As a partner in a band, he characterized the constant give-and-take between self and group as a "nasty democracy." The band "goes through all kinds of career decisions, creative decisions, song selection, employee decisions, and it's a really good thing to share success with guys, it's tough to share decisions. It's like walking through partly hardened concrete sometimes just getting the decision done. But that's the way we've always done it, and it works for us." As a band member, Martin feels that the open and casual environment of home recording, unlike the impersonal, structured, and walled environment of a large commercial studio, allows for spontaneous and creative artistic expression by the band:

the stuff that we are recording [in a home studio] is unbelievable, it's really great. I think it's all about the fact that it's not big and there's not any walls around us. There's a vocal booth [for the singer], but there's no other walls, we're all sitting in the same environment like we're at a jam session, which makes it less formal and you feel like musicians and not like we're making something.

As a musician with his signature playing style, Martin instructs celebrities and emerging artists, often in bartered, mutual mentoring relationships, in the development of their own signature playing styles.

Martin's commercial success through country radio airplay has released him from the corporate production formula, affording him and the band an increasing measure of artistic independence. The band's commercial success had rested on its strict adherence to the norms of commercial production. In recent years, the band has made fewer artistic compromises and increasingly records music that reflects their own tastes:

So we have compromised with some material and with the length, things don't need to be much over 3 minutes long because we're selling so many ad blocks per half hour at radio and we're doing these types of things. So yeah, we've made compromises.... So now we don't care. We have material that we are recording now that has been pitched to us or written by us before that we would not record that we are recording because we want to, and it's great material.

In addition, the band's business model of home production of music that pleases the band has, according to Martin, become economically more viable than studio-produced music for radio airplay: "I know we're going to be able to sell 500,000 and if actually we're making the money on 500,000 we'll make more money than we've ever made off of album sales. We could have what could be considered a numbers failure by Music Row and be going, 'we've never seen money like this before.'" Martin acknowledged that working as a generalist on both the creative and business sides of music production is a relatively new development in Nashville, compared to Los Angeles, and is challenging for a musician who had matured in the context of major labels and musician specialists. He explained:

As far as being a professional in the [Nashville] music business, you can be a specialist, you can be a songwriter, a record producer, a singer, a studio musician, this is just the creative side. In Los Angeles you need to be the artist, the producer, the choreographer, the songwriter, you need to have this whole thing that's so packaged and there's great talent out there, but it's not a super organic thing. So it can be a little more formulaic, but it's much more of a one man thing. I've [hypothetical Los Angeles artist] got a studio at home, I sing these songs, I write these songs, I do this, I'm going to be the next greatest pop star type of thing. Where here [Nashville] you've got this guy owns the recording studio, this guy is the musician, this guy is the songwriter, this guy is the plugger, and they're specialists.

A lifelong union member, Martin finds the performance rights organizations more helpful than the union. The band's performances are union acts, but Martin grudgingly remains a union member "because you can't work unless you are a member," opining that the union has been ineffective in setting scales for musicians and in generating employment opportunities. Furthermore, at the time I interviewed Martin, the union lacked a health insurance program for its members, and Martin's band, as a company, maintained its own costly group health insurance plan for the band members. Also a song-writer and publisher, Martin was pleased with the advocacy provided by the performance rights organization (PRO) with which he was affiliated. Referring to another PRO, the one whose songwriters' work the band has recorded, Martin stated: "they've been friendly to us. We need a party for one of their songwriters, they'll foot the bill and all that stuff."

Strategic Orientation

Martin's pursuit of success is focused on making a living at being creative. His pursuit is grounded in self-determination through continuous self-learning, remaining close to the song, gaining the respect and admiration from his peers and family, engaging the fans, and networking with collaborators. Martin has been successful in that he is able to sustain himself economically through his own creativity:

> My thing about success is being able to find an avenue that is stimulating and creative and ... that will generate some income. If I could make less money and be more satisfied I'd do it anytime. And I'm not super caught up with my perception of success. Do I really care? Maybe a little bit how people view me, but does it make me any happier? Not usually.

A self-trained musician, Martin continuously broadens his occupational skill portfolio through self-instruction. He expanded the range of his occupational skill portfolio from the base of his artistic pursuit of songwriting. By networking with colleagues and specialists, Martin mastered artistic support tasks as he transitioned from specialist toward generalist. Beginning in the late 1990s, he embraced and mastered the new home production technology, effectively adding the engineer occupational "hat" to the rack of several hats he wears. He acknowledged that the new music-production technologies have displaced many musicians, but he mastered the new technologies in order to increase his own productivity and actualize his artistry:

> I had to learn the technology, I had to spend the money and do that type of stuff ... that was a big learning curve. However, I was passionate about it and I knew once I learned that I would love it, and it was great. I like to do physical fitness, so the manual for this ProTools, which is the industry standard for hard disk recording, it's a good 700 or 800 pages. So I'd get on the treadmill every morning, and my technique was to spend a little time with the machine just kind of ramming and jamming and being rough with the program, and then spending another 45 minutes or an hour reading the manual, and then also sitting down with the manual and the machine and applying things I learned. But I've got it, I'm a ProTools guy, I can do some damage. So we set up my [home] studio.... Okay, for a studio design and for homes, one of the things is sound travels,

bass frequencies travel, sound waves travel, and they travel through things that they touch and they hit.... And that's usually what would affect my family, and that's the noise they would do that would affect me. And how do you do that? You get things that don't touch. It's actually in the center of my house in the downstairs, there's its own concrete slab that's poured that doesn't touch the rest of the house, and the walls are built on that, and the ceiling is built on it, and it's got its own ductwork and own things. So it's an isolated environment and it works great for my family.... I don't hear them and they don't hear us. It's perfect.

Although recognition from his peers—his fellow music professionals—matters most to him, engaging the fans is hardly an afterthought. Direct audience engagement—over his life course and that of his fans—figures prominently in Martin's business model for achieving a self-sustaining, creative life. Throughout his career, his audience has transitioned from teenagers to families:

It seems like when we were younger, and maybe this is marketing and maybe this is the latest and greatest thing, but when we were younger we had screaming teenagers and right now we have an incredibly diverse age range. You could be looking out there and see grandpa and grandma bringing grandson and granddaughter to the show, and their sons, and it seems very family-oriented. I see a lot of whole families and couples. I don't see individual guys getting together because this is the hot concert or a pack of girls, I see family groups and couples.

Pathway

A self-described "Christian" and political "conservative," Martin took a movement-inspired pathway in commercial country music toward becoming a free agent. The son of an engineer and homemaker, he moved from Midwestern City to Nashville in the late 1970s in order to launch a career as a studio musician. Music did not permeate the household of his youth, but Martin's father had played the tenor guitar as a hobby and encouraged his son to pick up the banjo. Martin became smitten with the banjo and trained himself to become an accomplished banjo player. Inspired by Earl Scruggs and bluegrass music, Martin's passion for the banjo carried him to Nashville, where he soon discovered that the banjo would not launch him on a lucrative career in music:

I would say that when I moved to Nashville my principal instrument was banjo. When I got here just nobody really cared. You'd think banjo, Nashville, country music, but it's just not a money maker ... well you know banjo is hot now, after I spent 23 years trying to hide that, and it's now hot again and it's one of the integral parts of certain contemporary acts.... So yeah, it's all cyclical.

Although he was not a fan of commercial country music, Martin felt compelled to find an optimal tradeoff between art and commerce in that genre:

> I love a lot of music, but I've always been drawn to bluegrass and to swing.... So it's usually things around that, and traditionally not commercial music forms. I've just never been drawn to what's on the radio. However, I've made a career of being on the radio, so it's been an interesting thing to where I can still be creative, do my creative thing however under the rules of what's going to generate income.

As he immersed himself in the commercial country music scene as a performer on the road and in Nashville show bands and as a session recording musician, Martin fell in with a band in formation that would become an award-winning and commercially successful band, and he has remained with them for more than two decades.

Martin's transition from performer-session musician to recording artist entailed self-discovery of his own voice. Soon after his arrival in Nashville, he was advised by his confidant, a renowned music professional some ten years older than he, to find his own voice. His confidant not only mentored him but also referred him to jobs to help Martin break in:

> He's the guy that kept on talking to me about, saw me develop as a musician, and a guy who had chops and I could play but was not finding the individual, and he was the one who kept talking to me about okay, now what you need to do is you need to find your own voice and you need to do the thing that is unique that other guys aren't doing, take your good technique and figure out how to play it like yourself. Not just transcribe everything else and play it. And so that was really important to my development.

And, working as a session musician revealed to Martin his desire to develop and express his own artistry. Looking back, Martin reflected:

> As it turns out being a session player and being able to make enough money to make a living isn't all that desirable because the guys that are super, super individual, you cannot be an individual on this record and then the next record on the radio be the same guy. You have to be a little bit more like a chameleon, and a little bit more like a journeyman player, and be much more rounded and what I was doing was I was taking all these different styles and I was going the opposite direction of having this one voice. And so where I was headed was I needed to be a recording act,

and I needed to be making records for myself, for my band, for one person. Everything that I was working for was not to be doing what I thought I wanted to do, and that was making records for a lot of people.

Roughly six years into his Nashville stint, Martin seized the opportunity to help launch a band that would set out to get a record deal on a major label to record its own work. He had been performing live in Nashville with a show band. At the last session of the season, the show band members decided to become recording artists and invited Martin to join them. Having signed with a major label, the band had their first hit one year later. They would remain with the same label, enjoying significant commercial success, for almost fifteen years.

A quarter-century after Martin's arrival in Nashville, the band broke from the label and became home-producing free agents. They were now playing for themselves and their fans, as Martin explained:

We're free agents, and we're like let's record some catalog. I grew up playing bluegrass music, as did [other band members], so we're recording a bluegrass record as well as a contemporary country record, and I think we've got plans, we've started a Christmas record, anyway there's about five projects that we're recording and we're recording them all at the same time. So we'll do a bluegrass song and then we'll do a Christmas song, and then we'll do … this beautiful country ballad. And it feels like you've washed your palate every time you play a different style of music. I think that's also some of … what's making this stuff sound inspired.

Jerry

Jerry exited the major-label commercial country world in a huff. Having worked his way up from musician, to staff songwriter, to a successful producer and then VP in a major label over a thirty-year period, Jerry left the label in the recessionary early 2000s and established his own, independent publishing and music production company. His initial transition during the 1990s to becoming a major-label VP would soon frustrate him and later compel him to strike out on his own:

As soon as I got over there [major label] they got bought by another company … and they took away all the car allowance and all the stuff from every one of their executives … But the worst part of being over there, there was some good stuff, first of all you've really got this power thing and so now I'm a producer and a hit songwriter, I'm this happening music guy in town, I don't know if I really see myself that way but I'm kind of getting cocky.... And people need you so all of a sudden, everybody likes you. It was the first time I'd ever experienced that, and it's a heady experience and it's also hard to deal with in some ways. But when I got to [major label], there's about five or ten people on top of me in the pecking order in the corporation that these guys, the budget guys and the other, it seems like their entire job is to make certain that I can't do my job. So you know they hire me to be creative and to do all this stuff that I'd been doing on my own quite well, to bring in talent, to sign people, and I did some of that, I signed some huge hit writers that are still rolling real well today and was responsible for a lot of that, but everything I had to do you have to justify in a corporation and I hated that. Hated it.

During a life-navigational conversation with a sagacious friend in the early 2000s, Jerry, a self-proclaimed "gun-toting Democrat" and "populist," confessed his immense frustration with corporate risk aversion and budgetary constraints on his artistic expression and came to the realization that establishing his own company would free him to express himself artistically:

I hate corporations, I mean I really hate them ... [my friend] said why don't you just do what you do the very best and be a publisher, which I'd never been. So I thought about it and thought about it and I said you know what, you're right.... If I want to do something, I can do it, I can just make a decision and do things. There's nobody up there to tell me what not to do, I can make mistakes, I can do whatever, I can sign people that I want to sign, I've got a great money partner who doesn't question anything, and we're going to expand and we're going to try to expand in ways we believe the music business is going.

Vision of an Enterprising Artist

In establishing his own publishing company, Jerry not only fled the corporate music world. He pursued a vision of a publishing company as an economically viable vehicle for promoting his own artistry and songwriting and nurturing young songwriters. As he put it: "I run a publishing company ... and it also has a production arm ... we also produce records and I write songs. So basically I've done the same thing since I moved to Nashville in different capacities. Basically it's just kind of making things up, creating songs and creating product. I'm in the creative side of the business."

Jerry's vision expresses his musical tastes and the necessity of remaining economically viable: "As long as it's rootsy, I like it. That's what I finally figured out. I love garage band music, and I love the Ventures, and I love James Brown and old great country music. If it's kind of human and real, I'm there." Running a company, however, compels Jerry to create music that will please the consumer: "my focus is now on what makes this company money and what makes me money, and that's some form of country music. As I've gotten older I've really devoted myself to that, and I don't branch out too much anymore to this other stuff."

Jerry's vision of the creative process, and his commitment to the next generation of songwriters and artists, are partly reaffirmed by his critique of the corporate model of music production. His earlier transition from staff songwriter to award-winning producer dovetailed with an increasingly impersonal and rigid corporate culture emerging in the songwriting workplace. Jerry described this transition that occurred during the 1990s:

> Then [the publishing company] was bought [by a large corporation].... It got more and more corporate, and the more corporate it got the less all the writers liked it. [T]he way [the publishing company] started and what was wonderful about it was this freedom. Companies are always a top down thing, reflective of ... the top guy. And [the top guy], who was the creative guy there, made an environment for a long, long time that was terribly creative. It was wild, and the writers had control of everything, which made it wild, because writers are crazy. The creative people are liable to do anything, there was a lot of sex in the offices, smoking dope in the balconies, butt prints on the Xerox machines, and parties all night, drinking beer, but at the same time there was these guys challenging you to write great songs ... but as [the publishing company] got bought out and then bought out again, we started noticing all the changes, and we got pushed more and more out.... There's still a studio there but it's a whole different cold and clinical place, which is reflective of the years that we're living in. It's not nearly the place that it used to be.

In contrast, Jerry attempts to nurture his songwriting staff. In response to my query about his role in mentoring young songwriters, Jerry stated: "It's a big part of my job. My job really is sales and mentoring. PR and sales and that kind of stuff, raising the profile of this business, trying to make it win, keeping all the plates spinning, and at the same time seeing young writers. I do it every day." For example, he will continue to support the young songwriter, including when she faces personal hardship:

> I mean, if they get in a jam, which corporations don't do anymore, so we try to be the anti-corporation. Like one of our writers is doing real well right now, but has gotten into a jam, going through a divorce, single mother, so she came and asked for some money, five grand or something to get her through Christmas, and we can do that for her. She's getting a lot of cuts right now, so we know we're going to get the money back, but even if she wasn't it's the thing to do.

As a business owner, songwriter, and mentor to young songwriters, Jerry endeavors to maintain a creative process in his shop that expresses his tastes and cumulative wisdom, on the one hand, while encouraging the self-expression of his songwriting staff, on the other:

I'm a steward to these writers here, since I write songs myself I've got an empathy, an experience that I have to be careful with, but at the same time I can talk to them about their songs in a way that they know what I'm talking about. A lot of times with publishers, the writers are sitting there thinking well what the hell do you know about writing a song? Well I know how to write a song, and they know it.... At the same time they're thinking well hell, he's writing his own brand of songs, and if you don't write like he does he doesn't like them. So I have to be careful with that, so I usually don't give specific advice, but I give advice all the time to writers on what to do and what not to do. Sometimes they listen to me.

Strategic Orientation

Jerry is climbing a "personal ladder," a self-determined, self-satisfying, and dogged ascent in the music business, and over the life course. He discerns his ascent, and it is periodically reaffirmed for him, from moments of peer and market recognition of his artistry. He responded as follows to my open-ended question about how he defines success:

> Jerry: It's such a flaky business and it's so quick lived, success, and it's such a business of rejection that I don't think you ever get a aah, I'm here at last, I'm finally here.... I see parallels with sports all the time with our business. It's a young man's game here, and the older you get you better get wily and figure out ways to play the odds. You better find a way to get on the business side.... There's been two or three times I knew I'd taken a step up the ladder, really knew it. But most of the time I just felt like that's neat. Here's a phenomenon for you: the first song I ever had recorded in Nashville was by a [famous blues man] ..., it was a song I wrote with ... my protégé ... [my protégé] called me and said [famous blues man] has recorded our song. I could hear it playing in the background. Well we'd been working on this, that's a huge deal for me, I remember the moment.... It was this huge feeling of elation. I'm on the phone hearing [famous blues man] do my song. The moment of elation lasted 20 seconds and the next feeling I had was I got to get another one of these. Like cocaine. I got to get another one. Within 20 seconds it didn't feel great any more, it felt like I need another one, this is not going to be nearly good enough. Now. I think all of these things, anybody that's successful in this town feels the same way....
>
> DC: The ladder that you said when you moved up, what is the ladder?

Jerry: Well, maybe it's a personal ladder. At least in my case it was, and maybe with everybody. I never had a goal of being the head of a record label or anything, I just wanted to stay in the music business. As a kid that was my goal. I never really had a goal until the mid-'90s of making any money, it never was a priority for me. I never had any money, there was times it was really tough, where I had nothing to eat. I'd eat the same chicken stew for a week. All that stuff you hear about, I went through that, and it was hard. But it never was as important to me as just being involved in the middle of music. So the answer about the success thing is I didn't ever feel successful, but I could feel myself climbing up.

Jerry was nominated for a Grammy roughly a decade after his initial arrival on the Nashville scene. For him, this was one of those rare reaffirming moments in which he had climbed up another rung of the ladder. It also inspired him to ascend further up the ladder:

It brought me to tears when I got nominated for that Grammy, it was one of the times that it moved me the most in the music business. I went to the mailbox and opened that up and it was a very emotional experience for me when I think about the shit that I'd been through. It was just a big deal to me because it confirmed to me that if you just try hard enough that you can do stuff. So from there I made a couple of other records ... and then I said okay, now I want to really make a Nashville record and make some money. And breaking into this market, even though I'd had all this stuff, was still very hard as a producer because nobody wants you to do it. Everybody wants you to do whatever it is that you do.... Somebody brought us [Jerry and a producer friend] an act called [new band] and these guys were playing on the road ..., so [Jerry's friend] said why don't you do the leg work and we'll produce this together, because [Jerry's friend] was on a roll, and he'd seen that I'd done this other stuff. So I got a team of writers together, we wrote some songs, we changed their name to [band].... I got them a record deal [with a major label] ... and ended up doing really well and they sold a Gold or Platinum or something on the first record we did for them and I wrote songs for them, so now I'm making money, now I'm really making some dough.

"Making some dough," however, is not the objective, but the consequence, of engaging in self-satisfying artistic expression. In response to my question about the importance he assigned to having his music please other music professionals, Jerry stated: "Financially it's very important. But if you're speaking spiritually or whatever, what I have to do first and foremost is please me. If I please me usually I'll make money from it."

Pathway

Jerry's journey to his current position occurred along a movement-inspired pathway. He grew up in Southern City during the racially segregated Jim Crow era of the South, his exodus from Jim Crow being catalyzed by the new musical movements of his high school years during the 1960s. The son of a used car dealer and a homemaker, Jerry's musical roots were in the Baptist church, where he had sung in the choir in his youth:

> Everybody was Baptist there. That was a big deal for my music. I knew how to play country music from the church, because if you've ever been in a Baptist church the songs are very much like country songs. The same exact thing. So because I had an ear for knowing how that worked, that really helped me when I played country music. It was the same melodies, same chords and stuff.

But it was the musical movements of the 1960s that inspired him and his generation in their early adolescence to become rock stars:

> We had the piano in the house, but ... it just was there, so I started playing it when I wanted to. Really I sort of picked up the guitar, probably like a million other kids my age, about 12 or 13 years old I picked up an acoustic guitar, I got a Mel Bay chord book, and I learned some Kingston Trio songs on it, because they were the easiest ones and they were in the book.

A self-trained musician, Jerry gravitated toward a wide range of musical genres, including rock, R & B, the Beatles and, later, Western Swing, all the while maintaining and developing an expertise in country music.

Jerry crossed the racial divide. Against his father's expressed wishes that he not play music that was associated with African American culture, he listened to and played R & B in black and white clubs in Southern City:

> I was captivated by the records that I would hear, particularly old R&B records and the country records. I grew up around country music and I liked black music, Bobby Bland and these kind of guys, so I went after that, and I learned to play that way.... [A]lso just because of Top 40 radio at the time, we didn't truly delineate between country music so much and rock 'n' roll and rhythm & blues ... there was one Top 40 radio station and [many musical genres] ... would all be on the same radio, on the Top 40. Now there may be a black radio station in a big city and there could be a country station, but Top 40 radio had all that, and when you played a dance in [Southern City] you'd play a Chet Atkins song and then you'd play maybe a Beatles song ... and you'd play rhythm & blues stuff.... I didn't know anything about desegregation and any of that.... I would go to the black part of town, me and a couple of my friends, and we would

go sneak in the back door and we'd be the only white people at all in the clubs. It was a little bit scary to us until we realized nobody was going to hurt us, and we'd watch the black stuff and we would take that and we'd emulate it. As a matter of fact, there was kind of a ground-breaking record called James Brown Live at the Apollo Theater.... Well that record really changed my world again, and I had a band with some other guys ... we learned the entire record, we were just four or five little white guys and we learned the entire record. We'd been playing country music and everything, so we kind of had this mixed up together, and I played in a club [in Southern City] ... and there were four bands. It was a teenage club and we'd get one week a month and we'd play there ... all of us were friends, we'd all just go watch the other bands.... Anyway, they were all good players ... who were dedicated in doing it, we were all 15, 16 years old, ... about 30 percent of the people in the little bands went on and made a career out of music.

I asked Jerry what it was about the James Brown record that moved him. Jerry replied:

That's a good question. I'd never heard anything like that. I'd heard records before, but I'd never heard a show like that, and I'd never heard anybody sing like that, and I'd never heard music played like that ... it was just the way they performed their shows was incredible.... I didn't see them at the Apollo, but I made it a part of my education from then on to see as many James Brown performances as I could after I heard that record. So I went to hundreds of them, and I went to hundreds of Ray Charles shows, and we would follow them around.

Jerry was part of a small group of musically gregarious high schoolers in Southern City. He explained that he and his musician friends were more musically adventurous than their high school contemporaries:

It was like our secret at first. It was our almost cliquey thing. We were listening to Bob Dylan too, we listened to a lot of music, we were kind of on the cutting edge of that, I mean the musicians were. We would like stuff and then the [other] kids would like it later. A lot of it, by the way, came even to us through the British bands. By the way, when all this is going on, in the background is playing country music which I took totally for granted because I heard it all the time. We played it, but it was just like that stuff because it was there. And there were blues artists around that we took for granted.

As Jerry reflected, he recalled that the musical movements of the 1960s were a dynamic and inspiring, vanguard alternative to what he and his contemporaries considered to be "manufactured" music that had come to dominate radio. He likened the contemporary era to the transitional era of his adolescence:

> People would play things for me and there would be like a guy somewhere and he'd go, "have you heard this guy Bobby Bland?" And I'd go "no," and he'd play it for me, and I'd just love it, as soon as I heard it I started after it because I was just drawn to it, I don't really know why other than I still believe it's tremendously good music. If you think about what was on the radio at the time, it was very similar to country radio now, it was just kind of really manufactured where it seemed like older people were spitting out what they thought was rock 'n' roll for kids to buy, and rock 'n' roll from the '50s had gotten really corporatized and so I didn't like that, so I started looking around for things I liked. I think kids are doing it again right now, I think that's what's going on out there right now.

Jerry struggled through the 1970s and his young adulthood continuing to learn and play a wide range of popular music genres, and battling a sense of hopelessness as he strove to climb his personal ladder. He roamed and rambled as a road musician and in show bands in Southern City beer joints, Europe, and Los Angeles, and he co-wrote a few songs, networking with his Southern City musician friends and professionals he would encounter on the road and transitioning from musician toward songwriter. Jerry characterized this "dark" period of his life as one of hopelessness and, yet, as one in which he honed his expertise in traditional country music and widened his repertoire, inadvertently laying an educational foundation that would serve him well in his ensuing Nashville years:

> I kept coming back to [Southern City] and that felt like a failure, and I didn't realize the benefits I was getting from playing in these beer joints. Who could? It was just a terrible grind. But we went through a period in the beer joints, we started somewhere in the middle there, maybe '75, '76, I met a guy ... who was way interested in Western swing.... Then I found a clique of guys that liked that. Then all of a sudden the honky tonks got more interesting, because we could go and play that stuff, and the people we were playing for mostly at that time in the '70s were kind of Korean War veterans if you think about it, they were in their '40s and '50s, there were some World War II guys there, but mostly it was kind of in that world, '50s kids. So they didn't mind Western swing, but they wanted to hear Mel Tillis and the things that were on the radio then, too. We played a little of that, but we started getting these big bands together. We'd take less money and we would have two or three fiddles and have an old-fashioned _____ band. We'd have a couple of fiddles, we'd have a steel, we'd have an upright piano player ... and it was really good. Again, we

found a way to start making good music and we'd kind of stick together instead of the pick-up things I was describing to you earlier....

I started really exploring all that, and learning how to really play good country music, because before then I had just been hanging on.... Then it got good to me, and I started playing that swing stuff, then we started playing Ray Price and things that were really to me significantly good music. As good as James Brown was five or six or seven years earlier to me. Once that kicked in I really learned a lot, I mean I learned a ton, what everyone should be playing in country music, what everyone should be doing for that traditional, particular style. I already had a rock 'n' roll kind of base, I knew kind of how that went, I knew how Stax music went, because I studied all that stuff and played it all in these different bands, and never knew I was getting this education. It never occurred to me maybe you're building yourself for something really cool. I just kind of did it because I didn't know what else to do. I felt hopeless, I felt really hopeless. I thought this is a dead-end street but I'm staying on it because I don't want to do anything else. I'd try to get off it and it just didn't work for me. And you know, the dark side of it is you're up all night and I never did like that, you go to bed when the sun comes up. Too many women, too many drugs, too much alcohol, it's all out there for you and I was the wildest guy there. I was very much the wild guy. Just for the grace of God, I don't know why it didn't kill me. So the period was dark, when I look back on the '70s I think man, I don't know how I made it through it.

Some of Jerry's Southern City musician friends of his adolescence had begun to break in as songwriters and musicians in Nashville during the 1970s. The career success of his friends lured and facilitated Jerry's eventual move to Nashville in the early 1980s. Jerry's subsequent career success as a Nashville hit songwriter did not immediately materialize. He endured harsh living conditions upon his initial arrival in Nashville:

Really I didn't have any money, so I'd go right down the street to a parking lot, and it was in the middle of the winter, and I'd just stay in this parking lot in the truck. I'd get a little bottle of whiskey, and it was real cold, and I did this for months off and on, or I'd go out to the truck stop in the parking lot. I'd spend the night, I had a blanket in the truck, I'd turn the heater on and get it real, real hot in the truck until it got so cold it'd wake me back up, I'd take a little swig of whiskey, get it real hot, three or four times a night. Looking back it was kind of rough, but it was okay.

It took some four years of playing on the road and working non-musical day jobs before he would network his way into a staff songwriter position at a Nashville publishing house that employed some of his Southern City musician friends. Jerry got his break when he parlayed a non-musical day job at a publishing company into a staff songwriter job. Jerry co-wrote a hit song with his staff songwriter friends which resulted in his promotion from a non-musical support job into a staff songwriter position at the publishing house.

IN FROM LA

James

An award-winning and commercially successful rock star, James's mid-career move to Nashville from LA in the 1980s occasioned his transition from major-label artist and songwriter to independent stardom. The transition and relocation were compelled not only by his desire to revive his band and career and reconnect with the fans, but by his continuing desire to poetically engage humanity:

> I was always a believer that humanity can move forward [by] ... pushing the boundaries of knowledge. Not just in a scientific manner, but the pursuit of greater spirituality, greater comprehension, both intellectually and intuitively, of some greater purpose of existence than just unfortunately the way it is currently in the Western civilizations, to be a consumer. I mean to me one of the most insulting epitaphs would be "he was born, he consumed, he died" ... it's the equivalent of saying "he came, he used up space and resources, and he left" ... what kind of a legacy is that for a human being? ... [President] Kennedy ... said the artist has a quarrel with the world, he has a love affair but a quarrel with the world because he sees what could be, he sees the potential, and he sees our inadequacies and he points them out and calls us to task on it, and that means he's not very popular a lot of times. And that was the thing that stuck with me, he said but the country, or the person, who has disdain for that ... has nothing to look back on with pride, and nothing to look forward to with hope.

James enjoyed commercial success from the film and television licensing of the music he had made during the late 1960s and 1970s. When the band dissolved in the 1970s, James set out to emerge from an ensuing slump by taking a reconstituted band on the road. To make matters worse, his career slump was occasioned by an acrimonious rivalry with former colleagues who had formed a new band which was attempting to capture James's original fan base. Furious and concerned that his rivals were ruining his reputation, James set out to revive his career and reaffirm his reputation. His revitalization strategy entailed becoming a "cottage industry" of new music production, publishing, self-promotion, and merchandise sales:

> When I saw what had happened to the name, that really didn't sit well with me.... And so we went on basically a crusade that lasted ... the better part of five years, of non-stop touring. Six shows per week, 20 weeks at a

pop, in North America criss-crossing back and forth starting in the worst clubs imaginable and working our way gradually back out of those clubs into small theaters and so on, also going to Europe several times, etc. And also once we saw that things were looking more promising, started this whole process that resulted in us being a cottage industry, which is okay we're going to start a merchandise corporation, we're going to have to put out some new recordings in order to let them know we're not just a retread from the past, and so that whole process slowly took shape.

James's move to Nashville served his touring for reconnecting with the fans and producing new music. A center of the music industry, Nashville was a viable community of artistic talent and resources that was optimally located near urban markets for live music and touring bands. James explained why he moved to Nashville:

[Nashville] certainly knows a thing or two about music industry related things, and also, for instance there's a reason why Federal Express is in Memphis, because it's almost smack center, which means that from there you can—it's like the hub of a wagon wheel, and from Nashville in a 600-mile radius, which means from Milwaukee to New Orleans from Dallas to Pittsburgh— ... cover like 70 percent of the population base of the lower 48. There's a reason why the country guys get on their buses and overnight 500 miles or wherever they want to be. This is a good place to operate from if we're going to be making a lot of our coin on the road, rather than being in Los Angeles, which means that ... you can play Phoenix and the desert cities only so often, that means you got to hop all the way to where the population is more dense and everything.

Vision of an Enterprising Artist

James's move to Nashville signaled his transformation from major-label artist toward an independent and self-sustaining enterprising artist. His transformation entailed an expansion of his professional skill portfolio to include a range of artistic support skills. He expanded his portfolio gradually, acquiring the skills over thirty years of career experience. His family "cottage industry" is his artistic enterprise, a self-contained band:

As time went on additional skills were required in order to kind of mind the store as it were, run our own little cottage industry, meaning that we got into publishing our own music, into recording our music, both solo projects and [band] recordings, in my recording studios, first a little one at my residence in Los Angeles, later here in [the Nashville] area. So some technical skills were developed with respect to recording equipment, operating mixing boards, etc.... I became kind of a paralegal/para-accountant. There were a lot of non-directly music related skills that were required ...

for our [enterprise]. So by the time we got into the '90s, ... it was a fairly complete self-sufficient combination of skills and equipment, etc. So we had in essence recording studio, publishing company, a merchandise corporation, a website, owned our own tour bus, a large truck with a triple sleeper, 105 cases of equipment, and we became self-sufficient to the point where the only thing we hired on the outside was a booking agency. Everything else was in-house. Truck and bus drivers, lighting directors, sound engineers for the live performance mixes, production managers, etc. So all of these developments happened over a course of about three decades.

The cottage industry generated an increasingly diverse array of revenue streams, especially after the move to Nashville:

[Nashville was] where we fine-tuned and expanded the whole ... organization and where we diversified the revenue streams, because aside from publishing and writer publishing royalties, recording things in our studio, which were then licensed to other recording companies for advances and so on. Obviously the personal appearance revenue, the merchandise revenue, then we started a website with selling merchandise off the web. I had a ... building erected that accommodated the truck, the bus, lots of storage for equipment, plus tons of merchandise. Things started to expand, we designed a catalog, full-color catalog with [40] or 50 different items. [A family member] ran the office.

A lifelong union member who had only passively joined the union at the beginning of his career, James also discovered the social welfare benefits of union membership when he moved to Nashville. Soon after James arrived in Nashville, a union representative approached him and helped him to calculate the many years of pension benefits he had accrued. He also qualified for union-provided health insurance benefits. Fortunately, James had meticulously saved his paperwork, giving the union the documentation it needed to recalibrate his pension benefits and strengthening his relationship with arts trade unionism:

Then later when we moved here to Tennessee, I was contacted by [a union rep] ... and he introduced himself and we had a lunch and we got on very well, and we started talking about stuff that had been really off my radar screen, which was well all those recordings that you continue to get royalties on, particularly the catalog recordings, [major label], are they contributing into your retirement fund the way they're supposed to? I said you know I don't know, they send me those annual earnings reports and I don't know whether it's correct, I don't know what the rules are. I said well let's put our heads together, and to cut to the chase as it turned out nobody at [major label] really knew who in the band ... needed to get paid based on this and the other thing. By the time we sorted out the number of songs recorded ... and reworked the formula, it was totally out of whack.... So [union rep] set out to—he says if you have the original recording contracts, I do ... and I've got all the royalty statements. He said okay, that's what we need.... By the time it all got reworked, my benefits I figured out, changed from whatever it had been previously to if I was to retire at 65 and I was to live for at least another 12 years, that would be about a million dollars' worth of benefit payments. Okay? So that's when I became real interested in the unions and what they can do.

The cottage industry would become self-sustaining to the point that James no longer had to go on the road. He eventually stopped the bus tours, but continued to play limited engagements: "When I told the guys I will no longer tour, that doesn't mean I will no longer play, it means I won't go on that bus and stay out and so on. By that time I sold the bus, I gave a lot of stuff away to crew and band members because of many years of loyalty."

Strategic Orientation

At the heart of James's poetic engagement with humanity is an emotional tie to his fans. His cottage industry, and his successful effort at reviving his career and reputation, depended on fan loyalty: "without the emotional ties that exist to this day, but certainly back then, exist between the band and its support base, the fans, without that all of these efforts of ours would have been just spinning our wheels. If nobody shows up there's no way up."

James's emotional ties with his fans originated in the social unrest of the late 1960s and the Vietnam War. His music resonated with a generation who opposed hierarchy, prejudice, and war and yearned for a vision and pathway toward freedom:

There was a great support base out there because these were the people who when we first came on to the radar screen of the music industry, in '68, '69, '70, '71, they were often in Vietnam because of the draft, or they were on the college campuses demonstrating against the war in Vietnam, or whatever they were doing, this was a crucial component of the sound-track of their life, they went beyond I remember this song because I danced with so-and-so at the high school prom to this tune. It was far more than that. These were the songs ... with a degree of bite to them lyrically, which so often we heard from people our own age say you know you're saying what I wish I could say, you're saying it for me.

His fans originally learned of his music over FM radio, as FM increasingly aired socially critical rock and played whole albums and lengthier songs than the short popular ballads aired on AM radio. James described "the emerging power of the FM so-called underground radio stations that concentrated on playing sometimes entire albums, but certainly were not scared off by 20-minute long songs or 5-minute long songs." Furthermore, James explained that he was of a generation of musicians who were challenging the risk-averse major labels to record self-contained rock bands and distribute the new socially critical and nonconventional rock:

We did not sound what they would now say this stuff isn't radio friendly, which is double speak for it doesn't sound like what is already on the radio, because we just retread the same thing until it's worn out and then we're ready to take a chance on something slightly more adventurous. So back then ... the established record companies ... were a bit clueless with respect to what was going on. They were still in an A&R man, get the artist in here, we'll pick the material, that sort of thing mode and here were these guys writing their own music and experimenting with weird sounds, so-called psychedelic sound. So the AM hit radio oriented radio stations there, they were still of is it catchy, can you dance to it, is it bouncy, that sort of thing, and that's still where the majority of people, particularly non-teenagers and so on, were getting their daily fix of music. But the counterculture had now spread beyond just San Francisco, Haight Ashbury, that sort of thing.... You could do things on a shoestring with FM stations and more and more young people that demanded more than just another 3-minute long catchy tune, started to listen to these laidback instead of the speed rapping AM, you had hey man, that was a cool cut, it was a whole different thing on FM. So FM and our music were compatible.

James illustrated the emotional depth of his relationship with his fans with a story about a Mississippi fan:

It's maybe the pinnacle of one of the things that's the most meaningful as a songwriter. I get this letter unsolicited some years ago.... Well this fellow writes to me, I don't know him from Adam, he's now in charge of [a Mississippi state government agency] and how they're performing and everything else. But back then I get this letter and he said ... I want you to know that I'm so-and-so, I'm a lawyer, I have a great family, two kids, one wife, I have a very good life, but what set me on my path to who I am when I was in Mississippi growing up with a very different attitude than I had surround me was your ... album, because you spoke for me and you let me know that I was not alone, and what that album said gave me— and now I defend the little people against the bullies of the world, and I want to thank you for that. It was stuff like this that gives you an idea of how the music penetrated beyond oh this is a nice catchy tune I can hum or dance to, there was more meat to it. And I think that was definitely a significant component with respect to the response that we got in ever-increasing numbers of people returning.

Pathway

The son of a self-employed seamstress and a salesman, James took a movement-inspired pathway toward independent stardom. During his adolescence in Northern City, James was moved politically and musically by the socially critical folk music tradition and blues that were reviving during the civil rights movement of the 1960s and the Vietnam War:

> I always sensed that ... there must be more than this, and ... it started to take more of a well-formed shape when I became more and more engaged in the here and now, meaning the conditions of the world in politics, when Kennedy was elected, and particularly when I was of draft age and all of a sudden the Vietnam War was of interest to me.... I think my— kind of a clearer vision of the path that I envisioned for myself, that I wanted to try, really was kind of crystallized through the experiences of the folk music revival in the early '60s, but specifically or particularly my experiences at the Newport Folk Festivals in '64 and '65 where I saw young men and women, my age or thereabouts, give or take a year, who continued the tradition of the Woody Guthries and Pete Seegers, but with their own newly written songs about the here and now, about the Civil Rights Movement, about the Vietnam War thing and other issues they had with the status quo.

James gravitated toward socially critical music as he listened to Bob Dylan and researched the Lomax's collection of blues:

> When Dylan's songs, particularly during his Times They Are a' Changing period, when certain songs, "Mr. Tambourine Man" and others, were played as folk rock electrified by The Byrds, I immediately took to that, I thought it was great, I liked everything that I heard them do. When I wanted to express something that I wrote lyrically it was invariably done in the idiom of the blues, because I had listened to all the field recordings, which went far beyond just the blues but had a lot of blues in them of John and Alan Lomax, Library of Congress recordings which I'd gotten out of the music department of the main library in [Northern City], and listened to all of that, it gave me a bit of an education about Texas blues and other areas, but particularly Mississippi Delta blues, and before even the emergence of that type of blues there was this whole rich archive of what were innocuously called work songs, but which could be levee building crew work songs, railroad building crew work songs, and prison gangs, in Texas Sugarland prison farm, Angola, and others. And it was there through those songs that I learned to read between the lines a little bit because obviously the African Americans had lived in this highly oppressive existence in that part of the country knew that white ears

would hear what they were singing, so they couldn't be too blatant and obvious in whatever call it criticism or commentary on their condition. So they, some of the texts were kind of like a code speak, but they were also steeped in reality, and while I don't remember all of the verses, which were pretty graphic, ... it was a song that the field workers, they worked them from sun-up to sundown, after sundown they couldn't see what they were doing, so they worked them in that incredible heat and humidity until they dropped. I mean the number of people that died was horrific.

By the mid-1960s, James and his new wife moved to Los Angeles not long after James's parents had already moved for personal reasons to Southern California. The self-described "itinerant folk musician" had fallen in with a rock band near Northern City that relocated to Los Angeles. The rock band subsequently broke up after failing to make a hit record and interpersonal friction undermined the band's capacity to collaborate.

Soon after the band broke up, James's fortuitous encounter with a producer resulted in the formation and initial success of his new hit-making band that propelled him and the band into stardom. The producer happened to be the new husband of James's wife's friend who was their neighbor in their rental apartment building. The producer encouraged James to reconstitute and revitalize his previous band by forming a new band:

> Next door to us at this little apartment that we rented another couple moved in and it happened to be a girlfriend of [my wife's] ..., and her new husband was a record producer for [a major label]. We got to talking and he was curious about [James's previous band]. I played him some reel-to-reel tapes that had been cut at live performances and he said hey if you're still in touch with some of these guys and put a new line-up together, get some tunes, we'll do some demos. That's what I did.... So we [now] had the five of us together and we started rehearsing in this garage underneath the little apartment that [we] had rented, and got our material together. I had some new songs I'd written, a couple of things we carried over from [the previous band], and when [the producer-neighbor], who stuck his head in there every so often to hear how we were doing, said I think we're ready to go in the studio, we did.

The producer got James a record deal with the major label:

> We went in the studio, cut ten or twelve tracks, and he took them to [major label] and they said they wanted to have a meeting. We were at this point just hand to mouth, some of our gear was in the hock shop, so≈there was no money for a lawyer and we didn't have a manager, so [producer-neighbor] and I sat next to each other talking to the record

company president, who told me outright, he said you know I don't understand this stuff, but my daughter, 16 years old I think she was, she likes it. So great. So we worked out what was basically just a slightly altered typical one-sided recording agreement when the artist has no clout and the label does a take it or leave it kind of contract.

Set up as they were for large orchestral recording sessions, Los Angeles recording studios in the late 1960s had not fully adapted to the recording needs of the new self-contained, socially critical rock bands. James's new band found a new studio and within six months had released a top-charting album through FM radio play that launched the band into stardom:

First we went into the studio where [producer-neighbor] had previously produced a couple of things.... But it was a very sort of commercial institution, I don't know how to put it. It was the kind of place where orchestras recorded, all sorts of other thing. Almost like a company studio like [a major label] would have in New York. We were very dissatisfied with what we heard coming out of the speakers because the engineers were company engineers, punch in, eight hours, punch out, and they were doing a "this is too loud, the needles are going into the red. I tell you what, you guys turn down in there and then I'll turn you up in here. Lovely." So we would come in and get this very loud small sound. We spent ten days in this thing and did not like anything we heard. Well, meantime a friend of mine ... who had been the manager at this ... folk club [referred James to] ... a couple of guys over there in Studio City, they got this converted restaurant and they built their own echo chamber and they got tube mixing board and they're really good, their rates are reasonable. I said wow, we've got to check that out. So [producer and band member] went over there and they checked it out, they said we're going to cut in there. Okay. We brought all of our stuff in there and in four days, four days for $9,000 we recorded and mixed all eleven tracks that are on the first ... album.

Doug

An award-winning producer-writer-composer-musician, Doug has been producing a commercially successful, self-contained, artist-centered pop band for more than twenty-five years. Originally a major-label session musician and performing musician with touring bands, he expanded his artistic activities to include songwriting, composing for movies and television, appearing on the screen, and producing throughout the first two decades of his LA-based career. A union member since the start of his career in the 1960s, by the time he joined the LA-to-Nashville musical migration in the 1990s, the multifaceted musical professional belonged to the AFM, AFTRA, and SAG and had his own publishing companies with ASCAP and BMI.

Doug continued to produce the artist-centered band when he moved to Nashville for personal reasons. He and his wife wanted to be closer to their elderly relatives. They also felt that during the last twenty years, since the time when Doug had worked briefly in Nashville at the start of his career, Nashville had become a more family-friendly place with sufficient cultural amenities for raising their two young children. Nashville now had "more things to enjoy. In fact, when we moved we said we're going to do something with the kids, we're going to go to the symphony, be members, just to have something. Because in '69 they didn't really have that kind of thing to offer, things that you get in a city.... There wasn't a museum ... [and] we wanted to be closer to grandmothers, because we wouldn't see them but once a year for about ten days, they'd fly out to LA."

Nashville also offered Doug the professional resources of a music-recording city that would afford him opportunities for widening his portfolio of professional activities. Doug already "knew a lot of people" in the Nashville industry. Soon after his arrival, Doug took on the A & R position of a new custom label that was started by the artist whose band Doug continued to produce: "in the meantime [the artist] had started a record label, and in the fall of that year the guy that was running the label asked me to be the head A&R, ... it's sort of the creative end of the record business. Not as much the business end."

Vision of an Enterprising Artist

In the course of his career, Doug has diversified his professional skill portfolio and the range of his streams of income-generating artistic activities. He actualized this vision of enterprising artist by constantly updating and expanding his own skill-set and developing long-lasting professional relationships with successful artists.

The Los Angeles music industry was an important space for Doug's professional development. During the LA phase of his career, he availed himself of the many learning opportunities available on the job and at the university as he extended his expertise beyond playing into producing and composing. He described his approach to self-instruction, explaining that broadening one's skill-set as one matures not only is personally satisfying, but also buffers the music professional from the constant threat of displacement by a younger music professional:

It's just as a player I didn't like to waste time, I wanted to do, and you get in a studio situation with a lot of producers, they don't manage time well. I said you know, I can probably do this. Because you're not trained to be a producer. You're usually an engineer or a musician.... It's something that I felt like you have to be open to any possibility if you want to make a living in the music business. At the same time I went and took classes, because I hadn't been trained in music, I hadn't been to a music school, I had private [music] lessons. I took classes out at UCLA in orchestration, film scoring, different music classes, master classes.... Whenever I would have the time available just to go to the classes. And there were a lot of people that way ... even though they were working in the industry.... You would be offered a job and you say well maybe I need to read up on this or ask questions. In other words, on the job training is what it is. When we were doing [movie] I wanted to get into orchestration so I asked this well-known jazz trumpet player what books I should read, and they told me, and it was true ... because I was never trained as a composer, which I wish I had been, but I still loved music so I didn't want to limit myself.... And as a player, you watch NFL players, there's always a younger guy that's going to take your place. So you have to broaden your horizon.

I asked Doug how a mature music professional discerns the pressure of displacement by the younger generation. He replied: "When you don't get the call, and somebody else gets the call.... It's because it's rock 'n' roll. Rock 'n' roll is youth. I had a friend that was a great bass player that several years ago was asked to play bass with this young group and they told the producer we don't want him out here. They didn't think he could do the job. Yeah, it's rock 'n' roll."

The risk of joblessness for freelancers like Doug also stems from the fragility of the interpersonal relations that bind an act or band. Doug's current long-lasting association with the artist-centered band is his second long-lasting artistic engagement. His first engagement as a player and composer in a major act endured during the 1970s until the principal artists parted company with one another. Soon after the breakup, Doug joined the artist-centered band that he has been producing for more than two decades. Doug explained that in the absence of an employment contract, the freelancer can be dropped by the artist at any time: "Even though I've worked with [the artist for many] years, there's no contract. If he wants to [he can] stop or get rid of me, so to me that's still freelance. And the same thing with [the artists of his first engagement], if they decide to change they can do that."

Doug illustrated the tenuousness of interpersonal relationships with the example of the breakup of his first engagement: "it's hard working with a ... couple when the relationship is going south. Bands are really family, I'm talking about royalty artists, when they break up they don't talk to each other, because it's like a divorce. They're that close, you know, they had a dream together, just like a husband and wife. So you'll see bands playing together that don't talk to each other." I asked Doug to what he attributed his long-lasting relationship with his current employer. He replied: "I think that I'm able to give him what he needs and wants, in a congenial manner, because I've seen this before too, producers work with an act and they have a big hit record, and then they don't work again. It's because there's friction, which I've never believed that friction is necessary to be creative ... we were friends before I started producing ... I was friends with everybody I worked for."

Strategic Orientation

Doug feels successful when he is satisfied with the music he makes and supports his family by pursuing his passion. He is satisfied when his music meets his self-imposed standards of quality, when he earns the respect of his peers, and when he engages the fans:

> it has to be satisfying, you have to be happy. That's one of the things that was so nice about being in music, because it's very satisfying when you're playing, and it's really not a job. It's not a 9-5 job, which is nice. But to be successful, to be able to take care of your family. And for me, to make the fans happy with the music, and also to make your peers respect you for what you do.

During his stint as a music executive, Doug encouraged the musicians to be themselves in their artistic expression. He contrasted this emphasis on individual self-expression with a more formulaic approach taken by music executives who produce commercial music for radio airplay:

> I enjoyed being a music executive, but I never was one that told an artist, all I told them was just to be who you are, whereas some executives will say you need to be like this so we can get you on the radio or something. So I'm not a big fan of that. I think the true artist has to be, that's what makes everybody different is they're an individual. You take it from things that you're influenced by and you put all that together, and then it comes out who you are.

Doug's passion for music was his original inspiration for embarking on his musical career, rather than medicine, the other career he had originally considered pursuing: "when I had to make that decision about medicine, it was that I'd be cheating myself if I didn't give myself a chance to play music because I loved it so much.... I thought about if I can make a living playing, if I had to play joints to make a living, that's what it had to be."

Entertaining the fans is especially meaningful for Doug, and he hopes to make them feel good at a live performance. For him, influencing the fans' feelings is more important than the musical interplay between the players. Referring to the emotional impact of his music on the fans, Doug explained:

> That it makes them [the fans], when they leave, that they're smiling, they feel like they've experienced something. It's just because I work in the whole [artist's name] thing, the escapism, and part of our mission is that they escape during those 2½, 3 hours that we play. I feel that way. Because I played in bands where all it was was about the music, and people appreciate that, but if you're a player it's just really you're not

trying to entertain the audience, what you're trying to do is have the interaction between the players.

Pathway

The son of two college-educated healthcare providers, Doug took a movement-inspired pathway to becoming an enterprising artist. He was raised in a small town near Southern City, the site of a lively rock and R & B scene during his adolescence in the 1960s. His parents neither encouraged nor discouraged him from pursuing a musical career.

Born and raised in the Jim Crow racially segregated South, Doug described his political beliefs as "left of center" and "Democrat" and his religious beliefs as "personal." He was drawn to R & B music during his adolescence and transcended the racial divide: "As far as music was concerned, I've never had the barriers, socially in society growing up in [Southern state] I was separated, but as far as music, most of my heroes were black." In his white segregated high school, Doug was one of a few students who pursued R & B music: "there were people like me. I went with two friends to the James Brown concert in [Southern City] in '63 …, and we were the only three white people there. It was new to the white audience."

The self-trained musician broke in to the Southern City music-recording scene during his high school and college years of the 1960s. Doug toured with a rock band that was based in Southern City and was soon hired by major labels as a studio recording musician in several Southern recording centers of R & B and rock music. Within three years of his college graduation, Doug was hired into his first long-lasting engagement as a band member of an LA-based recording act for which he played and composed music for film and television.

Once in LA, Doug had to hustle and network for session work to supplement his income from his work with the recording act. Although LA afforded musicians many networking opportunities, Doug was not a hustler:

> When I moved to Los Angeles … you could hang out at certain studios and hang out at the Troubador and see just about everybody. The Troubador was a club like a showcase club.… I remember one time in particular … I had to hustle to get that [recording session] job … I'd worked with [the producer] a whole lot, he's an old friend, and at first, in other words he was sort of dragging his feet to get this thing together, the music end of it, and I just had to keep hounding him. I said you know, you need me. Which I'm not that kind of a personality, but I had to do that. And there's been other times, but that's one main time. We had just moved … to a new house, and had two babies.

A few years into his first engagement, he worked briefly as a session musician on a career-launching recording session for an emerging artist. Five years later, that emerging artist had established himself and would circle back to Doug after the breakup of the recording act—Doug's first engagement—and hire him for what would become Doug's second long-lasting and current engagement as the producer of the artist's band.

A TRANSFORMATIVE GENERATION OF ENTERPRISING ARTISTS AND THE RESHAPING OF MUSICIAN COMMUNITY

Seeking an artistic alternative to commercialized popular music, the transformative generation helped to transform the Nashville musician community from one that was organized around the major labels, large studios and publishers, and radio airplay toward a community of self-promoting and self-contained bands that directly engaged their fans and audiences. The unfolding of Martin's, Jerry's, James's, and Doug's careers reflect the emergence of a new generation of independent enterprising artists and self-contained bands in Nashville. Inspired by the cultural and social movements of the 1960s and 1970s, this generation's movement-inspired careers also constituted a cultural break from mass-produced popular music. Indeed, Jerry and Doug had defied Jim Crow by attending James Brown concerts in their adolescence; Martin and James were originally moved by folk, blues, and bluegrass roots music. In this emerging musician community, enterprising artists helped to customize artistic expression and to lead and produce bands in a widening array of musical genres.

Sociologically, the profiles of the four enterprising artists in this chapter partly illustrate the theory of artist activism presented in chapter 2. The purpose of this theory is to explain how an artist's strategic and risk orientations and pathway shape his assumption and enactment of any of three artist activist roles in re-creating artistic community. The profiles in this chapter illustrate how an artistic peer fashions the role of enterprising artist, the most individualistic of the three artist activist roles addressed by the theory.

The four profiled enterprising artists shared common visions of an enterprising artist, strategic and risk orientations, and pathways. They envisioned the enterprising artist as an occupational generalist who created and helped to sustain creative micro-communities of musicians, songwriters, and artists directly engaged with music consumers. Their strategic orientations were grounded in a success orientation toward self-satisfying expressive freedom and in an audience orientation fixated on the music consumer. Although all four music professionals did not discount the importance of fame and fortune; their primary objective was to make and express their own music, and to do so in a way that earned the respect of their peers, their fellow music professionals. Nonetheless, in order to achieve artistic freedom, and to sustain themselves economically as enterprising artists, each of the four enterprising artists traded off a measure of art for commerce by directly engaging their fans and music consumers. Their vision of enterprising artist also rested on a risk orientation toward personal risk factors, such as one's competence and personal drive for self-improvement and seizing opportunities, as well as interpersonal risk factors such as sustaining collegial relations with one's close artistic collaborators.

As members of the transformative generation of enterprising artists in Nashville, the four musicians profiled embarked on movement-inspired pathways toward becoming an artist activist. With their personal risk orientations, they expanded their portfolio of artistic and support skills through continuous and lifelong self-instruction. As movement-inspired artist activists, their skill portfolios were inclined more toward artistic functions than support functions as they directly supported the artistic expression of their immediate artistic collaborators in their engagement with fans.

In sum, the transformative generation of enterprising artists helped to re-create musician community in the changing Nashville music industry. With the corporate consolidation of popular music production in Nashville, their movement-inspired careers unfolded, coincided, and supported a new musician community aligned and attuned to an increasingly entrepreneurial organizational logic of music production and distribution there. By reconstituting a post-bureaucratic musician community consisting of self-contained bands, they modeled a new artist activist role—enterprising artist—that would influence the formation of the contemporary generation of enterprising artists in Nashville.

CHAPTER 4

Identities in Play

The Contemporary Generation of Enterprising Artists

Musician-songwriter-producer Will Kimbrough was awestruck by his heroes who heard him perform his songs at The Bluebird Café when he first arrived in Nashville in the late 1980s. The young Kimbrough had migrated from South Alabama with his band, Will and the Bushmen, into a veritable "pantheon" of great songwriters whom he admires to this day:

> One of the first things I did in Nashville when I got a publishing deal with EMI was I got put on a showcase with other writers and I wanted to play this new song I'd written, I was like 22 or 23, and I was singing this song and I had my eyes closed because I was nervous and trying to remember new lyrics, and I opened my eyes and you know how close, when the stage is set up in the Bluebird you can look to the bar and the bar is like where my kitchen is there, and so I open my eyes and there's Townes Van Zandt and John Prine there smoking cigarettes and holding drinks, and looking at each other not really talking because you don't talk in the Bluebird but they're talking with their eyes, like this kid's playing this lame song, and I remember thinking this is Nashville, I'm here, there's Townes Van Zandt and John Prine, they live here too.[1]

An enterprising artist, Will Kimbrough has gone on to have a robust career in a wide range of Americana music as a successful songwriter, award-winning instrumentalist, band leader and soloist, and producer of his own and others' music . A self-described "modern-day Renaissance Man,"[2] the Nashville-based, DIY artist produces music in his backyard home studio, a free-standing cottage crowded with gear, wires, computer, Internet, and a floor-to-ceiling, multicultural collection of vintage and contemporary string, keyboard, and percussion instruments.

In this chapter, I examine the *contemporary generation of enterprising artists* in Nashville. Presently in their late teens, twenties, and thirties, the contemporary generation has been mentored to become enterprising artists by the earlier transformative generation discussed in the previous chapter. This new generation enters the musician community of enterprising artists that had been forged by the transformative generation. The contemporary generation harbors the same strategic and risk orientations as that of the transformative generation: a strategic orientation toward the pursuit of artistic freedom and a direct engagement with music consumers; and a personal risk orientation of "indie-DIY" self-determination and continuous self-instruction in a widening portfolio of artistic and support skills, as well as close attention to collegial interpersonal relations with immediate collaborators.

A NEW GENERATION OF ENTERPRISING ARTISTS

The contemporary generation pursues an artistic mission of identity expression that extends the artistic mission of the transformative generation. Generational differences in artistic missions resulted from changes that occurred in the societal context of political and cultural movements as each generation entered adulthood. The transformative generation, inspired by the anti-establishment political and cultural movements of their adolescence, was critical of formulaic corporate popular music and forged a musician community of self-contained bands and enterprising artists in order to individualize and customize their artistic expression. Emerging in a Nashville and nation subsequently characterized by dramatic increases in immigration and identity politics (see chapter 1), the contemporary generation enters a diversifying musician community of enterprising artists that encourages the artistic expression of multiple social identities through diverse musical genres.

The Nashville music scene is emerging as a community of identities with the migration of hero-worshipping, DIY, diverse musicians. The continuing influx of the artistically and demographically diverse, contemporary generation of enterprising Nashville artists has increased the range of genres alongside of Americana, country, and Christian music that are produced in Nashville. The recent relocation of Jack White and the Black Keys from the Upper Midwest, for example, and the rise of the Kings of Leon from Middle Tennessee have strengthened the presence of indie rock and vinyl recording; Lori Mechem and Roger Spencer's establishment of the Nashville Jazz Workshop and Rahsaan Barber's recent creation of his Jazz Music City label and production company have augmented the racially diverse jazz scene; the relocation of Delgado Guitars and luthier Manuel Delgado from Los Angeles and the migration of Latin American musicians accompanying Latino immigration have encouraged the performance of Latino musical genres in Nashville; and the creation of Lovenoise music promotion company has contributed to the development of urban music in Nashville.[3]

The profiles in this chapter of four diverse, contemporary-generation enterprising artists depict a wide range of popular music styles and genres in Nashville:[4]

- Art, an African American neo-soul, performing and recording musician-songwriter-producer; son of a 1960-era Nashville civil rights activist; mentored by a white senior California migrant to Nashville; college educated in an area music-business program.

- Susan, a white, country-Christian, performing and recording singer-songwriter; daughter of Midwestern farmers; college educated in an area music-business program.
- Tina, a multi-ethnic, pop/rock, performing and recording singer-songwriter; mentored by senior LA migrants to Nashville and by an established contemporary indie rock star; U.S.-born daughter of an Asian immigrant father and U.S. native mother; high school grad.
- Jason, an Asian American, performing musician-club manager-critic-producer; U.S.-born son of Asian immigrant parents; college educated in an area music-business program.

Their diverse profiles nonetheless depict the common "indie," generalist and entrepreneurial, occupational role each of these early-career artists enacts to hone, articulate, and find their own voices, and to express their artistic identities. A risk orientation based primarily in personal risk factors of self-confidence, individual creativity, and perseverance underlies their strategic orientation of self-promotion and forging and sustaining a direct engagement with their fans, largely independent of arts advocacy organizations, such as unions, and major labels. They also express an interpersonal risk orientation based in cooperative collaboration in song writing and, depending on their career stage, in producing the work of others.

In contrast to the movement-inspired pathways taken by the four artists of the transformative generation profiled in the previous chapter, all four of the contemporary-generation artists have launched their careers on family-inspired pathways. The transformative generation learned and forged the role of enterprising artist over a two- to three-decade period of their careers. The contemporary generation enters the community of enterprising artists often inspired and prepped by their families and equipped with a budding portfolio of artistic and art-support skills that they acquired in music college and expect to expand upon through lifelong, continuous self-instruction.

Art

A native Nashvillian and neo-soul artist, Art is deeply engaged in Nashville's emerging urban music scene. The genre allows him to be himself: "That's one of the hallmarks of being in the genre. It is you being you. It's almost like expressing who you are as if folks were coming to your living room at the house, and you were just sitting down and just hanging out, being you, being comfortable in your skin." Trained in school, college, and on his own, Art, age twenty-something and African American, is a self-published and PRO-affiliated songwriter and arranger, a non-union recording and performing musician, self-employed producer, and an emcee of a live show.

Nashville's cultural opening inspired and facilitated Art's participation in neo-soul and his subsequent contributions to the diversification of music genres produced in Nashville. Art's father was one of many Tennessee A & I college students who defied the whites-only ordinance by sitting down in Nashville's racially segregated downtown lunch counters in the non-violent movement that led to downtown Nashville's desegregation by 1962.[5] His father inspired him to reach out broadly to humanity through music. Some fifteen years into his career, Marv (pseudonym), a white, established gospel music producer who joined the 1990-era California musician migration to Nashville, arrived in Nashville in the late 1980s, five years before he would discover Art during Art's senior year in high school. Marv helped launch Art's career by recording and getting him some radio airplay and supporting Art's admission to and education at an area music college.

Six years after his college graduation, Art had just signed with an indie label as a vocalist, songwriter, and musician when I interviewed him.

Vision of an Enterprising Artist

An emerging and enterprising artist and producer-arranger of his own and other indie artists' work, Art's objective is to develop and promote his and others' artistic uniqueness via Nashville's "underground" music scene. The underground or indie music scene resists corporate homogenization and affirms a non-union production model, including home production, based in customized artistic development. The indie scene, for Art, proceeds with a business and distribution model based in self-promotion in niche markets via the Internet and touring. Art described the creative advantages of producing music in the indie sector, including artistic expression of diverse social identities:

> A lot of artists feel very strongly about maintaining their creative control and their creative identity, which sometimes gets a little watered down, or skewed, by the majors.... [The indie sector] makes the artists feel comfortable to be free in who they are. They don't have to change to fit a certain demographic that the artist's roster has kind of set. It makes it possible for you to do the music you love to do without reservation, gives you a little bit more of a breathing space, it's not as cookie cutter or mechanized or strategized.

Art also noted the business advantages of working in the indie sector. An expanding indie sector affords ethnic-racial minority musicians more economic opportunity than what the major labels offer:

> Most of the groundbreaking pioneers of the genre were signed to major labels under R&B contracts ... the reason they were signed to major labels is because [the labels] were looking for something different in the R&B realm, and they wanted to be the first to do it. But what they found was in signing one D'Angelo, there were ten more, so those ten more just did it through the indie process or independently, and didn't really look at how much money could be made off of being signed to a contract, they

just looked at how much money could be made period. The reason we have such a push on the independent side is because it allows you to keep as much profit for yourself.

Art's enterprising artist is an occupational generalist who expands his individual portfolio of musical and support skills through continuous self-instruction. In becoming an indie producer-arranger, Art has, for example, expanded his knowledge of keyboards, customized studio recording environments, and assembling tours. As a band member at the start of his career, Art learned keyboards in order to develop his skills as an arranger. He said to himself at the time:

I need to start writing my arrangements for the band, for myself, and to do that I'm going to have to get re-engrossed in a universal instrument that transfers across, whether it's guitar or piano. It was easy for me to decide on piano because I already kind of had a working knowledge of it, and I loved the sound of the piano, so I didn't take formal lessons if you will, but keyboard players that I had access to would just impart little tidbits and I would build off of those.... I just started burying myself in a practice room and I would take some of my favorite songs and I would go down there and listen to them and try to find those chords.... So I started learning how to write charts, the number system, learned how the classical number system transfers to the Nashville number system, and learned how to write shorthand, if somebody said write me a chart for this right quick I'd just sit with a post-it note and scribble something out and say that's it right there.... Next thing you know, I'm getting calls to arrange parts and arrange stuff for bands.

Art also expanded his tour management skills, which he acquired by observing the management of an international tour he joined three years after he graduated college:

I got to see what the process of putting together a tour really is, and it was an education for me as well because when I get ready to do a tour as an artist now I know what things are going to be very critical. Like the rehearsals and if there's choreography, all those dance rehearsals, then the dance rehearsal with the band, and the band is arranging the music to the dance numbers. How much is going to be on stage, all of that stuff, and then just watching it grow and unfold and then that first performance you're like wow, okay, it's cool ... we would sit on our break times and watch all these guys with cell phones and laptop computers making all of these logistical decisions on how we were going to be moved from one city to the next, because we're talking a tour staff of about 30 or 40 people. There were 8 vocalists, a 9-piece band, sound and light techs, front of house guys, the backline crew and all of that, and wardrobe. All of that together moving at one time, just watching the decisions that had to be made and how we were just moved from city to city and from venue to the hotel. It was an eye-opener, it was like how do you get these buses to show up, we've just finished a show and have to be at the airport in like 30 minutes, how do you do this? Definitely a learning experience for me.

As an emerging indie artist and producer-arranger, Art works with multiple artists and studios, not only to network widely but also to customize his work with other artists. A year after he graduated college, he started his own production company in order to "work with artists and help them develop their aspirations as an artist or as somebody that wants to foster a career in music." In producing other artists, Art seldom works in the same studio and selects the studio recording environment that brings out the best in each artist:

Different studios have different vibes that are very critical for whatever kind of music that you're doing at the time. It's like certain stuff we would do in a studio where the lighting is a little brighter because we want a little bit more of a lively texture to everything that we're putting down.... Then there are other studios that are a little bit more subdued and darker ... the vibe there is ... making sure that we're getting the right mixes or the right whatever so the aesthetic is different. It definitely plays on your mentality how you approach the work that you're doing.

The business model underlying Art's vision of an enterprising artist is geared to direct sales in a niche market. Art contrasted this model with that of the major labels:

If I were putting numbers to it, like say I was signed to a major label, my break-even would be 100,000 to 200,000 units. That's just to break even on the recording budget. That doesn't even go against what they've pumped into you in terms of imaging, media training, all of the things that they do with a new artist and you have to pay back all these consulting firms and whatnot that they've had working for them, because as the old saying goes, the artist pays for everything first before he takes a check home. So your break-even is about halfway to a gold status before you can even think about doing anything different. Whereas for an indie artist your break-even point is however many units it takes for you to recoup how much money you spent to make the record. Everything after that, profit. You're already getting your writer's shares if you've got public performance, whether it be licensing and having it put on background music CD's that go out to restaurants or venues or whatever the case may be, or whether you're getting radio airplay, or they're using your music on TV shows or something like that. But yeah, at this point it's not about how many units you sell, it's about satisfaction of the art form being exposed, and I've seen artists that had a break-even point of 20,000 units, 2,000 units, and you can sell at $10 a pop, just do the math on that, you can make a $20,000 project and recoup it in 2,000 units. So you can basically sell ten to twenty shows worth of CD's if everybody were to buy one, or even half, and recoup everything that you piped into your record, and then go right back to the process of doing it again, and also minimalize your recording budget because you recorded it in the basement of the house, you already owned the gear.

Art does not belong to a labor union because he is not compelled to join and he can charge union scale without joining the union. He explained why he hasn't joined a union:

Mainly because I wasn't doing so much work that required it, and in a right to work state like Tennessee is, you don't necessarily have to be under a union to get jobs. They definitely do sometimes help to foster that, and they also kind of help to protect you in terms of wages and things like that, because there are a lot of nonunion activities that go on, but they pay you like the bare minimum. A union basically holds people accountable for making sure that number one, whoever the case might be, whether it's an artist or whether it's a band or whether it's a producer, they hold potential clients accountable to make sure that they're paying you worth your time. And also providing decent working conditions.

Union membership is effectively required in financially large music projects. According to Art, the union is especially helpful "in instances where there's a lot of money involved, like when you've got televised things going on, or when they do festivals and things like that, unions come in very handy then because it keeps everybody balanced in their workload to rest time, helps to kind of iron out the kinks from creativity to commerce."

Strategic Orientation

More than making money, achieving "peace of mind" that he is doing his best in making music is Art's chief objective: "Success for me has never been a measure of a dollar figure, ever. It's in peace of mind, knowing that the work that you do has been the best that you can possibly do within your scope of skill or your knowledge if you will." He gauges his success by knowing that he earns the respect of his peers, family and friends for his artistic expression. When I asked Art how he gauges his success, he replied:

By the peace of mind that I have and the joy that I feel being able to continuously work, consistently. And knowing that I do have the respect of my colleagues, my friends, and my family for what I have done and what I'm still doing.... That's better than having any mound of millions of dollars, because you can take your respect to the grave. You cannot take no money.

After Art mentioned that being recognized by both his peers and the fans was important to him, I asked whose recognition mattered more to him. He responded that peers and fans recognize him in different ways. For Art, peers inspire and legitimize him as a professional artist, and from fans he achieves personal validation and immortality of his artistic expression:

They mean very specific things to me at times. Having the recognition of your colleagues means that you're respected as a musician for what you stand for and the work you put down as an artist. Being recognized by your fans means that you've made a connection with them musically and artistically and in some way in their life that they appreciate and they want to foster that relationship.

Pathway

Art has taken a family-inspired pathway toward becoming an enterprising artist. The son of a minister-postal worker father and a mother who was a structural analysis engineer, Art told me that both sides of his family instilled in him a passion for making music:

My dad was a minister, so there was always music around the house, whether it be gospel or R&B, soul, jazz, my dad was a lover of music as well. So having that music around, I grew up just kind of engrossed in it. Sometimes to the point of getting in trouble because I would listen to all of his record collection, and it really developed an ear in me for a certain texture in music. I really figured out early in life that this was something I wanted to do.... My mom's family is very musical. My mom's side of the family basically were all church musicians down in southern middle Tennessee.... Uncles that played guitar and bass, Hammond organ, drums and all that. My deceased grandmother was a well-known vocalist in the church.... So I guess it's in the genes somehow, but I was the only one that was crazy enough to pursue it.

His father's musical eclecticism, as well as his father's strong integrationist position and civil rights activism during the Nashville desegregation movement of the early 1960s, inspired Art to develop a broad embrace of humanity through music. A non-violent protester who sat down in Nashville's downtown lunch counters in the early 1960s, Art's father encouraged him to immerse himself in the wider community:

My dad, having gone through all that and then seeing us actually sign into law the civil rights act, the voting rights act, and watching the desegregation of public schools and whatnot, he would say to us if we're going to really root out our problem, we also have to be a part of the daring culture that will cross the line, cross the tracks, and embrace what is unknown to us or what seems uncomfortable, because the only way you're going to get comfortable in an uncomfortable situation is to face it.... And music seemed for him to be one of those delineating avenues, because I mean he'd seen James Brown when he first started in concert, the Temptations when they first came, the Beatles, Stevie Wonder when he was then called Little Stevie Wonder. He said those crowds would be mixed but segregated.

Art's father helped him to transcend racial barriers by introducing him to multiple music genres, including country music. When Art was eight years old, his father took him to a Grand Old Opry country music concert at which Art and his father seemed to be the only African Americans in the white audience:

It was definitely a shock for me to know that most of the patronage of country music was very white. Almost to the point of being scarily white, like not necessarily being afraid of the people but just being afraid of how skewed the demographic is. Now don't get me wrong, there was a wide age range, because there were kids there my age up to ... senior citizens that were just living out their golden years, they'd go and travel and come to the Opry. I think we were probably the only black people there.... And we would talk about it afterwards, it was like don't be afraid or anything, nobody's going to harm you, but we very likely were the only people of African descent.

Art pursued music throughout his elementary and high school years and would be discovered in his high school senior year by Marv, a white, established, California-transplant gospel producer in Nashville of the transformative generation. Marv had been referred to the band by his daughter, a schoolmate of some of Art's band members. By the mid-1990s when Marv discovered Art, music production in Nashville was desegregating and white producers were increasingly working with African American artists, as Art explained:

There was ... a wave of creative movement going on that said we're going to kind of go against the grain a little bit because we've been stuck in this box for so long as a genre and as an art form, let's stretch some boundaries a little bit, get some different textures and some different interpretations of the same music and just see what happens. A lot of music just began to take a whole new life because country artists were now pulling in mass choirs to provide backing vocal work on their records and you began to see the use of the symphony orchestra on major record projects.

After Art's band broke up, Marv continued to develop Art as an artist and got him some radio airplay in the late 1990s. He advised Art to attend an area music college in order to learn about the business side of the music industry, and facilitated Art's admission and education at music college: "[Marv] said if you really want to do some serious career development you've got to put yourself in an environment where not only can you work on your creative craft, you need to be developing your business mind and also get around folks that have a like passion as you for writing and producing." Having graduated college, Art ceased playing as a club musician and set his sights on becoming an artist and producer-arranger:

> I had determined I'm not going to be a Nashville club singer for the rest of my life. If I'm going to be an artist I've got to start doing what artists do, and what artists do is they network, hone their craft and their skills, and make sure that every opportunity that is presented to them to do something that will escalate them to the next level.... The turning point for me was leaving a consistent gig that was making me about $300 or $400 a week, which isn't bad ... now I want to not just be known in Nashville as a quality musician and artist that does something special, I'm ready to be known around the world.

For Art, that "something special" was making music that would help people to transcend social boundaries:

> It was a gradual process, but once you come to where you really under-stand what that is for you personally, that's kind of the eye-opener. For me the eye-opener was that I've wanted to do music that would delineate the lines.... Race, socioeconomy, and status and all of that. Beliefs, even gender, age, all of that. Just take down all of the curtains and see every-body in the same family. Quit looking at poor folks as poor folks, rich folks as rich folks. Look at them as folks.

Susan

An emerging singer-songwriter, Susan moved from the rural Midwest to Nash-ville in the early 2000s in order to launch her pop-country musical career. Raised a fundamentalist Christian, and a self-proclaimed Republican who is "definitely pro-life," the white, twenty-something artist mainly writes secular music that reflects her Christian and rural background, but does not evan-gelize her audience. She has not yet landed a record deal, and is endeavoring to reconcile her artistry, morality, and commercial career interests, as she ex-plained: "I grew up in a small town, I'm a Christian person, I want to show that in my music without being a Christian artist. And I've had labels say you're too proper, consider Christian music."

Susan strives to express wholesome family values in her music. Her lyrics cannot offend her younger cousin Mark (pseudonym):

As a writer I do explore other options and I do try to push myself a little outside of my comfort zone to write a few things, but I'm not going to be writing songs full of cuss words, that's not who I am. I always said I gave it the Mark test, this is a cousin of mine and when I came down here he was still fairly young but he was really into music.... And I always said I think about that, I think if he were sitting there watching it on TV and singing along with it, would I be proud that he was doing that, or would I say what am I doing, I'm teaching him to say that.

As she pursues her dream of becoming a singer-songwriter, Susan also struggles to reconcile her professionalism, family values, and the gendered behavioral norms of male-dominated, collaborative songwriting. Susan is miffed but resigned to routinely taking preemptive measures to limit sexual overtures from her male co-writers:

I think it's just always difficult being a female first of all in the music business. There are great people out there, and there are some not so great people out there. Sometimes it's difficult, if you know someone has a reputation it's kind of difficult to keep telling them no, I'll write with you, but let me bring in a third writer without offending them, but at the same time you just don't know, if I write with someone new, especially a male that I don't know I'll get a room at ASCAP.

For Susan, having to conform to societal norms of female beauty is another challenge of being a female artist:

I think in our society you're supposed to be this perfect whatever. You've either got to be so different there's something that's just undeniably oh wow, that person can do whatever they want because that's their thing. And I think we're coming around more to where we're accepting people more for who they are, but it is an industry based on looks. I work out every day for myself, to be healthy, but I also consider it part of my job. It is part of my job to look a certain way when I'm doing a show, things like that. So that gets kind of frustrating at times because some of these guys will say oh that doesn't matter, it's all about how you sing. And you're like no, unfortunately it's not. That can just be kind of frustrating because it's very time-consuming.

The norm of the single female artist also conflicts with Susan's ideals: "I do have a very serious boyfriend, and that's kind of looked down upon, if you're a female you're not supposed to be married, you're not supposed to want to get married, but that's important for me because it really helps me balance everything."

Vision of an Enterprising Artist

Susan envisions herself as an "indie" artist. The small labels, she argues, give the new artist more attention than the major labels, although major-label careers often are more lucrative than indie careers:

> For me personally I've always been more of a small atmosphere type of person. I've worked in the big corporate label, I've worked in the small publishing company, and I need to be able to make a phone call and get to the person that I need to get to. So I think the appeal of the independents is great, where they only [work with] three or four artists, they can focus on them. They may not have as much money to push them, which is a disadvantage to them, but I think the rise of independents is fantastic ... the independents ... can focus more on [the] artist, they can spend more time with them.

Susan's pursuit of an indie, self-promoting artistic career occurs in a supportive, technical, and social context. She embraces home-recording technology and social media for music production in distributed work groups:

> Anyone can record in their homes now. I can record, and I have a computer and a microphone and one other piece of equipment. I don't know what I'm doing with most of it, but I can make stuff that sounds decent.... I write on my Mac book every day. I seldom will write out a lyric. If I'm writing physically with pencil and paper, it's because it's ideas, but when I sit down to actually compose a song it's on my computer. We e-mail lyrics back and forth. Publishers have work tapes and lyrics within minutes after the song is finished. And studios. I mean, you can do so much for so little money these days ... where before to cut that record from start to finish you have to get it all right, and sometimes you got some amazingly creative accidents that stayed there. But today you can still save those accidents and you can say give me another track, let me try this or that.... You can have a producer sitting in Nashville in their studio and an entire string section in London playing, in real-time he can be producing the session over the Internet. It amazes me to think you can do that. I have a lot of co-writers, we e-mail a lot of different lyrical ideas or melody things. With Garage Band you can bounce anything to iTunes to make it an MP3 and send it.... People don't actually have to be in the same room to finish something.

Although the Internet, in Susan's view, is a double-edged sword, its self-promotion advantages for the indie artist far outweigh its threats to the industry posed by illegal downloading of music. According to Susan, the Internet has:

> affected labels, here a few years ago when all the downloading first started, you'd drive up and down Music Row and every other house was for sale, every other publishing company, whatever. I think we as an industry are starting to come around to that and starting to embrace it. I hope it's not too late. I think we should have embraced it more a few years back instead of trying to fight it as hard as we did. But I mean with MySpace and some of those outlets, and CD Baby. I've used CD Baby for years. I'm on MySpace, and I can't believe some of the people that find me and some of the opportunities out there. You can sell downloads on MySpace now with SnowCap. You can put your music on iTunes through CD Baby, your own personal website, and I just think it's incredible. And artists can truly start a career, launch a career, and have a very successful career independently with that.

Susan's professional development is supported socially by a cohesive, interpersonal network of occupational peers and mentors, as well as performance venues that help to develop new indie artists. She does not belong to a union because she is "not playing on studio sessions," or to the NSAI, which she otherwise admires, largely because she cannot afford to pay the dues. Susan described the occupational cohesion among songwriters she experiences in songwriting: "every day there's an opportunity. I can write first thing in the morning, … and there's always somebody to call to bounce ideas off of. There's inspiration everywhere here."

Her vocal coach and a senior songwriter, whom she calls her "Nashville dad," are important sources of support and professional development. Susan's vocal coach helps her find her unique voice:

> He's a phenomenal vocal coach, and he's really helped me a lot, he just pushes me to extremes. We're singing Christina Aguilera, I mean this is not what I do, and then Aretha Franklin. But there's always a reason for it, and he's taught me how to use my voice and … if I can't put my voice back together enough to get through a set I can call him and he can do it over the phone, so he's helped a lot.

Susan's "Nashville dad" is about twenty-five years her senior and instructs her in the art of songwriting:

> I've got a good friend that I met … in 2000 in my first trip down here, just kind of randomly met this writer and I consider him my Nashville dad, he's been here for years and he's always taking care of me, he's always ready to teach. If you had him in here you'd be here all day, you probably

wouldn't get a single question answered because he'd be telling you how to write songs. He's been great, he's helped me a lot.

Susan avails herself of the many live-performance, professional development opportunities that are available in Nashville's bars, clubs, songwriter nights, and showcases. She recently settled on The Happening and The Courtney, live-music venues in which she feels comfortable as an artist and which generate audiences:[6]

> For me, ... I find the ones that work. When I started out I played The Louise all the time, that was pretty much the only venue I played as a writer. Now I love The Happening, and probably 90 percent of the shows I play are there. If I'm going to do a showcase, I used to use Jammin', the last one I used was The Courtney, and that will be my place from now on. Again, it's a balance of where are people going to go, are they going to want to drive downtown to park if I play a writer's night down there, or is The Happening easier? The Happening is non-smoking, everybody can come to that. And just different things like that. For me The Courtney had, I felt, a better setup and better sound for what I needed. I tend to stick to the same places because I know what I'm going to get.

Although Susan hesitates to describe herself as an entrepreneur, she acknowledges the gratification she feels from reciprocating and facilitating the professional development of her peers. Helping others to develop as artists would be a gratifying way to expand her portfolio of artistic and artist-support activities as an emerging enterprising artist:

> I'm really not an entrepreneurial type of person ... I mean I always have things I want to do next, and essentially I guess I do kind of have my own business in the fact that I'm promoting my own career, but I've never really delved into starting a label or a publishing company. If anything, I would say it would be more of an artist development type of thing, because I know that.... And I love doing that ... if I were to start a business it would be more artist development because I love that, I love guiding people and helping people, because people did it for me.

Strategic Orientation

Susan aims for a life and career as a self-sustaining artist who is expressive on her own terms, and directly and deeply engaging of her fans. She does not sneer at having commercial success and gaining industry recognition, but she conceives of success as perfecting her own artistic expression: "I think for me personally it's being proud of what you do, and again I'm going to say being able to make a living or have a career doing what I want to do and what I love to do, making music." Furthermore, she strives to achieve a deep artistic engagement with humanity, by connecting directly with her fans and listeners:

> I don't want to sit here and say I'm writing songs specifically for that person, because you do have to write what you feel and what you think is right, but it is. It's the worst feeling in the world to go out there and sing and have the crowd just not get it and not connect with you. On the flip side, it's the most amazing feeling in the world to be singing along and see people throughout the crowd singing lyrics to your song. That's the payoff for me I guess, is when I'm out there and the crowd is into it, and they're connecting, and you're touching somebody somehow. That's why I do what I do.

Consistent with her objective of perfecting her own artistry, and the gratification she feels from facilitating others' professional development, Susan's own professional development thrives on supportive peer recognition, especially that of "other writers" who

> have looked at me, or publishers, and said I've seen so much growth, that's encouraging. When they can look at you and say keep doing what you're doing, you're growing each time you come in here, that tells me that I am doing the right thing. Because there are days you don't know, there are days you wake up and go am I crazy, I'm 25, I feel like I'm 18. I don't have a job, what am I doing? So that's been great.

In contrast, recognition from "the industry" intensifies the art-commerce tension she feels in having to comply with aesthetic guidelines for commercial success. Susan reflected on this tension by contrasting her feelings at a songwriter night with a peer audience with how she feels at a critical industry showcase:

> When you do just a songwriter night, ... I send out millions of emails and you might get one or two industry people that show up just because they're interested, so they may come out, but generally you've got your fans who follow you, and you've got your friends who are there to support you. I always joke about we would sit up here and play for each other, we'll do it. So if the room is empty we're still going to do it. And a lot of times I do go out to somebody's show because they came out to mine. You just support each other. Showcases are where you're going to find the more critical audiences and again that's kind of a term that's thrown around, sometimes in the right instance and sometimes it's really not a showcase. At my last ... showcase ..., it was a full band show, and I invited ... a lot of the industry people. People from every record label, every publisher that I knew, and I had a really great turnout. That is the time when

you sit there and you're not really connecting with the crowd as an artist, because you are there to be critiqued and ... you hope that enough of your fan base and enough of your friends show up and act as your fan base so that you can connect and ... give the record label people, the producers, the publishers, the writer from the *Tennessean* and *Country Weekly* ... a true picture of who you are as an artist.

Pathway

A self-trained musician who grew up in a supportive farm family, Susan sang in school and church prior to high school. Upon entering high school, Susan began touring, opening and headlining at county fairs throughout the rural Midwest with a regular band. She toured during the summers while in high school and during the year and a half at the local religious college she attended before she moved to Nashville; once there, she completed her college at a Nashville-area college music-business program. Her parents strongly encouraged her to pursue her musical career:

> I've just always been singing, ... In school they would say what do you want to be when you grow up, let's take these tests and find out what you want to do. I always did those and thought okay, cool, I'll go into pharmacy, I always had something in mind. Then my parents just said do you really want to sing? ... they've always been very supportive and ... helped me find outlets to try it out and see if it's what I wanted to do, and then I just fell in love with it. I grew up listening to Faith Hill and Martina and Reba and all those ladies, and just going to concerts when I was young. Always kind of in the back of my mind knowing I wanted to do it.

As she embarked on her family-inspired career pathway, Susan protected the family farm from any lawsuits she might incur as a touring, and increasingly enterprising, musician: "I ... have a limited liability company where I can run pretty much everything I do music-wise I run through that account. My parents and I started that when I was touring just to avoid lawsuits if anything should happen with equipment falling on someone. We didn't want my dad to lose the whole farm essentially. So we do have that, and of course we ran all the merchandise through that."

Susan became a performer-songwriter when she moved to Nashville. Prior to her move, she performed with a cover band, but had begun to write her own music late in high school. Her Nashville friends advised her to write because writing-performing careers were the vanguard careers in Nashville. She mustered up her courage to pursue her new career path:

> [E]verybody kept pushing me, the industry is changing, you've got to write, essentially that's how you're going to make a living if you want to

do this. I really started thinking about it, I thought I've got to try this.... Then slowly I came around, but I really didn't consider myself a writer until probably six or eight months ago. It took people saying ... you can actually bring something to the table, you're not just an artist. So then it kind of gave me a confidence boost.

Susan is now actively immersing herself in the collaborative community of co-writers:

It really is challenging. Like with Al [pseudsonym], ... he and I have done it so much and we're such good friends that I can just walk in the room, ... I don't have to have any melodies in my head, I can just walk in and we'll find something. So sometimes it's really easy like that. Other times if I'm writing with some of the big writers, you kind of go in and you're the kid, you've got to prove yourself.... I don't have a publishing deal yet so I'm pitching my stuff to a lot of publishers, and I'm fortunate to have quite a few of them say well we'd love to set you up with our writer, and then you try those and hopefully you find your other Al, ... or whoever that's going to really click with you.

Tina

An emerging, pop/rock, performing and recording indie artist who was raised in Nashville and recently graduated high school in her junior year, Tina is the daughter of an Asian immigrant father who owns his own business-service enterprise, and a homemaker mother, a U.S. native of European descent. Tina identifies with both of her parental ethnicities and addresses the theme of being true to oneself in her music:

The overall theme behind what I've been doing lately is just kind of staying true to yourself. Like there's a song called [title] on my EP, and it's like people sometimes will try and change you, whether it's in the music business or just in general, and it may not be for the better so it's like either stand your ground and know why you don't want to change, or look at what they're saying and see if that's something you want to do. But to at least have some kind of belief in what you do and staying true to that, and not letting somebody try to break those dreams if somebody has a dream.

She replied with an independent and entrepreneurial spirit to my request to elaborate on her artistic theme: "It can be anything from a kid that's in high school and is having trouble fitting in with the other kids, or it can be an entrepreneur that wants to start a business but people around him say well why don't you just work for the bigger company or whatever. Those are a few examples of where you'd want to stay true to who you are and not change."

Tina attributes the threats to individual artistic self-expression and pressures to conform in the music industry to the media. I asked Tina, "are there certain specific forces that you feel cause individuals to not be themselves?" She replied:

Yeah, I think like in the music business, the media. You see the paparazzi that chase everybody around, and they become so worried about what everybody else thinks around them. Especially with successful artists, I mean, look at Britney Spears. And that goes along with what you were saying earlier about making music that pleases others. Because at that point all they're trying to do is please what the paparazzi or the papers say and then maybe that may change their music, I don't really know. So I think that media, people around you, in school, having a certain image, I think it's all like an image. They put on this façade of the way they think people should be instead of being an individual.

She attributes her own individualism to the values her parents imparted to her and her brother: "they taught us to be individuals and to be thinkers. So that's kind of always been with me, so I've always kind of done my own thing and said people can like it or they don't have to. This is who I am."

Beginning at age fourteen, Tina has pursued her professional development in a sequential apprenticeship with three producers. The first two were age fifty-something, established, award-winning writer-producers of the transformative generation who had migrated from LA to Nashville during that musician migration of the 1990 era. Her current producer is a thirty-two-year-old Nashville-based musician in an internationally successful rock band:

Well my producer right now has really been the best producer I've had by far, but he's been a really big influence not necessarily on my style, because I always had like a certain sound that I wanted, but he's really been able to like hone in the sound and really take everything to the next level. I'm really grateful to have somebody like that because that's kind of what I've been looking for in the last several years in producers, but they just haven't had the time to commit, and he's been able to really give me direction. From his experience he's been really successful in his band, so he's learned a lot in his travels and touring.

Vision of an Enterprising Artist

As Tina endeavors to break in to the music scene, she weighs the indie route against the major-label pathway in terms of cost and distribution opportunities. I asked her what are the "biggest changes" in the music industry that had occurred in recent years:

I think the biggest changes are first of all it's a lot less expensive to make a record nowadays, especially in Nashville.... That's the biggest change, and with that to be able to create a record on your own, the power is somewhat not as present with the labels because if you can make a record on your own, people say well then why would I want to be with a label? And the purpose of being with a label other than the recordings of it, if you financially can do that, would be marketing and distribution and promotion.... With a major label it's already a built-in process that's been there for 50 years, and it builds in promotion teams and they know all the radio companies and DJs who are going to spin the records on mainstream radio ... that is the advantage of having a major label. But now the disadvantage is they've restructured deals because of all the losses, record sales have gone down 25 percent or something this year, which people don't notice the digital sales continue to plummet, but with that said I think that labels have deals that are called 360 deals that they're restructuring now where they take basically a percentage out of your touring, out of your merch, out of all different aspects of an artist, whereas five or ten years ago that wasn't happening.

As she breaks in, Tina continues to widen the genres and demographic markets for her music, as well as expand her individual portfolio of production, management, and distribution skills through continuous self-instruction. Although her primary artistic genre is pop/rock, she has diversified her genres to include country music and music that is thematically inspired by the Asian cultural tradition of her father's ethnicity. Adding on country music increases Tina's chances of getting a song cut:

I've written some country stuff as well on the side, or a song that ended up turning out more country than we expected, where the co-writer really likes it and their song plugger wants to pitch it ... actually there's a new one that we just finished which I'm pretty excited about. My producer just signed with [a production company], they're like the best people to be working with for country.... So crossing my fingers, hopefully I'll get some country cuts.

Recording Asian-themed pop music in her father's native language gives Tina access to an additional niche market:

So a lot of times I learned songs in that language, and my dad will help me with pronunciation and stuff. Ever since I did that it's been great because on My Space it's a great tool as far as like an online presence. I posted a song that I recorded with actually a Nashville session musician and I've had like I don't even know how many plays on the song, but all of a sudden I've got like all these people contacting me, [Asian] people, on My Space and online saying I love your music, where can I buy your CD? So I'm thinking about at some point if I can find the time to make a record, because obviously there's some kind of demand for it.

An efficient enterprising artist, Tina has been expanding her technical skills. She has begun to do computer-based engineering on her laptop:

> For me as an artist I can hear which passes were the best, so then I would comp my own, so that's kind of engineering.... I have an M Box, which I run Pro Tools with that, and I'm about to probably get some other different types of recording equipment, probably update Pro Tools ... actually the amazing thing with technology now, I have Garage Band on my laptop, and ever since I've had my Mac I'm able to record on that as well, it has built-in speakers into the computer. So it's amazing, I mean it's obviously not the same quality as a record, but to get the idea across and for the song to kind of stand on its own it's a really good tool to use.

Tina engages her burgeoning fan base via social media and is attempting to rationalize her increasingly unwieldy process of fan communications. I asked her if she has much interaction with her fans over the Internet. She struggles to achieve a direct personal engagement with a growing fan base:

> I'm trying to think of a new like plan as to how I can do it because up until this last like two weeks I answer all the messages, like all the comments and everything. I'm behind a couple of hundred messages. That's a job in itself on top of all the other things I'm doing, like travelling and trying to do shows and writing.... Every once in a while I put up a general message and say I just want to let you know I'm listening to all the comments, keep them coming, thank you, I appreciate it, if it takes me a little while to answer back I hope you understand.... So I'm always afraid if somebody doesn't read it and they'll think why didn't she answer back. I just worry about all that, I'm very meticulous when it comes to all that kind of stuff.

She recently produced her first project and intends to hone her production skills. Becoming proficient in producing, she explained, increases her capacity to be artistically independent:

> This last project was the first project I produced on my own. I definitely have room to grow since I'm really young. I have a producer right now that we're working with and he's in a rock band, so he's getting ready to hit the road, they're doing like a U.S. tour and Australia and stuff. So since he's kind of out of the picture for a couple of months I decided I kind of wanted to take the reins myself and get some experience with producing,

giving direction to the musicians. I think it will help a lot down the road when he's not always around.

Tina described how she, as an independent artist, produced the record by memory without a score or the Nashville number system:

It involves a lot of things. It depends on like what scale, like if you're on a record they have people like all different kinds of jobs that would take the role of like an average, normal producer for an independent project. So for a label they have like a creative team of people that will contact the musicians, do scheduling, book the studio, all that kind of stuff. But for like the project I just did, I kind of lined up all the musicians and then as well as being in the studio, giving direction to them and saying this is the feel or vibe of this song and also even down to like the notes they're playing, if you hear something that doesn't sound right, figure out why, or if it does sound right but if you want it to go in a different direction it's your job to kind of push and bend the musicians.

An enterprising artist, Tina is crossing the DIY threshold as her art-making business scales upward. She is looking for a manager to help her support her artistry, but she acknowledges that she needs even greater scale in order to attract someone to manage her artistic enterprise:

I'm at the point right now where I would really like to get some management in place, because I'm doing so much on my own and it's just a lot of work. I mean, all the aspects, you've done a really good job at trying to cover everything. When people think music business they think write songs and somehow they make it to the radio, but it is truly a business.... Generally a manager won't make any money until there's an income being made or money is being made, and right now that's not happening. I really have to find someone who really believed in what I do to get that to happen now.

Strategic Orientation

Tina conceives of success in artistic and commercial terms. She loves making music and, at this early career stage, views artistic expression primarily as self-expression. She hopes to develop her fan base and ultimately to be recognized by the industry by writing hits and winning Grammys:

The first and foremost thing behind all of that is I make the music because I love making music, and I make it for myself but also in hope that it's commercial and other people like it. So as far as music professionals, it is important that it's something that they see as commercial, but it doesn't necessarily mean they have to like it. So it may be some record executive that doesn't even like certain types of music, but he's really good at getting it to the next step.

For Tina, songwriting is personal expression, although she also writes with her fans in mind: "I have a certain message that I want to convey to the listener because it's an expression of who I am and whether it's visually or it's through the music I want them to be able to see that, which is why I do it." Tina explained that her fan base is developing on the coattails of her successful producer. Her fans also hail from her father's ethnic Asian community. I asked her to characterize her fan base in demographic terms, to which she replied:

At this point I really can't. On My Space it's really broad. I'll get requests from the teeny bopper demographic, and I got put on [my producer's band's] page on the top friends, they put me on there, they have like thousands of fans or whatever, so I get lots of requests from them. Their biggest demographic is like the soccer mom kind of demographic, just because of the kind of music they do, it's like arena rock. So I get a lot of those fans to my page, and I get a lot of the [Asian] community, so it's pretty broad.

In response to my question about how she gauges her success, Tina replied in terms of market indicators and recognition from the music industry:

I guess getting some songs cut by an artist, getting a record label behind you. I mean, I wouldn't think that if I get a record deal in a month I wouldn't say I'm where I want to be, because even after you get a record deal it's still not guaranteed that the record will come out or that it will do well. But it's the first step. So that would be some kind of success to me. Releasing a single and it doing well, that's success to me. And like ... playing a show in front of 30,000 people and being on TV.... And down the road, record sales. Grammys.

Pathway

Tina has taken a family-inspired pathway toward becoming a successful artist. Her parents' enthusiasm and wide-ranging musical tastes inspired her passion for music, as well as her aesthetic quest to achieve a subtle and unique fusion of her parents' diverse cultural traditions in her own musical expression:

I would say since I was a little kid my dad would always play a lot of [Asian] music around the house, ... so I grew up with a lot of different influences. My mom listened to anything from Wynona to Celene Dion, so I just listened to everything as a child, so that influenced me. I always kind of wanted to infuse that into music just because I think in today's day and age to really stand out among other artists you really have to have something that's unique and different, and so I'm still trying to find a way of doing it where it's still commercial at the same time, because the kind of music I would like to do is very commercial kind of music. So I'm still figuring it out, and right now it's very subtle influences in a lot of the melodic structures, because they have a lot of minor and chromatic scales. Some of that just kind of comes out naturally in the music, but it's not always, unless it's somebody that really studies music and really listens to every little thing I do vocally, they notice those kinds of things. But the general public probably won't say oh, she must be from [Asian nation] when they hear the music. So I'm trying to find a way of infusing it the next couple of projects that I do ... I don't want it to end up being like, Shakira's music is very Latin influenced, or Colombian, I don't want it to be that extreme. I just want where it kind of catches your ear, where you hear a little [Asian instrument] sound and wonder what that instrument was, or hear a rhythm on [Asian percussion instrument] and are just kind of intrigued by it.

Jason

The U.S.-born child of immigrant Asian parents, Jason had dreamed of becoming a rock star or club owner during his childhood. The thirty-something enterprising artist remains wedded to the indie music scene as he transitions from guitarist in a successful touring and self-recording rock band toward club management and indie artist development. From his position as assistant manager in a live music venue in Nashville, Jason is widening his DIY portfolio of club management, music production, marketing, and artist development skills, networks, and professional activity. The self-proclaimed "workaholic and control freak" remains indie because "That's where the money is.... You have control, you can do whatever you want still. You don't have to pay out to anybody, you can sell your CDs online, the Internet you can do yourself. You just do it yourself."

Vision of an Enterprising Artist

Jason envisions and enacts a dynamic and ramifying club manager role. The club manager is embedded in a set of interdependent networks and exchange relationships with co-workers and artists. His club management, and his sideline in artist development, are mutually interdependent. In addition to booking, scheduling, and promoting music and events, stocking the bar and kitchen, and cooking and cleaning for the club, Jason provides critical feedback to artists and labels, advises managers of other clubs, engineers live music, writes and plugs his own songs, and plays on simple gigs.

For Jason, artist development is an important means for generating food, beverage, and door sales. For the indie artist and label, the live venue is a major vehicle for self-promotion and music distribution. He provides artistic criticism to artists and labels, as well as booking advice to managers of other clubs about the economic viability of performers:

> Bands are always wanting feedback, how did I sound from that songwriter's night? The songs are still too long, let's get straight to the meat.... I have even the labels go, Jason, what do you think of them? I go she doesn't sell it to me ... I mean like I've had other music venues' managers hanging out going what do you think about this person? I'll go the show is great, nice guy, don't book him. Why? No sales.... But again, I'm not the manager but they want the critique. This is the music business, you're going to have to have tough skin.

For Jason, providing advice is integral to maintaining mutually supportive exchange relationships within the Nashville club community:

> I believe in support, you've got to help wherever you can. One day I will need help, and besides money, one day I might need your help. Half the guys are electricians, so it's like man, I know one day I'm going to remodel a house or build a house, I want you guys, can you cut me a deal? It's little things like that. That's how you get somewhere is helping someone out, you're a community, that's what you do.

In the competitive and volatile community of live music venues, which change hands frequently, Jason envisions his relationship with the club owner as a long-term "family" relationship:

> This is the kind of business where friends or family have to get involved. That's what I thought about doing. I'd love to open up my own venue. Of course it didn't happen that way.... I would like to but I think I've been adopted into the [club] owner's family.... I'm happy where I'm at. Basically we've incorporated his ideas and my ideas and [another co-worker's] visions, it's pretty much there.... We're just close. Good friends.... But if he wants to get rid of it and sell it, I wouldn't mind trying to buy it out or becoming full-time owner. Or if he decides to open up another one, I'd be like what city and state, make sure my son's taken care of, hopefully he's in college by then and I can go off and do my own thing.

In the meantime, Jason is actively developing the club as a diversifying, multipurpose "flexible" venue for live music, artist development, and, possibly, a new club-centered label and production company. New home-recording technology and the Internet help promote the venue as well as enterprising artists who are directly engaging their fans:

You can do stuff in your own house. At the [club] we have a 24-track recording device which we can record live shows, which helps in the marketing of our venue....

[W]e charge a fee. If you want to do an electronic press kit, you want to do a live CD, we've got it right in-store ... But then our thing would be here's your thing, you can use this, record it, mix and master, whatever, package it, do your CD release party here. Or talk to Jason, ... he can help you get to the next level.... But we could always go into [Club] Records, which we could take your music, sell it ... I would run the label or be part of the A&R ... I'd be like hey guys, you sound great, CD's good, how about this—let me start selling your CDs online from our store, you can have your parties here, we'll work on the Internet stuff with you, work on your merchandise, go from there.... I mean we're trying to launch an Internet radio station as well.... It's just a very flexible venue.

Strategic Orientation

As a club manager, Jason is oriented toward managing the relationship between a band and the fans, a central feature of the strategic orientation of the contemporary generation of enterprising artists. In Nashville, according to Jason, managing this relationship is tricky: "[The] Nashville crowd is fickle. You can't compete, you can't have competing fans, you can't be overplayed.... I guess it's just all driven by the bands and the fans. You just have to think smartly how to book, and hopefully it happens."

Internet technology, claims Jason, is vital for linking bands and fans:

MySpace is the most important thing right now because everybody's on it. If something was to wipe out MySpace we're all screwed. Used to be when email first came out, hot mail would be the one, you'd keep all your hot mail addresses. That's my back-up in a sense.... I'm still a fan of just give me a call. But yeah, MySpace, Internet, you can sell your stuff on the Internet, with live streaming I can do shows, college bands if they're playing in Nashville they've got old school friends in San Francisco that can watch the show from their home.

Jason feels successful not only when he receives a "steady paycheck and the doors are still open," but also by the gratification he feels from helping a band to resonate with their fans:

Here's the best example I've had recently. It's a bluegrass band ... really good band.... But they did a cover of a song by ... a rock group, and they turned it bluegrass style. When I first heard it, I said that's a good song, the harmonies are there, but the orientation of the instruments was wrong, that's why you guys can't vibe on it, I see what you're trying to do. I told them let's change this up, let's let this instrument do this and this instrument do this, record it and try it. Lo and behold, six months later they came by, they were on the road, they dropped off a CD, I put it in and I don't tear up too often, but that song and the way they did it made me tear up. I called them and said it sounds good, they go Jason, those changes made a world of a difference. I go good, that's what I want to hear. They love the song, it's a hit wherever they go, it's just beautiful. That makes you feel good.

Pathway

Jason's mother, more than his father, helped launch him on what has unfolded as a family-inspired career as an enterprising artist. Jason, whose father is an architect and his mother a nurse, described his mother's influence on her children's interest in music, and Jason's pursuit of a musical career:

When I was a kid I found her guitar in the closet, an acoustic Yamaha. It was in bad shape. I just started strumming away and she asked if I wanted to take lessons. It took off from there. Did the free guitar lessons and then progressed up to better lessons, and then I ended up going to [a Nashville-area college]. So I thought a guitar performance measure could work as a session guy. My mom's always been the one that's always loved the arts. My sister has done ballet and piano, I tried to pick up piano but I just stuck with guitar.

Jason described the pivotal moments on his experiential pathway in self-training and formal music lessons in family-metaphorical terms. He never joined the union because it was reputed to not provide a return on dues in job referrals and health insurance. Instead, his pathway consisted of stints with a successful indie rock band, who he considers "family" despite its unfortunate dissolution, and apprenticeships with fatherly mentors, including his current boss and club owner.

Beginning in junior high school, Jason apprenticed in an instrument repair shop. Larry (pseudonym), the repair shop owner, mentored Jason in music and navigating life:

My biggest mentor of all time is [Larry]. My dad didn't really abandon us, he had to go find work somewhere else.... So [Larry], who gave me my first real job at a [repair] shop, took me under his wing and he was more a father to me.... He was there every time I needed help.... I would go to school, after school I'd go to the shop and he'd be there. I'd talk to him about anything, he'd tell me his stories, we'd go run errands, go fishing. He was just basically my dad. If I needed help, he was there for me.

During his college years—he graduated from a Nashville-area college in the mid-2000s—Jason and some friends formed an indie-recording rock band that had a successful eight-year stint performing original work on a national and international touring circuit. Three albums later, the band met its demise with the exodus of the lead singer, who embarked on a solo career. Although the breakup embittered Jason toward his exiting band member, the band experience, for Jason, was a positive and powerful training experience in a wide range of artistic and art-support skills, and he remains close with the other ex-band members:

> Well, I like to brag about this band.... We were the band that had it all covered. What I've seen is you've got bands that are great musicians, bad businesspeople. Or good businesspeople, bad musicians, but they cover up for it because they make it look so good. We were all perfect in a way that we used the gifts that we had to make it work ... my bass player was more the arranger of the music. So he was good at that, he was good at doing promotions, and he made sure at rehearsal that we worked on what we should ... my other guitar player, his background is in radio so he knew the marketing side, he knew what he wanted to do and he was the producer of the band. [another band member] was our socialite, he would be the one being seen everywhere.... I was behind the scenes, making the phone calls, making everything work. I made sure that the calendars were straight, the budgets were straight. I was the go-fer, I'd go out and get CDs, folders, anything. We all had a good business sense, so we knew it was a business, we knew to run everything like a business, but at the same time we had to go out and be seen, because this is how this town works. So we were out everywhere. If we weren't rehearsing we were out supporting local music, and if not that we were with our families.... Not only did we have ourselves looking good, we had ourselves marketed right, we wrote good songs, we put on good shows, we support the scene, and we have our shit together.

After the band broke up, Jason moved into club management. He heard about the opening of some new live-music venues from another band, and was referred to his current job by a live-music sound engineer with whom his ex-band had worked at another Nashville venue.

EMERGING ENTERPRISING ARTISTS

As they embark on their careers as enterprising artists, the contemporary generation reproduces and extends the musician community forged by the earlier, transformative generation of enterprising artists. They reproduce the community of enterprising artists by adopting and enacting the enterprising artist role created by the earlier generation who mentor the new generation. This is a role of artist activist grounded in a personal risk orientation, in which employment risks and opportunities hinge on one's perseverance in perfecting one's artistry, continuously expanding one's individual portfolio of artistic and art-support skills, and promoting oneself in live venues and through social media. Based on a personal risk orientation, the enterprising artist acts on a strategic orientation toward the pursuit of artistic freedom in a direct engagement with the fans, the music consumer. By widening their skill portfolios and becoming occupational generalists, they reproduce the community by producing not only their own music, but also one another's music.

In the context of Nashville and national identity politics, the contemporary generation extends the musician community as the increasingly diverse generation of emerging artists express their social identities in a widening range of musical genres. Following the entrepreneurial lead of the earlier generation, the diversifying contemporary generation creates a more inclusive community of enterprising artists who produce music on their own, in close collaboration with other enterprising artists, and in direct engagement with their fans.

Reproducing this diverse community of enterprising artists occurs discontinuously. As the eight profiles of enterprising artists in this and the previous chapters show, enacting this "individualistic" role of enterprising artist rests not only on artist perseverance and self-expression, but also on sustaining collegial relations with one's immediate collaborators and successful engagement with one's fans. Interpersonal rivalry, animosity, and competition for fans can overwhelm enterprising artists and jeopardize their community.

Some enterprising artists, and closely aligned impresarios, have taken it upon themselves to create communal social spaces for other enterprising artists in Nashville. These enterprising artists, acting with an *inter*personal risk orientation, create social enterprises—clubs, music schools, production companies—with the explicit social mission of encouraging artist professional development, collegiality, and employment referrals. These "artistic social entrepreneurs" are the second type of artist activist theorized in chapter 2. Throughout the musician migration to Nashville, they have envisioned, modeled, and instituted an array of communal social spaces for their fellow enterprising artists.

CHAPTER 5

Creating Social Spaces for Artists

Pathways to Becoming an Artistic Social Entrepreneur

Throughout the last few decades, artistic social entrepreneurs have arisen to create communal social spaces for the growing community of enterprising artists in Nashville. These social spaces encourage artist professional development and collegiality and provide job-referral and networking opportunities for artists. Nashville's Bluebird Café, for example, describes itself as a

> songwriter's performance space.... A typical nightly performance consists of three or four songwriters seated in the center of the room, taking turns playing their songs and accompanying each other instrumentally and with harmony vocals.... In 2008, original owner and founder Amy Kurland sold the legendary venue to the Nashville Songwriters Association International (NSAI), a 40+ year old, not-for-profit organization devoted to the service of songwriters and the craft of songwriting. More of a donation than a corporate sale, Kurland saw NSAI's mission to "educate, elevate and celebrate songwriters" as a way to continue the Bluebird's relationship to songwriters and to the community.[1]

Driven by compassion for others, social entrepreneurs often develop social enterprises where there is a "significant institutional void" by "using market-based methods to solve social problems."[2] According to one exhaustive survey, social entrepreneurs are "individuals or organizations engaged in entrepreneurial activities with a social goal."[3] The social goal of an artistic social entrepreneur is to build and sustain artist community and provide professional development opportunities for artists of any or all career stages.

In dynamic and diversifying Nashville,[4] these purveyors of artist community serve enterprising artists whose bands and micro-production enterprises are sustained by collegial interpersonal relations with immediate collaborators, but which may founder on the shoals of dysfunctional interpersonal relations, as discussed in chapters 3 and 4. I refer to *artistic social entrepreneurs* as occupational peers and closely aligned impresarios who socialize risk for their fellow artists by creating communal social spaces—e.g., schools, taverns, clubs, performance venues, university-based music programs, independent production companies, co-working spaces, and renovated loft studios—in which artists network with one another for work opportunities, inspire original

93

music, and hone their skills. In these social spaces, artists instruct one another in what are often, as Robert Faulkner and Howard Becker put it, multiple and "fragmented" repertoires of the local music community.[5]

In this chapter, I examine pathways to becoming an artistic social entrepreneur. Previous research on social entrepreneurs has emphasized the impact of one's stock of human, social, and cultural capital on one's mobilization of requisite resources for launching and sustaining a social enterprise. Less sociological attention has been given to the influence of career-biographical factors, such as family, religion, education, and pivotal career turning points that may inspire and compel one to become a social entrepreneur and to envision and shape one's social enterprise, let alone an artistic social enterprise.[6] The profiles of four artistic social entrepreneurs in this chapter illustrate how their strategic and risk orientations and career pathways shape the social enterprises they envision and influence their assumption and enactment of their roles as artist activists.[7]

Artistic social entrepreneurs are the second type of artist activist theorized in chapter 2. Their strategic orientations toward community-building are somewhat more "collective" than that of the "individualistic" enterprising artist. Like the enterprising artist, the artistic social entrepreneur engages in individual entrepreneurial action. Unlike the action of the enterprising artist who directly engages music consumers, the action of the artistic social entrepreneur is directed at enhancing the professional well-being of large groups of peers.

Artistic social entrepreneurs and enterprising artists are also distinguished by their risk orientations. Enterprising artists are focused primarily on a personal risk orientation of perseverance in the continuous expansion of one's portfolio of artistic and art-support skills. In contrast, artistic social entrepreneurs are focused primarily on an *inter*personal risk orientation. The interpersonal risk orientation of artistic social entrepreneurs is expressed in the social spaces that they envision to sustain collegial interpersonal interactions among peers. These interactions include peer mentoring, teacher-student mentoring, and social networking for launching careers and job referrals.

Two types of artistic social entrepreneurs, based on the level of institutionalization of their social enterprises, emerged from my interviews with Nashville music professionals. The first is what I term an *organizational entrepreneur*, an artistic social entrepreneur who operates an ongoing formal organization, such as a music school or nightclub, with a hired staff and a large number of regular participants who are also linked to established artist advocacy organizations, such as unions and professional associations. The second is what I call a *portfolio entrepreneur*, an artistic social entrepreneur who maintains, produces, and promotes an ongoing but dynamic roster of indie artists, collaborates and contracts with freelance partners and employees on a project-by-project basis, and has little or no connection to artist advocacy organizations.

The comparison of the four artistic social entrepreneurs indicates that organizational and portfolio entrepreneurs differ sociologically in the pathways they took to become artistic social entrepreneurs. All four hailed from families of business owners or families who otherwise inspired entrepreneurialism in their children. The differences pertain to the embrace of artistic expression. The two organizational entrepreneurs took what I term a *family-inspired pathway* to artistic social entrepreneurship. In this pathway, the organizational entrepreneur hailed from a family that practiced both entrepreneurship *and* artistic expression as a career or economic livelihood and that inspired and financially supported their child's artistic social enterprise. The two portfolio entrepreneurs, in contrast, took what I call a *movement-inspired pathway* to artistic social entrepreneurship. On this pathway, the emerging entrepreneur was swept up by an artistic movement during her childhood and adolescence that inspired her to overcome strong familial inhibitions on pursuing a career or economic livelihood based in alternative and avant-garde artistic expression.

Artistic social entrepreneurs are not themselves necessarily professional musicians. Of the four entrepreneurs profiled in this chapter, one each of the organizational and portfolio entrepreneurs is a professional musician, while the others are music-loving social entrepreneurs closely aligned with the musician community.

Sustaining an artistic social enterprise for peers is not a foregone conclusion. Artistic social entrepreneurs endeavor to sustain their communal social spaces with steady revenues from music consumers. In this highly competitive arena of niche markets, the artistic social entrepreneur competes for the revenues from a large number of "omnivorish"[8] consumers who may not steadily consume the avant-garde music of the niche market served by the social entrepreneur. The two types of artistic social entrepreneurs model different organizational approaches to addressing consumer-market uncertainties that can differentiate and destabilize the emerging community of enterprising artists.

ORGANIZATIONAL ARTISTIC SOCIAL ENTREPRENEURS

Ellen's music school and Roberta's club sustain communities of musicians and songwriters of all career stages. Ellen and Roberta are white and college-educated, and have taken family-inspired pathways to becoming organizational artistic social entrepreneurs.

Ellen's School: A Community of Mentoring Musicians

Ellen founded and has directed a music school for several years. The school offers a broad curriculum of courses on playing multiple genres of popular music for students with a range of playing experience and competence. It is supported by tuition, concerts by the faculty of area professional, union musicians and occasional touring musicians, fund-raisers, and grants from arts agencies.

As a social enterprise, the school promotes the personal and professional development of its students, aspiring music professionals. One faculty member, a producer-arranger, explained that professional session work does not provide learning and apprenticeship opportunities and that the school is an important source of mentoring for aspiring professional musicians:

> It's a unique school.... The faculty is heavily working professionals.... As a result you [the student] can take a course there and by osmosis get a lot more information than you're paying for as far as the course goes. That's been where I've mostly imparted my wisdom on anybody that wants it. Normally in the work environment I'm working with my team of people that I generally hire.... As a producer I'll put a budget together and get that okayed ... but generally I have the hands-on for these smaller projects, these instrumental things that I do that may involve from 6 to 20 people ... there's very little mentoring that goes on there because they're my peers and above. But occasionally someone will ask if they can come to a session, somebody from the [school], but normally that's where [at the school] I do the mentoring.

As members of this socially diverse artistic community, the faculty shares a common repertoire of music and its members frequently perform and record together in school-related and other professional venues. As this white faculty member put it, referring to her fellow musicians:

> They really love the music ... probably 90% ... are never going to get rich playing ... music ... but what ... keeps the community going is the necessity ... to keep the word out there and keep the music in front of people, so that another generation can carry it on ... and that's why the [school] has been such a boon to us, because it's a community center for us to go hang out, have coffee, see your friends, talk about the music, teach the music, be in an ensemble, playing the music, just reveling in this wonderful art form that's going to have to keep being nurtured or it will go away.

The school also helps out-of-town musicians to enter and become integrated into the Nashville music scene. Recalling his initial entry and pathway to becoming a faculty member, this African American musician stated: "I met [Ellen] after I moved here. After I moved here I started to do just what I did in [previous location], get out on the scene, go sit in with people. And [Ellen] was one of the groups that I sat in with, and you just strike up a conversation, one thing leads to another, you just start to develop a relationship."

Ellen's Vision

Ellen envisions the school as a cohesive community that nurtures personal development, positive relationships, and individual artistic expression. As she explained, "I created something that I had always wanted, that I wish that I would have had. This whole thing is an apprenticeship, being able to study and play with your mentors, and that's not what you get when you're in a college or university.... You grow in a situation like this rapidly because you're playing with guys that move you along." For Ellen, the school is not only an apprenticeship in music professionalism, it is an apprenticeship in sustaining meaningful human relationships. She likens her school to a family:

> This is a social place for people, they come for social reasons, it is a family, we socialize a lot with each other. We have jam sessions ... [that] are social events for people to be together. It's just real interesting what it's done for people.... This is my family ... there's a lot of love through here. It's really quite incredible to watch the kids. Some of the young ones that I've seen, that I've mentored that've gone on to college, they've got full rides, and they call me and say thank God I studied with you ... and I'm thinking, alright, I've done the right thing.

Ellen's humanistic vision is reflected in her holistic approach to mentoring. Mentoring helps the student not only to hone his technical skills, but also to strengthen his self-confidence in artistic self-expression:

> And I'm loyal to these people. If there's something wrong I call them up. I seem like I'm a psychologist sometimes, because if I see the tears come on, which happens, they're on stage, they're scared, there's a lot of issues that come up. I don't really address it too much on the stage, I pull them off and talk to them.... The light goes on, or they got into the moment and tears come, or you make them get into their lyric and say what is that about, what's that to you.

Ellen's humanism extends to fostering meaningful relationships. She takes delight in the facilitative role the school plays in strengthening interpersonal relationships of its participants:

> We mentor a lot of people. We probably mentor everyone that walks through the door to a certain extent ... so I see a lot of lives change.... A lot of lives are changing big time.... I've got one lady that's a psychologist, she's 65, and she came here about three years ago. She didn't sing real well, now she sings real well, her look is completely different, their marriage is completely different ... much better, much better. Her husband plays piano ... and they basically want to retire because all they want to do is play the piano and sing. So that's like a big one.

Ellen's Strategic Orientation

For Ellen, career success is achieving artistic freedom, realizing her dream of making her music, encouraging others to realize their dreams, and leaving a legacy of dream fulfillment that is passed down through the generations:

I think it has to do with dreams. Fulfilling a dream and going after it. A lot of people think it's from who you played with and what you done. Yeah, well that's successful, but ... when it's all said and done ... do you feel good about what you did? To me ... it's your soul. It goes a little farther than that. I think it's like did you get to your dream, did you get to what you wanted to do in this life? ... I'm doing the music that I've always wanted to do ... I'm making people's lives very happy, I'm giving people their dreams. I just feel that I'm doing something very special with this school that is ... going to be passed down.... And hopefully they tell their kids, so it's going from generation to generation.

As a prime mover of an artistic community that serves both students and her fellow musicians, Ellen's audience is primarily the consumer and peer professionals. Her audience configuration was expressed earlier, in her vision of the school as a family, in the testimonies of the faculty members about the school as community, and in her concept of career success.

Ever the enterprising artist, Ellen's audience also includes herself. Her concept of career success includes her own pursuit of artistic freedom, and she notes that directing the school has also helped to advance her own artistic career. For Ellen, the school is a source of social capital for networking in a national music scene:

I think this [her association with the school] has advanced my career quite a bit, because I've gotten an opportunity to play with national artists that I would have probably not have had the chance to play with. And I've also done many CD's since this has started, not only for some students, but for more professionals in this area.

Networking from the school has enhanced her own visibility:

the recognition that we're [the school] getting is from other musicians, and from our students, because they're telling other people about what we're doing and a lot of people want to come study with us. I might add, as an artist I'm getting recognized now.... Because my CD's are being played a lot right now.... I had an album that was released three years ago ... and there's a nationally syndicated show that ... he [the DJ] plays my CD like maybe twice a week. It's a huge, huge show that is hard to get on, and he loves my CD. In that way I'm being recognized a lot, because that's a huge honor to be in that show.

Balancing her own and others' careers, if at times unwieldy, is consistent with Ellen's risk orientation of pursuing a diverse portfolio of artistic and administrative activities. As an enterprising artist and generalist, her risk orientation is one of minimizing the risk of joblessness by simultaneously pursuing and seizing multiple, complementary professional opportunities. Regarding breaking in to the music scene, Ellen explained that "It takes a long time, and you have to have your fingers in a lot of pies."

Adopting this generalist strategy for minimizing risk, in Ellen's view, is a means for minimizing the risk of joblessness that results from the personal risk factor of low self-confidence. She advises aspiring artists to boost their self-confidence by spreading risk across multiple gigs:

> Again, have your fingers in a lot of pies. Do everything that you possibly can do, play every gig that you can play, do things that aren't comfortable for you, that may not be comfortable for you now. I remember one thing that I used to do is when I got asked to take the musical director position at [a] dinner theater, I'm thinking oh my God, it was an Equity theater, so all these people from Broadway were coming in. I'm thinking, what in the hell am I doing, you know? And he asked me point blank do you think that you can do this job? And I said yes.

As the school becomes self-sustaining, Ellen intends to give more attention to her songwriting and composing. Doing so will compel her to reorient her audience toward herself: "I came here to write, I was a composer, and as I've progressed with the school I've had to give it up. So what I came here to do is what I'm trying to get back to."

Ellen's Pathway

An enterprising artist, Ellen, now in her forties, had been writing, recording, and performing her own music, producing her own and others' music on her own label, and teaching music as she founded and assumed the directorship of the school. A graduate of a Midwestern college music program, Ellen had been playing music professionally since her adolescence. Upon graduating college, Ellen headed to Los Angeles to launch her career as an artist. Ten months later, declining session work and an earthquake compelled Ellen to relocate and pursue her music career in Nashville. Nashville, she felt, was a friendlier and more affordable music city with warmer weather than Chicago and New York. Ellen founded the school about a decade after her entry into the Nashville music scene.

Ellen's father, a musician and successful music-business entrepreneur, is the chief original source of her inspiration to pursue a music career and to establish the school:

> My dad is still playing, probably plays more than I do. He had a big band, he also owned a music store, a full-line music store, so I had every instrument available to me at a young age. I was in that situation of being a jack of all trades and master of none at that point because I just tried to do everything. I was immersed in it. As a little girl I played outside, but most of the time I was doing music. I took drum lessons, guitar lessons, piano

lessons, and my mother made me have dance lessons, and that was all in one week. But he's probably my biggest inspiration of why I'm doing what I'm doing, and the business part of it I see more of him in me than my mom because she taught piano for 40 years, but my dad's really a great business person as far as the creative side of him, he has created a lot of other businesses.... So he's a big inspiration of how my creative mind goes, it's like he sees something and he thinks about it, and he just makes it happen.

Roberta's Club: A Welcoming Community of Emerging Songwriters

Roberta's nightclub offers emerging songwriters a venue in which to be heard and to break in to the Nashville music scene. Performances consist of songwriter nights, where a senior songwriter performs with emerging and established songwriters, concerts, and benefit events. As an artist community, the club is committed to the professional development of songwriters, and it constitutes a base for Roberta to book shows at the club and other venues. It convenes music professionals both as performers—many of whom are members of entertainment unions and professional associations, and as an audience of fellow music professionals who support and learn from one another and who network with one another to attain co-writing, publishing, recording, and performance referrals and deals. The club, which makes and sells music merchandise and serves food and alcohol, also caters to a local lay audience and tourists.

Roberta's club is perceived by artists as a serious artist community that helps launch careers, as this emerging, singer-songwriter explained:

> I started playing there in high school, and I've had a couple of shows a year. A lot of times, a lot of co-writers will ask to come as a guest, if I don't have my own round I'll come in and play a couple of songs. And I like playing [at Roberta's] just because a lot of the other venues ... are out there to hear music but also socialize, and the good thing about [Roberta's] is for people to hear the song because it's a listening room.

Roberta's is also an important site for what this established songwriter referred to as "peer to peer learning":

> It [peer to peer learning] can take place while you're collaborating with somebody, they might have new ideas or heard something new. It can take place at any number of the venues where there's writer's nights. I go to [Roberta's] and I hear a song and I go man, that's great, I love how they made this musical change, or they found this phrase, way to say something. It all enhances your musical or lyrical vocabulary.... The other night I went and heard somebody at [Roberta's], and I got home about

10 o'clock and I was juiced. I immediately sat and started picking on my guitar and doing my songs. It's very motivating.

The club is an artist community that simultaneously promotes individual expression and nurtures a songwriters' community. According to this seasoned writer-producer-musician, commenting on Roberta's:

So when you do a songwriter in the round there, you're setting yourself up to be compared and it can either be nerve-wracking or it can be just joyous, and sometimes both in the same night. Very often you witness ego on display on a grand scale, but it also can be, if everybody is sort of into everybody else's thing and you have little harmonies worked out, it's a real community feeling too.

Roberta's Vision

Roberta envisions her club as a welcoming artist community for emerging artists to launch their careers. As she put it:

I think if you're serious about making it in the country music business you have to come to Nashville and be present. You say that, then they get to Nashville and all the doors are locked, there's no where you can get in. And so the clubs ... and ... the professional organizations ... are the only places that say to the brand new green person that just got off the bus, come on in. If you are that person I believe you have to get involved with all of those organizations. You need to get out and play and be seen and meet other people and ... make the contacts that their events have. And [my club] is one of the teeth on that gear.... So for the brand new person it's a place to get in the door, start to meet other musicians. Those other musicians are going to help you make more contacts. It's a place to make friends, socialize, find co-writers, and find guitar players, try out your material.

Her welcoming artist community rests on her beliefs about fair treatment of emerging artists whose variable personalities often lead them to have career takeoffs that range in smoothness and length of time. For Roberta, fair treatment means paying attention to emerging artists and giving them a chance to be heard and become visible:

I want to make it fair. Some people are going to jump from point A to point Z in six months to a year, they're just going to have that much talent and the stars are going to align and the right people are going to see them. And that's great. But some people can't do it that way, they have to go from A to B to C, and they hang around C for a few years and maybe get to D. And they could so easily be lost or ignored or forgotten if you aren't keeping real track of them.

Roberta's belief in fair treatment of emerging artists stems from her general belief about fairness and deep interpersonal relations:

> From a political philosophy of life, I think that people sometimes need a leg up, people need to have attention paid to them that you can't always tell who somebody is or what they have to offer by the first impression you get of them, and that fairness says that you take the time and you deal with the fact that sometimes it's difficult to listen to somebody's song because it starts out funny. I think unfair people go for the easy.... I would never put the guy who gets a call from the record label ... ahead of the guy that I already made the commitment to.

What is more, Roberta maintains that fairness also makes good business sense: "I've had far too many of these young songwriters come to tell me the story of how taken advantage they were ... and I'm not interested in getting rich off of other people's misfortune. You can put that in the fairness category. And to put it in callous business terms, it's part of my marketing strategy."

Roberta's Strategic Orientation

Roberta gauges her success by the many musicians' careers she has helped to launch: "I'm certainly very proud of those people who have successful careers and I've been a part of that, that really means a lot to me, that I have been able to participate in helping people earn a living." More than any financial gain, it is the status she derives from helping musicians to launch their careers that Roberta finds gratifying:

> If I wanted to make a good living I wouldn't be doing this. I mean I can take this same space and make it into a sports bar and put television all around it, or a karaoke bar, or whatever, and be doing considerably better financially. On the other hand, this has worked out pretty well for me. Not necessarily from a financial standpoint, but I have status and acclaim and a sense of satisfaction that I don't think I'd have, a different kind of satisfaction if I was running a successful sports bar.

Consistent with her vision, Roberta's audience centers on music professionals, more than music consumers. Music consumers, for Roberta, come to the club to learn about new music, they do not drive the content of the performances at Roberta's club:

> I prefer to bring them [fans] to the music rather than bring the music to them. I think that what we do here is really special and if presented to any person who's willing to listen to it with an open mind, they will love it and come to appreciate it. I don't want to bring [low-quality music] in here because I know it's what everybody likes to listen to.

Roberta's Pathway

Roberta's parents inspired her interests in music and in becoming an entrepreneur. Roberta's father, an enterprising, union musician-arranger, inspired her interest in helping musicians: "Well my father made a living as a [musician].... I think that directed me to the idea that musicians are the coolest people in the world."

Both of Roberta's parents inspired her entrepreneurialism. Her father had become a music contractor, and her mother was a hard-working entrepreneur who helped others to develop small businesses. She described how her mother's acumen as a small-business entrepreneur inspired her and informed her approach to operating a small business:

> She came home every day and talked about fixing the toilets down there or cleaning the bathrooms. She bitched about it, and I bitch about it, but it's what I do. I know, and any small businessperson knows, that you cannot make it in this business if you're not willing to get not just your hands dirty but your clothes dirty and your face dirty and all that stuff, all the time.

Roberta, now in her fifties, opened the club as a music venue about a decade after she graduated from a Northeastern college as a liberal arts major. At that time, she settled in Nashville, where her family and friends helped guide and finance her initial entrepreneurial pursuits in the restaurant industry. Increasingly, her social life and friendships would center around successful working musicians in the Nashville music scene and music club restaurant staff. With the strong encouragement of her musician friends, she set out to establish her club:

> I thought about doing the chef thing, started dating this guitar player here in Nashville and I was just out of college and people kept saying what are you going to do, I said I'm going to open a restaurant. They said well can we put in a stage and we'll play music? So I was hanging around with him in music bars, he and his friends wanted to get hooked up and sort of like getting carried away in a tornado, suddenly I was doing this. It was never anything that I had planned or that I chose more than ... having a good time moment in my life. And there I was. I was stuck with a restaurant that had a stage and a sound system in it. Within a year or so of that we had our first writers' night and it just got to me.

The development of Roberta's club coincided with the rise of the indie sector of the Nashville music scene during the 1990s, and the emergence of this new pathway for musicians to launch a career. In response to my query about any impact on her club of the rise of an indie sector alongside of the major-label sector, Roberta explained:

I think that the search for talent ... hasn't changed very much. There may be more, these new independent or small companies may be functioning more like the major labels did back in the '50s, '60s, and '70s, in that they take more time with the artist.... [T]he big companies got so driven by market and technology that if they couldn't make a number one record that was going to make them a million dollars in the first two weeks or three months, they give up. And one of the things you want is artist development, you want somebody who signs an artist because they believe in them and sticks with them, even though the first album doesn't do terribly well, because they know the second album will do. So I think that's something that these small labels are doing. How does it impact us or how do we impact them? You know we have what we would call baby artists, a signed artist that nothing has really happened for them, and they could be sitting here playing for three years before—and their claim to fame is they're signed to a label. I actually think that these small labels move more quickly. What used to happen with the big labels is their artists would play here to a certain point and then the day would come where we'd get a call, the label doesn't want me to play there anymore because now I'm too famous and it will look like I'm not a big deal if I'm still playing a little venue. It's funny because I haven't heard that in a long time.

PORTFOLIO ARTISTIC SOCIAL ENTREPRENEURS

Joe and Terry have taken movement-inspired pathways to becoming portfolio artistic social entrepreneurs. Joe, inspired by the Beatles and, later, by the "indie" music movement, is white, completed some college, and became an independent producer after a successful if volatile career as an artist on major labels. Terry, who is African American, a lawyer, and inspired by the hip-hop movement, is developing a neo-soul sound in Nashville.

Joe the Independent Producer: "Indie" Humanism for Emerging, Enterprising Artists

Joe is an independent producer and label owner who develops emerging artists in the rock, country, and other popular music genres. An enterprising artist, musician, and songwriter, he has previously enjoyed substantial market success with major labels that continues to help sustain his work as an independent producer. Joe has landed record deals for five artists over his career and, in the five years in which he has been producing on his own label, has twenty-seven releases on his label. Joe also supports his independent production work by his own live performances and by negotiating to have his own cuts included on the records produced and released by the other labels with which he lands deals for the artists he has developed. He has health insurance and a pension through his membership in AFTRA.

Joe is at the center of a small artist community that comprises the emerging artists, including some family members, with whom he works closely for one to three years as he mentors them and helps them to land a record deal with a major label or his label. An empathetic producer and mentor of songwriters, he described his approach to mentoring this way:

> I taught songwriting for a couple of semesters, and one of the things I drilled home to them was when you sit down to write a song you could be writing it to get something off your chest, to totally personal, to write something for a friend, to write something that you want to get cut and get on the radio in a specific format. You could be writing with an artist, and you're trying to basically amplify what that artist is about, or you could be writing for your own band and capturing whatever that is. Any number of those reasons. But when you sit down to write a song you damn well better know which one of those reasons you're writing for, because you're wasting your time if you don't know why you're writing something with this person today.

Joe customizes his working relationships with the artists based on their professional objectives. In one instance, he left an emerging punk band alone, providing them only with occasional feedback during their practice sessions in the studio across the hall from his office, until he advised them to begin recording:

> What I did with [this band] was more than anything listened to what they did, listened to how they did it, never entered any more opinion other than opening the door to the rehearsal room ... across the hall ... I'd open the door and say guys, that riff you were playing for the past half hour, it sounds like you've abandoned it, it's really good. I'd shut the door. That's about it. They were writing songs in a way that had nothing to do with the way I write songs, I was fascinated by it, they had their own thing going on and I was not going to touch it. But I did know when they had enough great songs to finally go in the studio, and that was my job.

In contrast, Joe was an integral co-writer with an emerging country band:

> Because they're a country format my job is to co-write with them as much as possible and aim everything at the center of country radio. Although it's also to help them achieve and maintain their own unique sound, which does sound unlike anything that's on the radio, but it's very commercial ... as sort of guide, mentor, and co-producer, co-writer ..., my job is to keep everything on track. Right down to sitting in folding chairs for

weeks at a time with my partner, rehearsing the band. Every song, every guitar stroke up or down, parts, harmonies, everything.

Joe's Vision

Joe fashions his production work and relationships with his artists after a humanistic, "indie" vision of artist development. Working with emerging artists is his calling:

> Actually it's my personal mission.... People helped me achieve certain things, and I signed with [a major label] in 1980 and made three albums [in the 1980s]. I re-signed to [major label] when I moved here, I sort of stumbled into another record deal totally unintentionally, and then went on to make another record for [another major label], and then at that point it was time to get off the road. I'm really glad that that was where I stopped, because I would have missed more of my kids growing up and all that. But after that I took it as my personal mission to help people get record deals basically, to develop artists, and that's what I've been doing ever since.

His humanism rests in a personal, fair, and non-exploitive producer-artist relationship that he adamantly distinguished from that of the corporate major labels:

> Some major label executives would tell you that indie labels are like the minor league teams for baseball. I don't look at it that way, I know they look at it that way, we look at our label as the end for artists, and we have a really interesting situation at our label where up till now all our artists' contracts allow artists to leave whenever they want to. There's no options, it's a 50/50 profit share instead of being the usual heavy handed we get all the money deal that record companies have.

Joe's humanism is an entrepreneurial humanism that denies the necessity of union representation for home-recording self-employed artists:

> Most independent records, if a band is making a record in their basement, they don't have to join the union to make the record. The union might prefer they do, but there's no point to it. There's nothing that they can do for the union or vice versa. It's not like they're apt to be taken advantage of by some producer somewhere and get paid less than they should to play on something, they're playing on their own stuff.

Joe's Strategic Orientation

For Joe, producing music is both self-expression and professional development for his fellow music professionals. Joe works in a world of personal and interpersonal relations with his fellow music professionals, especially artists, songwriters, and producers. The consumer is a remote, abstract mass market. As Joe put it: "I have to do the ... mainstream country writing, I enjoy it but I have to do it to feed the other stuff. That's what pays the bills. Once in a while an artist from [my label] could blow up huge, but that's not why I have [the label], I have it for art. So I have to have the commercial side to feed the other side."

For this producer-songwriter, success is getting a song cut on an album. Getting a song cut, Joe explains, reaffirms the songwriter's occupational identity and self-esteem:

> Any songwriter will tell you, they get very, very stressed out in between cuts. I know a guy that had huge, huge, hits for years and years and years with one particular act, she kept cutting his songs, made lots of money, then he went like six years without one song cut on anyone's record. And then all of a sudden had another number one with [major artist] again. He was depressed, he was ready to sell the house, he was miserable to be around. And then he was on top of the world again. When I'm on Music Row and I run into a songwriter and I say man, how are you, the response is almost always well I just got a cut on this record and I've got this single coming out.

For Joe, getting a song cut is a matter of talent, hard work, networking with fellow music professionals, and luck. He illustrated his point with the example of how one of his songs that was cut by a major band rose to number one on the charts:

> Given the fact that there's a certain level of talent that you're all at, 80 percent of the people at that level of talent aren't going anywhere because they didn't get lucky.... Now later [the major band] told me the story about the night they listened to [Joe's song], and they were listening to songs to cut for the next record, and they got to mine and it was a little demo we'd done, and they played it and the band said next, no, let's go on to the next one. And the drummer said wait a minute, I thought that was kind of cool, it had like a cool little rhythmic thing to it. And the lead singer said yeah, but it doesn't have any sort of a twist to it. Country songs have a little twist in the title a lot. And he said but I kind of like it, why don't we listen to it again. That's how close I got, okay? And they listened to it again and they said you know, we don't have anything else like that, let's cut it and see how it comes out. And they did. But I mean, when I finally heard that story, knowing that they had rejected it and then they were like ah, let's listen to it one more time, and that was the difference. And that story repeats

itself all through any songwriter's career.... All of a sudden because one person heard it, or maybe her daughter has the album, there's no calculation to make that happen.... It's not about the harder you work the more successful you'll be. In a way you have to make your own luck in that regard that you're working hard, but the luck still has to come.

Joe's Pathway

The son of a manufacturing business owner and a homemaker mother, Joe was moved by the Beatles and the Monkees during his adolescence in the 1960s. Over his parents' pragmatic objections, Joe would pursue a music career as a self-taught rock artist. By age seventeen, Joe had a notebook full of original tunes and his song about his girlfriend won first place in the songwriting contest sponsored by Eastern City's big radio station, affirming his professional identity as a songwriter: "That was the first time I ever thought wow, I'm a songwriter. It was definitely a point where in my mind it was like there's no doubt this is what I'm going to do."

Joe excelled as a philosophy major at the liberal arts university he attended briefly before transferring to a music school that he did not complete. At the same time, Joe was playing the clubs in Eastern City, persisting in his efforts to land a record deal. At age twenty-five, he landed a record deal with a major label, launching his career as a rock artist. By the mid-1980s, having discerned that Nashville was a music scene in which songwriters could have their songs cut on other artists' albums, Joe, now in his mid-thirties, initiated several visits to Nashville. By the end of the decade, Joe and his family had moved to Nashville to cinch his songwriting career.

Joe's parents could not wrap their arms around his artistic pursuits. As Joe explained:

> My mom and dad naturally thought it was a pipe dream, my dad took over the family business from his father.... I just said I don't want to do that kind of thing, I want to make stuff up. And my dad never understood creativity, still really doesn't get it.... But his idea of work is it's something that you have to love, but it has to be hard. He left at 6 in the morning to avoid the traffic ... and he came home about 7:30 at night having avoided the traffic afterwards. He wanted to work all those hours anyway. We'd have dinner, we'd play some ping-pong, then you go do your homework and he'd go back to work again at his home office. He worked his ass off.

His father, who had not completed college, wanted Joe to pursue a formal education in music if he was intent on pursuing a musical career:

> Me being creative, sitting around thinking stuff up, I think [my father] really equated with being lazy because you're not doing anything, you're not physically lifting anything, you're not going through sheaves of paper,

you're not working. He never looked at it as work. And he really insisted that I go to college.... A philosophy major, I got all A's, and then my dad said what are you doing with this philosophy degree, what, are you going to open a philosophy shop? I said I want to be a musician, this is what you want me to do. And he said isn't there a music school you can go to or something? I said yeah.... So I went to [music school] for a little while, and thought I just need to get out and make music, and so I quit and started making a record. So I made this little independent record ... I was playing [in] a duo, and I was working in a hi-fi store to support myself.

Joe transitioned from successful artist to independent producer-songwriter about five years into his move to Nashville. Joe had landed a couple of record deals with some major labels in Nashville, was a successful touring and recording artist, but was summarily dropped from one deal during a corporate regime change at the label. The other major-label deal ended when interpersonal acrimony with his partner broke up the group. Joe was now forty years old with a family to support. He explained his transition to producer-songwriter this way:

The guy who was running the company left and went to New York. Story of my life at [major label], and I had another new president. The guy that signed me said I hate to tell you this, but you're going to lose your deal, so are all these other acts that I signed, and I'm going to get fired. I said that's ridiculous. He said I've been in the business, I know what's going to happen, it's a regime change. That's exactly what happened, and I was devastated. Now I was up to about $12,000 a show on the road, third single was out, and all of a sudden I just get a phone call that I don't have a deal anymore.

The ending of the next major-label deal moved Joe into his career in artist development:

When that was over at that point I had no interest in continuing as an artist. At this point I'm approaching forty, so there it is, there's no point. To me that was sort of the cut-off date.... For me it [performing live] was a way to be in front of people performing, which I loved, to have the glare of the spotlight, the fame part of it, autographs and all that stuff, which I'll admit that I loved. But certainly I'm over it. And I gained a lot of perspective in the years after that, being able to look back at this whole section of my life and seeing how it affected me, affected me and my family, how much I missed my kids.... I just didn't want to do it anymore. So I concentrated on songwriting and actually producing.

After the first artist he produced had gone gold on a major label, Joe had become a producer. In response to my question about how he broke in as a producer, Joe, now in his fifties, explained the importance of interpersonal networking with partners who can secure contractual stability with a major label:

> Basically the way you break into producing in Nashville is you develop an artist and you bring it to a label, and you hope you don't get skomped out of it, which is the case for most people. What I did with my first artist is I went to one of [major label's] favorite producers and said I have this artist, I've got a lot of label interest, and I said how would you like to co-produce with me? He said you don't need me, this is the guy I had worked with at [other major label] for my record. I said yeah I do, because if I have you I'm not going to get knocked off this project. So we co-produced the record. And he returned the favor with the second, because he had heard about this band, and then we did the next album together. And then that started a career in artist development.

Notwithstanding his parents' objections to his having pursued a musical career without completing college, Joe's approach to running his business appears to bear his father's imprint. I asked Joe if he saw any such parallels between his and his father's approaches to running one's business, and he replied directly:

> My dad is the most honest, square, always gives everyone the benefit of the doubt, knew every employee, micro-managed everything. I remember being in his office once and he's the head of this huge company, ... and someone comes in and knocks on the door and says excuse me, Mr. [surname], can you tell me where the vacuum cleaner bags are? He had alcoholics that he would administer their Antabuse pills in the morning, he was that kind of guy. I have great admiration for him and for his work ethic. He worked his ass off.

Terry the Independent Event Promoter: Launching Urban Artists and Creating a New Sound

Terry is an independent event promoter and marketer in the urban music genre. His for-profit and non-profit, production, performance, and artist-development ventures cater to and promote urban youth and young adults and launch emerging, independent urban artists. Terry denied the existence of a unique Nashville urban sound, but his production and promotion ventures aim to carve out a Nashville urban music sound in a music scene that is dominated by country and rock music. As Terry explained:

> The infrastructure to have a successful urban label, meaning access to new and upcoming artists, access to the other side, which is the publishing, all that's right here in Nashville. It hasn't necessarily formed yet.... I

can foresee that coming in the next 5 or 10 years.... I mean we're ... in the final stages of developing [an urban music publishing company], because we hear so many great songs that are original from Nashville, but they don't have the resources to actually get them in the right hands like a plugger, so a big part of what we're doing at this next level ... is getting a lot of these artists paid, not necessarily by them being on stage playing for 20,000 people, but getting that one song or two songs cut by a [major artist] or something like that because of relationships we've developed with managers, and with the artists themselves. Like the major label artists, we have access to them and that's all you need is access.

Terry's ventures constitute a cohesive and dynamic community of emerging urban artists. As a community, Terry's ventures convene emerging urban artists and serve as their career-launch platform. This percussionist-songwriter-band manager explains how Terry and his colleagues help launch urban music careers: "[T]hey don't play, but they bring in artists.... They got started as a bunch of guys who decided to get together for one night and just listen to good music. And so that's what they do. And they help the urban artist, spoken word, hip-hop, R&B, even jazz, they give them a platform to perform. Those guys to me have been like mentors."

A singer-songwriter-keyboardist who participated regularly in Terry's live venue characterized the venue as an artistic "movement" that is unfolding in Nashville and seeking to expand to surrounding cities such as Birmingham, Chattanooga, and Louisville:

It's an event. But it's also a movement, because what we do is we allow people a platform to do everything under the sun artistically, whether it's a specific genre of music or even the genre of spoken word and poetry. I mean, we've had mimes come in and do things.... It's artistic expression at its most inclusive, but at the same time, also at its most ground-breaking and most grassroots.... It started as an opportunity for folks to get together and just kind of hang, and then a band kind of grew out of it ... which was kind of like a neo-soul, hip-hop band. [The venue] really began to make serious headway ... on the artistic scene through deciding to begin a weekly performance series that incorporated open mic and a featured artist that would come and do maybe like an hour performance. Somebody that was unseen and unheard of, but had that artistic thing that would kind of catapult them to the next level.

He went on to explain how he helps to build Terry's live venue by attracting a racially mixed audience. The marketing strategy for sustaining this community of urban artists is to transcend a racial social order among audiences and genres. The artist community and venue of a minority genre depend on generating revenue from large audiences who hail from both racial-majority and racial-minority music consumers:

I was a perfect fit for the event because I knew how to make people feel very comfortable in an uncomfortable situation. So when a mixed crowd would be there, white folks wouldn't feel uncomfortable because I would make everybody feel like family. They were like not everybody can do that, and that's a gift that you have to be able to get everybody on the same page, on the same brain wave, and we need that because if [Terry's live venue] is going to impact this delineation of genres and artistic expression, we need to have a mixed crowd. So I promote [Terry's venue] everywhere I go, too. I wear t-shirts on gigs and photo shoots and stuff.

Terry has extended his social mission of building community and launching artistic careers among at-risk inner-city youth in Nashville. Terry described the purpose and functions of his new youth venue, which is a collaboration with a local non-profit organization:

It is a free studio for inner city kids, and the way you get to use the studio is by doing community service, service learning, collecting service learning points. So we get these young kids that are kind of distracted in the school system but maybe talented musically, we'll get them to volunteer, do different community service things, get educated on the actual music industry on the business side and then as they earn points they can use the studio for free to record their music. It's a positive diversion from some of the things that we find our youth in these days.

Terry's Vision

Terry's commitment to promoting the artistic expression of urban youth and young adults rests on his belief in the values of freedom and positive living. With music, Terry explained, one "can advocate positive change through music because music can be used to move people in certain ways. And it's not all political stuff. At the same time it doesn't have to be about materialistic things or kind of destructive to the African American culture either. So that's why I say like positive."

As a youngster, Terry discerned a strong freedom theme in hip-hop music that continues to inspire his social mission. Hip-hop music was an artistic movement of his youth and adolescence:

The hip-hop generation is basically when hip-hop really made a mainstream push … in 1985, '86 when I first heard my first hip-hop records, I was 7 or 8 years old I guess. You had some guys like DJ Jazzy Jeff and the Fresh Prince, you had Eric B and Rakim, you had these artists, Run–D.M.C., you had these artists that you could see on MTV, you hear it on the radio, it's kind of mainstream and growing up with the music that previous to that I really couldn't identify with anything, hearing that music that I could identify with just because of the beat, just because of what they're saying and how they're saying it kind of tapped into me like it did a lot of other people during that time ... and a lot of people kind of gravitated towards that music, and I was one of them.... I think it was the freedom and the way they articulated their topics. The topics themselves were things that not necessarily you would hear in other types of songs. Being at that age it appealed to me, "Parents Just Don't Understand" by DJ Jazzy Jeff and the Fresh Prince. I mean there was a rap about how this kid was getting in trouble with his parents and they didn't understand that he was actually just trying to have fun and he wasn't a bad kid. It's a funny song, it's still funny now. But it appealed with the beat that was behind the lyrics. It really appealed to someone like me, I'm 8 years old and even the people older who are 15 or 16 at the time. So the subject matters and the music that it's associated to because there's a lot more up tempo, the whole culture of hip-hop which is the break dancing, graffiti, and DJ-ing the music, and then the words all collectively kind of inspired a sense of freedom ... the way these rappers and these emcee's were expressing themselves was just like a sense of freedom and it's definitely counter to anything that our parents could understand, and that's what you need.... So the way they expressed it and then what they were saying as well. So that's what kind of pulled me.

Terry also was inspired by the hip-hop value of positive living and community-building. He distinguished between positive and negative hip-hop sub-genres:

And I was always pulled more towards the political/culturally relevant type artists like Public Enemy, A Tribe Called Quest, these are bands that kind of had a certain angle and it wasn't the negative part of the culture like the NWAs and the Eazy Es which were articulating a much more darker side, but although it's reality too it wasn't my reality, I couldn't really relate to it and it never really appealed to me, I really didn't gravitate towards that. And then even now the artists that I listen to, I listen to a lot of hip-hop, ... like Kanye West, that is a little more articulate and a little more relevant for me than let's say a 50 Cent or something, which is just kind of exploiting ... things in the culture that don't lead to anything.

Terry's pursuit of positive living rests on his critique of materialistic greed and vice:

Not advocating for material gain, jewelry, houses, cars, kind of like the bling bling lifestyle ... not contributing to that and articulating more about expressing your real feelings or addressing, just articulating real issues in our culture like drug abuse, domestic abuse, poverty, and things of that nature. And not poverty from the sense yeah, go sell drugs and get out of the ghetto, but in the sense of why don't you save your money or work harder.

Terry's Strategic Orientation

Terry gauges and conceives of success as creative and engaging entrepreneurial expression in a financially rewarding, increasingly cosmopolitan, racially diversifying, Nashville consumer music scene. On self-determination and entrepreneurial freedom, Terry stated:

> Being an entrepreneur, you have the opportunity to have ultimate freedom, and to me ultimate freedom is the ability to be financially stable from your own like juice, put it like that, your own production. If you're working for someone at any time they can say we don't want you to work for us anymore, and there's a sense of control there that if you really thought about it it's kind of scary.

He likened the distinction between corporate and entrepreneurial work to the different life lessons he learned from high school football and wrestling, respectively:

> I mean it's kind of like the difference between, and I found this out in high school, the difference between being a linebacker on the football team, you can't win the game. I was very good at what I did, but it was very hard for me personally to win a game. We had a very good quarterback, it was very hard for him, because he played well every game, but when the line played well we won more games. It's all these things that are dependent on other things. I also wrestled. When I wrestled if I had a good day I won. If I had a bad day, I lost. That's how I look at entrepreneurship, it's more like wrestling.

Market success is directly linked to the quality of Nashville's downtown economic development. The market success of a Nashville neo-soul music scene depends on the increasing cosmopolitanism of white and black music consumers, and on increasingly racially mixed music audiences. Terry explained:

> Nashville [is] not necessarily the Mecca for urban culture; it's been a challenge to do what we do because [we are] so focused on urban life and lifestyles. The positive side to that is that Nashville is on an upswing as far as the culture of the city is constantly changing because the city physically is so much in a transition change. The resurgence of the downtown living and the different attractions that the city is trying to put in place to keep people downtown and keep them entertained. We feel that [our venues are] probably about three or four years ahead of [their] time but it will definitely come to a point where it matches up with what Nashville is because the type of individual that Nashville is attracting is not the same as it was twelve years ago.

Terry described the new white and black Nashvillians. He projected market growth among white consumers of neo-soul music in Nashville:

> We believe that ... because so much of that hip-hop generation were white youth, you have people who are 31 years old that are white that love old school hip-hop because that's what they grew up on. You can go to Atlanta and sit at a bar and play the type of music that we play [here] and you'll sit next to an Asian person, next to a white person, the white person might have on a t-shirt and flip flops, the black guy might have on a suit and be a partner in a law firm, and the Asian guy might be a graduate student at Emory. In Nashville it's a lot more separate in that you go to 21st Avenue and you're going to sit by Vanderbilt graduates, people that work at the hospital, or Belmont seniors or something, but you're not going to bump into a TSU grad or Howard grad just there. If you do it's obvious that there's not a lot of them in there. And I think that what's happening in Nashville right now is that guy that's in Atlanta who maybe grew up in Chicago, loved hip-hop, went to school in New York, is ... looking at Nashville as an option because it's cool enough for him now.

Similarly, Terry explained, Nashville is an increasingly attractive city for black graduates of college and graduate school to settle:

> On the black side I think people like myself where 12 years ago I'm not living in Nashville because I could live in DC. Where maybe a lot of my peers couldn't, I could, I mean with my resume I could move to New York, I could move to LA, and ten years ago I probably would have. But there are amenities in the city now that just didn't exist. Even the football team, the condo living, those kind of things that are sexy to a young single African American male, they're options now. So going to Meharry Medical School and being an African American, going to Vanderbilt Law School and being an African American, Nashville is an option. Where 10 years ago it really wasn't. So things like [our venues] are there to kind of balance out that full experience. And I've seen it. I've seen so many of our attendees are Meharry students, are Vanderbilt law students, are people that otherwise, okay I'm just here to study, once I graduate I'm leaving.... A lot of the ones that were not native Nashvillians, why would I stay here, I'm going to Atlanta to find a husband, I'm going to New York to find a wife. Literally.

Terry's Pathway

Terry's college experience with hip-hop culture put him on the pathway toward law school and social entrepreneurship in the arts. His college hip-hop experience helped free him from racial and religious constraints in his pre-college years that, he explained, inhibited artistic and intellectual expression and critical thinking. Family and clergy role models would inspire and encourage him to become an artistic social entrepreneur.

Terry, now in his thirties, grew up in a largely white suburb of a Southern city in a morally conservative religious household. According to Terry, attending an Eastern historically black college freed him to immerse himself in the hip-hop culture:

> I grew up in [Southern suburban city], which was very small when I was there, I mean my graduating class in high school was less than 1 percent minority, not just black but like minority, it was very, very kind of one way. But I loved the hip-hop culture, I loved the Northeast where the hip-hop culture was birthed out of. I just wanted to make it to New York and DC and have that experience. And when I was in college I had that experience and it was great.... I grew up in a very ... religious household as well, so that also kind of went against that too. Not necessarily going against religion at all, because I don't think any of the bands I listened to went against religion in any way, but it was still a sense of freedom that you were not restricted by this sense of spirituality or this sense of racism, which were kind of the confines I grew up in. So the Northeast for me just in this general sense represented freedom.

Terry found that the Pentacostal religion in which he was raised was intellectually regimented:

> I think in a way it was restrictive because you were given rules like this is what we believe as Christians, 1 through 10. If you break the rules you're not so much a Christian, and you definitely want to be a Christian. Okay, if you have a different idea it's, don't ask that or don't address that, just follow these rules and you'll be okay. So it kind of puts you in a mind-set of just follow the rules and you'll be okay versus challenging the rules or thinking for yourself outside of the box, which is just by its nature kind of suppressing because it kind of limits your thinking and what you can do or what you should do or what you can do.

In Terry's experience, the hip-hop movement encouraged critical thinking, in contrast to his Pentacostal religious upbringing: "I think in my church it was very much follow the rules, don't make a mess, versus hip-hop, ask questions, read a book and challenge the authority." Immersion in the college hip-hop experience released Terry from the racial and religious confines of his upbringing:

> I played sports in high school in [Southern suburban city] and there was a certain level of racism all throughout my existence growing up and the idea that—hip-hop is basically a male-dominated thing, so these

black men [in college] were kind of being free, saying what they feel the way that they wanted to say it, it kind of represented a sense of freedom for me.

"Freestyling" on the college green encouraged individuality and expression:

One of the ... elements of hip-hop they call freestyling, where the rappers rap off the top of their head, and I used to do that a lot when I was younger because it was like a cool thing to do and a lot of people liked hip-hop at that time, engaged in that, so you'd go with your friends, you'd listen to a beat, and you'd just start rapping about whatever.... At [college] on the lawn, they used to call it the main green on the campus, you'd see groups of guys rapping, freestyling, they call them ciphers where people are in a circle rapping. I used to engage in that all the time and it's fun.... [I]t's an opportunity for you to get things off your chest, to kind of express yourself on different ideas, even in certain situations kind of posture your manhood without fighting. It was very, very cool, very fun thing to do.

Family and clergy role models inspired and encouraged Terry to become an artistic social entrepreneur who is focused on youth development. He attributed his humanistic orientation toward youth development to his mother, a college theater professor at an historically black college, and to his football coaches:

I think at the heart I'm a teacher like my mom. I've always, even through college, have found ways to volunteer with different programs with youth. I know when I was growing up I was in a lot of different programs ... probably the most impactful were my football coaches from junior high school and high school that basically put me on the right path with the way that they communicated with me. A lot of times lessons I learned in football were not necessarily how to make more tackles, but how to respect authority or how to do your part in a bigger picture. Those type of lessons which were really instilled in me through athletics I think kind of laid a seed as well that you have an obligation once you get to a point that you can influence younger people you should, and you should do it in a positive way.

Family members and clergy encouraged Terry to become an entrepreneur. Terry knew that he did not want to work in a nine-to-five job like his father, a college-educated truck dispatcher:

I remember telling my dad when I was about 13 that I didn't want to be like him in the sense of getting up, going to work, and coming home, because it seemed boring. I'd go to work with him, he didn't look happy, he did it, he provided a great life for us, but he didn't look happy. My mom on the other hand, she has been a professor since she was a senior in college, before she even got her Masters she was teaching, and she still teaches. A very long career. And she's happy because that's her passion, that's what she wants to do. If she could do anything else she would have been an actress, but she teaches drama, so it's kind of like the same. That contrast for me kind of inspired me.

A minister and an uncle urged Terry to become an entrepreneur. The born-again minister, for Terry, is an exemplary entrepreneur:

He's an entrepreneur. He started the church in my grandmother's living room and now it's one of the largest African American churches in [Southern city]. He didn't own a house until he was 41, they lived in apartments all their lives. The house he lives in now is like $1.8 million.... He's actually a nice model as well as far as entrepreneurship when it comes to who do you see as kind of like a model. I don't talk to him necessarily about what I do, but just knowing the full story and the sacrifices that he made, and still makes, to be successful in his industry, which is being a pastor of a church but it's still an industry, we've learned a lot from that as well because the biggest lesson we learned is that if you sacrifice and stay committed to a vision it will manifest.

Upon retiring, Terry's uncle, a chancery court judge in a Southern city, exhorted him to become an entrepreneur before establishing his household. Terry initiated his entrepreneurial activities as a law student and, after working a few corporate legal jobs, followed his uncle's advice and became a full-time entrepreneur.

ORGANIZATIONAL AND PORTFOLIO ARTISTIC SOCIAL ENTREPRENEURS: VISIONS, STRATEGIC ORIENTATIONS, AND PATHWAYS

Both the organizational and portfolio entrepreneurs envision humanistic, artist communities that provide social spaces—spaces for fostering collegial interpersonal relationships—that generate professional development opportunities for artists, and especially emerging artists. The two types of artistic social entrepreneurs differ in their strategic orientations and pathways to becoming artistic social entrepreneurs.

The family-inspired, organizational entrepreneurs adopt a strategy of building and reproducing artist communities based in long-term, continuous mentoring relationships among a large number of regular participants and interlopers. Ellen's school and Roberta's club provide social space for intergenerational mentoring and for emerging artists to gain exposure among occupational peers, music-industry gatekeepers, and music consumers. Consistent with this vision and strategy, Ellen and Roberta tend to collaborate with artists who belong to unions and professional associations. Ellen and Roberta, then, are not only helping to sustain and reproduce artist communities, they also help to sustain the economic well-being of artists by linking especially emerging artists to artist advocacy organizations.

The movement-inspired portfolio entrepreneurs, in contrast, adopt a project-based strategy of developing alternative and avant-garde artists who work in new genres. Joe and Terry personally and proactively position artists by mentoring and collaborating intensively with a small number of artists. Their artist communities are based in meaningful but shorter-term relationships than those of the organizational entrepreneurs, have no connection to artist advocacy organizations, and serve the purpose of launching the artist's independent career.

Conclusion

Along with the musician migration and growth of enterprising artists in the Nashville music scene, artistic social entrepreneurs have arisen to create new social spaces that encourage artist professional development. As artistic social entrepreneurs, they help to reconstitute musician community in a corporate music scene that is rapidly diversifying and re-organizing into a multi-genre, entrepreneurial music scene producing music for identity-based niche markets.

Artistic social entrepreneurs help to reconstitute musician community by creating social spaces for enterprising artists. The emerging community of enterprising artists is sustained by collegial interpersonal relations among immediate collaborators in music production, such as self-contained bands and micro-production companies. Interpersonal collegiality, however, often founders from interpersonal dysfunctionality, as shown in chapters 3 and 4. Artistic social entrepreneurs preempt this potential void in a musician community by creating social spaces—social enterprises—that encourage interpersonal collegiality, professional development, and networking opportunities among occupational peers.

The two types of artistic social entrepreneurs—the organizational and portfolio entrepreneurs—socialize risk in different ways. The organizational entrepreneurs socialize risk by convening larger numbers of participants in longer-term relationships and wider networks than the portfolio entrepreneurs; portfolio entrepreneurs proactively launch the careers of alternative and avant-garde artists by collaborating intensively in shorter-term, focused, mentoring relationships with artists than the organizational entrepreneurs.

The different pathways taken by the two types of artistic social entrepreneurs indicate the vital societal role of entrepreneurial music families and artistic movements in producing artistic social entrepreneurs. Entrepreneurial music families spawn the next generation of "family-inspired," organizational artistic social entrepreneurs; artistic movements galvanize "movement-inspired," portfolio artistic social entrepreneurs.

Artistic social entrepreneurs sustain their communal social spaces for artists from the revenues generated by music consumers. Steady revenue generation is challenging in Nashville, a competitive music scene of niche markets that is differentiated by many social identities and music genres that are consumed by "omnivorish"[9] music consumers. Each of the profiled artistic social entrepreneurs struggled to create and attract large numbers of fickle "majority" consumers to sustain their avant-garde social enterprises for enterprising artists operating in niche markets.

Artistic social entrepreneurs, guided primarily by an interpersonal risk orientation, create communal social spaces that are fueled by a steady revenue stream generated by music consumers. The great impersonal risk factors—market vicissitudes, technological and political-legal change, and changing music consumption patterns—that differentiate and destabilize consumer markets and threaten musician livelihoods are beyond the artistic social entrepreneur's reach. "Artist advocates," the third type of artist activist theorized in chapter 2, guided by an impersonal risk orientation, are reinventing arts trade unionism and professional associations for the emerging community of enterprising artists.

CHAPTER 6

Artist Advocates

The Corporate and Entrepreneurial Generations of Arts Trade Union Activists

Artist advocates are creating an arts trade unionism that is attuned to the interests and aspirations of the contemporary generation of enterprising artists in Nashville. The hotly contested election for the presidency of Nashville Local 257 of the American Federation of Musicians (AFM) in 2008 reflected the rise of a new arts trade unionism. The cover-story characterization in the *Nashville Scene* of the Local 257 presidential election heralded a new approach to arts trade unionism. "To onlookers on the coasts, Local 257 had become a battleground far larger than Nashville's city limits, in a sort of proxy grudge match for control."[1] In this "election of historic proportions," as the Local 257 newsletter put it, insurgent Dave Pomeroy defeated eighteen-year incumbent and Music Row icon Harold Bradley for the Local 257 presidency in "what was widely viewed as an upset" in an election with "the most vigorous turnout in years."[2]

Eighteen months after the Local 257 election, Pomeroy, who hailed from the ranks of recording musicians, joined a rising, national "Unity Slate" of insurgent candidates who went on to win the top international AFM offices at the 98th AFM convention in Las Vegas in June 2010.[3] Bradley, who also lost his bid for re-election as international vice president, was honored by the conferral of "emeritus" status by the convention, and Pomeroy gained a seat on the international AFM executive board.[4] Commenting on the implications of AFM leadership change for the revitalization of the union, Pomeroy stated in the Local 257 newsletter that "the future of the music business is people owning their own stuff. We are reinventing ourselves so we can be the organization that young musicians look to for advice and ways to help them protect themselves."[5]

AFM leadership change also signaled an agenda to revitalize the sagging membership base of the union. The American Federation of Labor and Congress of Industrial Organizations (AFL-CIO) attributed the dramatic decrease in national AFM membership, which declined from 255,000 to 7,000 between 1955 and 2013, primarily to digitalization and technological displacement of musicians, as well as the focus of the union on achieving collective bargaining gains for the remaining recording musicians.[6] Local 257 had lost about 1,000 members during the decade of the 2000s.[7]

121

AFM vice president and Local 257 president Harold Bradley had encountered political opposition to his efforts to reform federal labor law on behalf of freelance performing musicians. He had chaired the international AFM Freelance Committee, whose August 2000 report made multiple recommendations, ranging between outreach among young musicians and the amendment of national labor relations law that would have allowed union "pre-hire" arrangements with live-venue employers.[8] These amendments—the Live Performing Arts Labor Relations Amendments—were introduced in Congress several times between 1989 and 2001 but never made it to the president's desk for his signature.[9]

In this chapter, I examine how a new generation of Nashville arts trade unionists are reinventing arts trade unionism for the contemporary generation of enterprising artists. Arts trade unionism is at least a century old in the United States.[10] Nashville AFM Local 257, for example, was founded in 1902 in the era of live music. With the advent of recorded music, corporate major labels, and mass distribution through radio airplay by the early 1950s, Local 257 had been transformed into a union representing both live and recording musicians and artists by a generation of arts trade union leaders who I refer to as "corporate-era arts union activists."[11] Throughout the corporate era, Local 257 has developed and enforced master contracts with corporate signatories that apply especially to the major-label recording industry. The new generation of arts trade union leaders—who I refer to as "entrepreneurial-era union activists," are endeavoring to revitalize arts trade unionism as the Nashville music scene transitions from the corporate era of major labels into an era of indie entrepreneurial music production and distribution.

The advent of new entrepreneurial-era arts union activism is embedded in the generational shift of enterprising artists in Nashville. In terms of generations of enterprising artists, entrepreneurial-era arts union activists hail from the ranks of the transformative generation of enterprising artists. As discussed in chapter 3, the transformative generation broke from the corporate era of major-label production and distribution during the 1980s and 1990s by forging the emerging indie community of enterprising artists in Nashville. The transformative generation is presently mentoring the contemporary generation of enterprising artists. As discussed in chapter 4, the contemporary generation of enterprising artists is the socially and artistically diverse generation of non-union, early-career artists in Nashville. They are occupational generalists who are honing their broad portfolios of artistic and art-support skills in order to self-produce on indie labels and self-promote their own work in live venues and over the Internet in niche markets.

Labor union leaders are often faced with the dual challenge of recruiting new members—"organizing the unorganized," and of maintaining internal "labor solidarity" among diverse union members. Previous scholarly research on U.S. labor union revitalization has addressed institutional factors—political-legal, organizational, technological, macroeconomic, and social factors—in accounting for organized labor's demise and revitalization. Less attention has been given to the development of individual artist activists and activists who envision and emerge as leaders to realize a new trade unionism that resonates with the new generation of artists of the new art world.[12]

In terms of the theory of artist activism, arts union activists are what I call "artist advocates," the third type of artist activist theorized in chapter 2. Their strategic orientation toward community-building is the most "collective" of the three artist activists—more collective than that of the artistic social entrepreneur and that of the "individualistic" enterprising artist. Artist advocates are the most "collective" type of artist activist in that they are uniquely focused strategically on sustaining the artistic freedom, career success, and livelihood of the whole occupational peer community, beyond that of individual occupational peers.

Furthermore, unlike enterprising artists and artistic social entrepreneurs, who act with personal and interpersonal risk orientations, artist advocates act with an impersonal risk orientation.[13] They envision union-organizational initiatives that are intended to align with the new economic interests of the contemporary generation of enterprising artists who "own their own stuff." These new economic interests in intellectual property are brought about by such impersonal risk factors as the rise of occupational generalism in the form of "hyphenated" occupational roles (e.g., singer-songwriter),[14] structuring of competitive niche consumer markets, geographical decentralization of self- and home-production of music, and the advent of digital distribution and self-promotion.

I examine and compare in this chapter the strategic and risk orientations, career inspirations and pathways of corporate-era and entrepreneurial-era arts union activists.[15] Specifically, I profile four Nashville artist advocates who are distinguished by the sources of their original career inspiration—whether movement- or family-inspired—and by the era in which they became trade union activists.[16]

In each era of Nashville music production, the profiled arts union activists envisioned, organized, and practiced an arts trade unionism that advanced the interests of professional musicians. Movement- and family-inspired activists were moved by a personal morality—whether it was pragmatic idealism or a religious or political morality—to actively empower, protect, and pursue the artistic and economic interests of their fellow musicians. In addition, arts union activists envision and enact a unique trade unionism that conforms to the socio-spatial logic of that era of music production, and is linked to the type of career pathway the musician has taken in becoming an arts union activist (see table 2).

In socio-spatial terms, the corporate and entrepreneurial eras differ in their organizational ecology, employment relationships, and degree of occupational specialization. In the corporate era, music is produced and mass-distributed by a spatially centralized, small number of corporate major labels, recording studios, publishing companies, arts unions, and performance rights organizations. In contrast, the emerging entrepreneurial era is one of a spatially decentralized

Table 2. Arts Union Activism by Type of Career Pathway and Art-World Era

CAREER PATHWAY	CORPORATE ERA	ENTREPRENEURIAL ERA
Movement-inspired	Extend union contract coverage to non-union sectors of music-recording industry	Promote individual union-contracting, professional development, and musician self-promotion in all music-production sites—studio, live venue, home
Family-inspired	Promote social inclusion of occupational and demographic subgroups of musician labor force in the union	Help corporate-era musician specialists to reinvent themselves as generalist, enterprising artists

array of a large number of small, loosely coupled, non-union, independent, often home-based music producers distributing music via the Internet to niche markets. Musicians in the corporate era are employees who are hired on a project basis to record others' work, whereas the self-employed musicians of the entrepreneurial era often are self-contained bands and other enterprising artists who self-record and self-promote their music in live venues and over the Internet. Occupationally, the musician of the corporate era is a specialist with a narrow range of income streams, whereas the enterprising artist of the entrepreneurial era is a generalist with multiple income streams from a range of music-related economic activities.[17]

Movement-inspired and family-inspired union activists enact their roles differently in each era. In both eras, movement-inspired activists extend union-contract coverage to non-union sectors of musicians (table 2, top row). In the corporate era, union-contract coverage was extended to the major labels who became signatories to a union music-recording agreement. In the entrepreneurial era, movement-inspired activists help enterprising artists to network and to attain individual union contracts with employers in live venues and home production sites. For example, Local 257 posts networking resources on its website and has developed union contract templates for live performances and for solo overdubbing by home-recording musicians.[18]

In both eras, family-inspired activists promote "labor solidarity" and social inclusion within the union occupational peer community (table 2, bottom row). The corporate era coincided with industry growth, occupational specialization, national arts union mergers, and the civil rights and women's movements. During this era, family-inspired activists endeavored to ensure representation and participation of occupational and demographic subgroups of musicians in the political and communal life of the increasingly diverse and complex arts union. In the emerging entrepreneurial era of declining union membership, the chief challenge facing union activists is union revitalization among different age cohorts of musicians. The challenge is not only to attract younger cohorts of enterprising artists who are skeptical of arts unionism, but also to help older cohorts of corporate-era musicians to participate in the union occupational peer community as self-reinvented enterprising artists of the entrepreneurial era.

CORPORATE-ERA ARTS UNION ACTIVISTS

Rick and Vicki served as arts union activists during the corporate era of growth and consolidation of the major labels in Nashville. Both are white and college-educated and identified strongly with their peer community of professional musicians. Rick took a movement-inspired career pathway that led him to envision and practice an arts trade unionism that promoted both the Nashville Sound and the individual expression of his fellow professional musicians. Vicki took a family-inspired career pathway toward an arts union activism that envisioned and promoted an inclusive and cohesive community of her fellow professional musicians.

Rick

Rick arrived in Nashville from Southern City as Owen and Harold Bradley were launching the Nashville Sound on Music Row in the 1950s. His arrival also coincided with the transition in the union role from performing-musician advocate toward advocate for recording-industry session musicians. Rick's career as an award-winning, Nashville session musician, performing and recording artist, and producer took off with the continuous growth of the Nashville recording industry through the 1970s. The lifelong union member became active in the union some twenty-five years into his career along with the consolidation and digitalization of the Nashville recording industry, and the advent of rock 'n' roll.[19]

Rick reflected on the rise and decline of the union. He linked the rise of the union to the emergence of a tight occupational community of professional Nashville recording musicians:

> I come from the old school, so it's very important for me to deem myself a professional and to be a member of the union, because that's the union slogan is that we are the professionals, and it puts you with a better class of players, or talented bunch of players, which means that you're always able to learn from playing with guys that are even better than you. Also, your career is like a pie, you work for multi[ple] employers ... if the phone doesn't ring you don't work, as a recording musician. It would be different if you were working as a road musician, but even that you're not on the road forever, so you work for different employers. It really takes a lot of faith ... [i]n your ability.

I asked Rick to distinguish the "new school" from what he referred to as the "old school." The new school of younger, more individualistic rock musicians, he maintained, was disinclined to join the union. Linking the "new school" to the recent decline in national union membership, Rick explained:

I think it [new school] has a different attitude. The union has lost [members] partly because the union ignored the rock 'n' roll players when they came along. All the old guys sitting in these locals, if there was some work that came in they got it ... they didn't like rock 'n' roll. So we missed recruiting that whole bunch of guys, and then we came to a point where they really didn't need us if they were successful. So right now some of the younger players, or even the ones here that are making good money, it's always what can the union do for me, not realizing that the union has already done it for them, that they're just the beneficiaries of the previous musicians and record producers, singers and songwriters who have built the business. But they have a "I want more" attitude and it's a little different, because the older musicians realize that the union, first they made sure we got the right scale, then they put in a pension for us, and so they recognize the union as a good thing.

Vision of an Arts Union

In Rick's view, artistic professionals differ from other unionized workers. Nashville musicians are mainly self-trained artistic workers who are hired by multiple employers for project work on the basis of their professional reputations, rather than on the basis of an individual credential portfolio of formal training and skill-level achievements. As freelance workers in a reputational labor market, they are dedicated to music, encourage one another's professional development in an occupational peer community, and are less militant than other unionized workers. Rick explained:

I think emotionally they're different people, they're artistic, they're creative, and I think that might be the difference because if you're a worker, you're not that creative, you're doing whatever they tell you to do. But these artists have to be creative to exist, and ... we're not the kind of people that normally go out and march and strike and do stuff like that. It's really different, because with everybody having their own recording studios we can't do a recording strike and the record companies know that.... But really we're different, we're artistic, we're creative, which to me is different from a guy who's punching the clock.

Rick continued by distinguishing between an arts union and a building trades union, both of which represent workers who do project work in occupational labor markets. The building trades union operates an apprenticeship and training program and a formal skill hierarchy through which individual workers ascend. The arts union, in contrast, does not evaluate the skill level of the individual worker. Rather, it is the employer who evaluates the artist's skill level on the basis of the artist's professional reputation:

They [building trades] start out with apprentices on up to masters or whatever, and we [musicians] can't do that. My prime example of that is the person that hires you determines whether you're an apprentice or a master. For instance, Chet Atkins is a prime example. You call him for a record session, we've got him listed here as a master guitar player, which he is. But all of a sudden he goes in and you want heavy metal. He's not a heavy metal player.... So we can't label people as apprentices as a cover-all, the people who hire us really label us, and it's a real big difference because if you're an apprentice in the electrical union or the carpenter's union, then I think you're assigned to do a certain amount of work and when you get all of that you move up to another one, and then you move up, and then finally hopefully make whatever master is or whatever their designations are. But we don't have those designations.

For Rick, the arts union primarily advocates through collective bargaining with recording companies to improve the terms of employment and promote the job security of its members. Through collective bargaining, the union often attempts to minimize the constant threat of displacement of artistic workers by the continuous changes in music production technology and to raise wages by extending union agreements to non-union sectors of the industry. Rick illustrated the challenge of changing production technology with the case of the VOM—the "virtual orchestra machine":

It's the machine that can replace an entire symphony, and also can replace ... a pit band, and of course they used that during the last strike of the Rockettes. And of course now they're trying to get it to say that it's an instrument, and we're saying no, it's not an instrument, it's a storage device. And so far we've won because it's more like a computer and a guy's banging on a computer, and we don't think that's a musical instrument.

The union's "unholy war," as Rick put it, with the non-union Christian music recording industry in the 1990s illustrates the union role in extending union agreements to a formerly non-union sector of the recording industry. According to Rick, the gospel companies were unable to escape from the union by recording in England because of the union's influence with symphony orchestra musicians and because the requisite musical talent resided in Nashville:

The musicians are here. When we had the unholy war, the problem we had with the gospel companies not being signatory ... what won the whole thing, [the union] told the musicians they couldn't work for anybody ... they won the war ... it was because of the rhythm players, bass, drum, piano and guitar. We seem to have a feel that they can't get anywhere else. Because one of the first responses from [a gospel music producer] was they'd record in England, which [the union]couldn't stop him there, but [the union] put out an alert that if [the gospel music producers] wanted to do two or three sessions that they had to make sure the people were signatory.

The union also provides its members with a retirement income through the union pension program. In recent years, Rick acknowledged, the union has run up against employer resistance to extending pension coverage to freelance club musicians who present the club owner with a union contract when negotiating the terms of employment prior to a live gig:

> You want to make it simple for them [employers], because if you give him two pieces of paper, give him a contract and then another form for pension, he's going to say well I've got to go see my lawyer.... That was where we were running afoul, we had too many pieces of paper. Because there's not that much money changing hands on a small job, a club job, or anything like that ... we don't have as many people [members] taking advantage of it as we should, and we keep trying to harp on it, hey, you can control your destiny. And the pension thing is the best thing that [the union has] got going because it's something that you can collect while you're alive.

Strategic Orientation

For Rick, success is gaining an excellent reputation as a professional musician and as a member of a peer community of talented professional musicians. Pursuing one's artistic expression, gaining a reputation, earning recognition from one's peers, and supporting one's peers are objectives unto themselves, as well as instrumental for one's ongoing professional development and for receiving a call for the next job:

> If you're playing really well, up to the best of your ability, then that makes you feel successful. If you're making enough money to make a good living and provide for your family then very definitely that's a bonus and you also are successful. Then if you're able to translate both of those things and help others, other musicians, and not have to go through the real hard times or collect money for them or do things for them, then to me that's another form of success.

Rick was proud of his international reputation:

> That's really the ultimate and it's something you can't control. If you were successful just in the United States that's something.... I think that for

your work to be played around the world is very rewarding, to go into another country and hear a record that you played on, or to hear an artist doing a song that you played on and doing that arrangement.

One builds a reputation by playing and learning in one's peer community. For Rick, the peer community furthered his professional development, expanded his repertoire, and opened up work opportunities:

I played all kinds of different music. I played in [a] Dixieland band, ... [a] dance band, ... [in a] big orchestra ... on the road with [a country artist], I played ... country music. So if you're playing with all these really good players like that, well you have to learn, it has to improve your playing, and it makes you very diverse. It gives you so many more opportunities.... I think it all improves your playing.

Pathway

Rick grew into his trade union activism on a movement-inspired career path. He was enamored with the popular music of his adolescence and, with the encouragement of his pro-union and musical family, embarked on a musical career. Rick recalled the beginning of his career:

I thought I wanted to be a banjo player because I heard somebody playing it on a radio station in Chicago, and [a family member] came to me when I said I want to play banjo, it's kind of a happy sound, and he said no, no, banjo is going out, you got to learn to play guitar. So my dad bought one at a junkyard for about $6.... Then when I was 15 my cousin came by and told my mother everybody in the union is working.... I want to take him on his first job and I won't let him have anything but a Coke and I'll take care of him. So my dad was a traveling salesman, he was out of town, so mother finally relented and I went over and played at [a bar], and I must have been awful. But we just played and had a good old time, a typical kind of a beer joint.

Rick's emergence as a trade union activist occurred organically with the growth of the Nashville Sound and the deepening of his membership in a tight peer community of unionized Nashville recording musicians. The consolidation of this peer community occurred prior to the advent of digital, multi-tracking, and solo overdubbing in the 1970s and home studios later, when analog-recording musicians would arrange and record music with the Nashville number charts as a cohesive, virtually autonomous (from the producer), self-determining, improvising musical group. Rick described the pre-digital recording process in which he participated with his fellow session musicians:

We're together right off the bat, we don't have to say well what are you going to play there? And if a guy [musician] says well I don't like that, I got something better, then you listen to it and if you like it you take credit for it. We all thought we were arrangers, honestly. We always wanted to be involved in the record and we always wanted to come up with ideas of what to do. And then you filter it to the leader [musician], and in the meantime the record producers in the booth are usually not even hearing this, and the leader thinks that's a good idea and he'll say let's try that. Sometimes the A&R man will never know it happened. But then if the leader doesn't like it he'll say well, that sounds good, but we'll save it for another time.... It is a group process, and we've had some guys here who were successful as publishers, and they would come in to do sessions and we'd be playing, and the guy [publisher] would come out and say well, what if you played this, and he would tell us what to play, and we'd never get the hits with him because his usually weren't as good as what ours were.... [The producer would] give us the format and then he'd sit in there and talk to the engineer a while and after about 10 or 15 minutes say what have you guys got, are you ready? He'd say play it, and if it was a minor change he'd say well I'd rather have the steel play instead of the piano on the intro, and then if it was a major overhaul, ... [the producer] ... still didn't dictate notes to us, he depended on ... whoever was playing all the lead to come up with the good notes. If he didn't like that well then he'd tell them I don't like that and try something else.

Rick's union activism rests on a cradle-to-grave commitment to his fellow musicians, a commitment that weathers the vicissitudes of consumer taste and industry market conditions and the ups and downs of musician careers. He illustrated his commitment with the example of a lifelong musician friend who ended up retiring as a cab driver: "He was a pop jazz player when I was growing up, and ... he was playing the commercial country music ... for many years. And then he ended up driving a cab after that went down. So he's the kind of guy that I'm trying to protect in whatever way we can." Rick took great pride in the Nashville local union's death benefit: "[The union has] the best death benefit. If you're a member twenty consecutive years you qualify for an $8,000 death benefit. It's self-funded, ... and [o]ther locals don't have that, they have maybe a $1,000, $1,500 in LA and New York.... A lot of them don't have it, the small locals don't have it."

Vicki

An award-winning performing, touring, and recording artist and musician, Vicki has worked in country, jazz, rock, and other popular music as musician, songwriter, teacher, producer, session musician, jingle writer, and radio show talk host. She first joined the union when she moved from Southern Town to launch her musical career in the Nashville music scene in the early 1960s. A lifelong union member, and propelled by the civil rights, women's, and peace movements of the 1960s, she would become active in arts unions for some two decades beginning in the late 1970s.

Her activism expressed a social ethos that stemmed from deep social relations among a cohesive group of professional musicians who had performed and recorded together for many years. Stymied by a recent, failed attempt to convince a younger colleague of the benefits of trade unionism, she contrasted the social ethos with a contemporary individualism:

> The fact that he's getting hired a lot tells me that he's good at what he does and he's professional, so he's a real good example of the kind of guy we'd like to have in the union, but ... I couldn't give him any real answers that would make him feel better about it. The fact is, there's so much non-union work now and there's so much technology, and everything's all over the map.... When I was coming up, joining the union was like you wanted to be with your buddies, you were all in this together, and you were protected. But now everybody's got their own things.

Vision of an Arts Union

Vicki's recollections of her becoming active in the union reveal her vision of an arts union as an inclusive, advocacy organization for her fellow professional musicians. The union itself, she recalled, was a tight occupational community, and her activism, especially participating as a Nashville delegate to the national union convention, allowed her to meet many fellow musicians whom she admired as musicians:

> The conventions were about three days long and they were always major things. Like every two years the wages and working conditions things would be up for renewal or not, and there were always resolutions and amendments and stuff, and that's voted on not only by committees, but by everybody on the floor. First of all, I was hanging out with my friends. Everybody on that board ... is a singer and/or a musician ... or whatever, and they're just very interesting people, and a lot of them were my friends.... I would always stick my name in the hopper, because I enjoyed going. You see a new city, and then our counterparts in other cities, especially in New York and California, were other singers and musicians like us, and quite a few of them were people that you'd hear of.

As she became active in an arts union with a multi-occupational membership jurisdiction, she encountered an intra-union rivalry between actors and her fellow singers. Vicki would become an advocate for singers:

> One of my friends in New York who's a famous singer and television performer said if we're not careful the singers get left behind ... the actors

had a lot of clout because they had these numbers so they could show up at their local elections and just bomb everybody out of the water. So with the blessing of the directorship we formed a singer's caucus ... all of the singers from all of the locals would break off from the group and have a half day thing themselves. People used to say when you walked down the hall you could always tell who was in the rooms because when you walked by the singers we were all laughing and drinking coffee, and singing a tune once in a while, and enjoying each other. When they walked down where the actors were they would be throwing chairs and screaming at each other. Everything was drama.

Vicki's orientation toward union inclusivity extended to gender inclusivity. An original member of the Nashville chapter of the National Organization for Women, Vicki was recruited into a national union committee position by her powerful union sister:

She was formidable, and she was the head of [a] national ... committee and they were taking nominations for additions to the committee.... She came over to my table and said she wanted to put my name in nomination. I said ... I don't know anything about [that].... She said you're a clear thinker, and you can learn, and I want more women on my committee. So I did. And that was fun, I learned a lot.... At that point ... she felt like they needed some new blood ... she had two things that she always worked on, and that was protecting the singers, whenever anything was going on on the floor if it didn't include the singers in terms of whatever was happening, up she would go to the microphone. The other thing was that she always wanted the women to have a bigger voice in everything.

As an advocacy organization, the arts union endeavored to improve the wages, working conditions, and workplace safety for its members. Vicki described some of the chief issues facing singers and others working, especially for corporate employers:

Say a variety show that had lots of people coming out to play and sing. If they're using special effects like the smoke machines, that's very hard on your lungs, it's some kind of chemical. The other thing is if they are using dancers, like when they're doing the Oscars or something, if they use smoke machines on certain kinds of floors it makes the surface slick and dancers would fall and injure themselves. So we had issues like that to bring to the table and say write some of these things in the contract, that this dancer is not required to dance on a floor that's unsafe, that kind of thing. We had a lot of issues, the singers did, about breaks and how long you could keep a chorus, after so many hours you've got to let them go to the bathroom and have a break. That stuff all had to be written and rewritten all the time because corporate management was always trying to get the last nickel out of everybody.

Vicki looked back with pride on her years as an activist: "The first year I was a ... board member I had a whole week of sitting in rooms with people, actors that you would have seen on the screen your whole life ... and some of them are wonderful, nice people, and singers that had been on the Bob Hope Show and Perry Como. It was great. And I was so proud to be a part of this group of people."

Strategic Orientation

If the union is integral to and reflective of a tight artistic community, Vicki's concept of success is the joy of playing music with her fellow musicians who sustain one another with deep mutual admiration. At the start of her career, she had never expected to be able to earn a living by succeeding in this way: "I think being recognized as a decent musician by your peers and/or people that you look up to or idolize, is real success ... getting to play music that I love with musicians that are wonderful, and actually getting paid for it, is pretty much far beyond what I thought I was doing when I started teaching school."

Although the primary orientation of her music making is toward her peers, Vicki also makes music for music consumers, friends, and family. She acknowledged the importance of "fans," "because if they don't like us, we don't sell any records," but was not oriented toward making music for music executives. Referring to her peer community, "There's a kind of an unwritten law that we all say ... that the worst audiences you can ever play for are ... Music Row or California ... music executives, and publishers, because they don't listen to anything. They're busy making their deals with each other."

Pathway

Vicki took a family-inspired career pathway toward becoming a union activist. The daughter of a tire-dealer and master-mechanic father and a mother who worked as a bookkeeper at the service station, Vicki grew up in a household imbued with a wide range of popular and religious music. Her parents played musical instruments, were more musical than other households in Vicki's small, Southern hometown, and encouraged their daughter to take music lessons and pursue a music career. For Vicki, her family imparted a social meaning of music based in family togetherness:

I don't know that I ever thought about doing anything else. So I don't know if it was one particular person or if it was a string of stuff. There was just never a time in my life when there was not music.... As far back as I can remember. My parents were both musical, my grandparents, everybody ... when I grew up we didn't have television, everybody had a piano and a radio, and there was always music around. Weekends were like times to get together with friends and play music, which is what my parents did.... They were both blue collar people ... the family was tobacco farmers.... It's very ordinary folks, farm folks and stuff, but there was always music around. My father played guitar, and played a little bit of fiddle. He could pretty much play a little of any string instrument, but mostly guitar. I still got a couple of his guitars.... He loved bluegrass and mountain music, and he loved hillbilly music. We listened to the Grand Ole Opry all the time. He loved Ernest Tubb and people like that. My mother liked the little bit more urban stuff, she liked Perry Como, Artie Shaw, Benny Goodman, and that kind of thing.... My father was exceptionally musical, and my mother had a really good ear, and she could plunk a little bit on the piano. She came from a bigger family than my father did. Everybody was Scotch Irish on both sides. A lot of talk, everybody read books, and sang, and harmonized. There was just always music around.... I've got a recording of my mother and me singing "Whispering Hope" when I was 10 years old. My father had a little recording machine, and I wound up being able to retrieve some of that stuff and have it put on CD. Again, the hymns were things, it was not unusual on a Saturday night for everybody to be playing the blues and singing and carrying on, and then by the end of the night after everybody had a bunch of beers and somebody got a little maudlin, they would sing "I Come to the Garden Alone," or old gospel things like "Amazing Grace."

Beginning at age five, Vicki took music lessons throughout school and entered college knowing that she would pursue a professional music career: "Well, I wanted to, and my mother wanted me to. My dad wanted me to become a piano teacher and move next door so I wouldn't move away. But yeah, I didn't really plan for it other than I got the degree and then I taught for three years." Vicki became politically "radicalized," as she put it, as her initial professional immersion in the Nashville music scene coincided with the Nashville non-violent civil rights movement of the early 1960s. Vicki's radicalization extended her family's pro-labor, New Deal populism:

Neither of my folks were ever union members.... Early on I developed a real trade unionist sense because the whole idea of the union to me was good.... One of my mother and dad's friends was a heavy equipment operator, he was like an uncle to me, and he was a union member. As he got older, ... and he was retired, ... he and I would sit and talk about union stuff, ... after I'd been in the union for many years. But he would sit and talk to me about what it was like before he joined the union. He was really sold on the idea of unions, and this was a [Southern] farm boy.... My grandparents and my parents went to the polls every time the door opened. We read the morning paper every day, cover to cover. I can't remember a time when we didn't have the paper at the breakfast table, and my grandfather always worked on every Democratic campaign.... On election days my grandmother would drop him at the polls and he'd be working the whole day. It was like Franklin Roosevelt was God in our house.... He saved the country during the Depression as far as my grandmother was concerned, and my father, too.... They thought he was a great man. My father wept, I remember very clearly when Roosevelt died, I was about 7, and my father was just in tears. So I grew up thinking being a Democrat was where it's at. But as I got older I grew into the idea that that was not a bad thing. As I've gotten older I've gotten more liberal.

Reading labor history and philosophy in college led to the further development of Vicki's pro-union orientation and her embrace of an integrationist and feminist orientation toward civil rights and group relations:

I read a lot of biography, I read a lot of memoirs, I read all kinds of stuff. I read detective novels, too. I just got interested in the whole history of unionism and part of it was because, I mean everything from the partisans in the Spanish Civil War all the way to the dock workers that were beaten up back in the '30s. I always kind of resented the fact that everybody that believed in integration and fair treatment all were considered Communist sympathizers or something. Early on I didn't like that, that was back in the early '60s. By the time the Civil Rights movement got here, and the women's movement, I was like ready to go out in the street and march. I didn't, but I did a lot of reading and thinking and talking.

Although she wrote pro-integration letters to the editor and wanted to march on downtown Nashville, she was constrained from marching by middle-class norms:

I remember seeing the sit-ins on West End Avenue, and also not being able to go down 5th Avenue. There were a lot of stores down there at that time that I shopped in because they were sitting in at Kresge's and the police had cordoned off the thing. Yeah, I remember all that very clearly.... I couldn't figure out how to keep my family life intact if I [participated in the march] ... nice people just didn't go out and march in the streets. They just behaved themselves and shut up basically.

Throughout the 1960s, Vicki participated professionally in the predominantly white, Nashville country music industry, all the while crossing the racial divide by mingling and performing in integrated music venues in Nashville in her off time. She emerged from the 1960s as an integrationist and a founding member of the Nashville chapter of the National Organization for Women:

I remember talking to some of the guys, not at recording sessions, ... and one of them was [a] drummer.... I remember having a conversation with him in '63, God what a year, about the Birmingham church that exploded, killed those little girls, and how appalled everybody was at that.... This was a blond-haired blue-eyed guy from East Nashville, but he had been in bands all over the country, and he had black friends, I had black friends, and we would sit and commiserate, people like that would sit and commiserate about it, but we didn't do it a lot around people we didn't know. It was always just the guys you hung out with at work, and I remember thinking, because I had been really troubled by all the stuff going on and people's heads getting banged.... But I remember that after that bomb in that church killed those little girls, a switch went off some way. I felt like I am now officially radicalized. That's it, I've had enough ... it was such a gradual thing. I mean I was the little Green Hills housewife, dressed to the teeth and every hair in place.... But then I'd go home at night and I'm seeing pictures of Vietnam on the 6 o'clock news, and then people getting killed, and then Robert Kennedy was killed, and Martin Luther King. And '68 was just awful for everybody, and it was such a gradual thing that I don't think I realized it until the '70s that I was coming through the liberation of black people and the liberation of women, plus Vietnam was all over it, so that whole thing was like such a big hunk of stuff. I just woke up in '71 or '72 thinking what? ... we started keeping track, some girlfriends of mine and I, about how many couples we knew got divorced during that time, from '69 to '73 or '74, and in every case the woman was saying I've been unhappy for ten years and I finally got the courage to walk out. All these weird things were happening, families were going asunder and all this stuff.

Vicki gravitated toward union activism as her commercial singing career unfolded during the 1970s, along with the deepening of her membership in the Nashville community of musicians and the transformation of her political orientation.

ENTREPRENEURIAL-ERA ARTS UNION ACTIVISTS

Bill and Marty have served as arts union activists during the entrepreneurial era of major-label contraction and the emergence of a community of enterprising artists in Nashville. Both are white and college-educated and identified strongly with their peer community of professional musicians. Bill took a movement-inspired career pathway that led him to envision and practice an arts trade unionism focused on facilitating the self-expression, self-promotion, and self-advancement of younger artists. Marty took a family-inspired career pathway toward an arts union activism especially aimed at helping his fellow specialized professional musicians to transform themselves into multi-faceted generalists and enterprising artists.

Bill

Bill's trade union activism expresses trade unionism for enterprising artists. His union work of engaging young enterprising artists extends his own wide set of enterprising artistic activities as recording and performing artist and musician, self-published songwriter, producer, engineer, record-label owner, and freelance journalist. A member of the transformative generation of enterprising artists, he entered the Nashville music scene in the late 1970s, played in clubs and as a member of a touring and recording country-artist band, developed as a major-label session musician, and launched his own artistic and production work. Bill became a trade union activist some fifteen years into his music career as Nashville entered the entrepreneurial era of music production.

Bill's union activism grows out of a pragmatic idealism about fairness in compensation. In the contemporary era of digital production and distribution and self-promotion, Bill's activism focuses on empowering enterprising artists to navigate through the challenges and opportunities of digital technology and self-promotion:

> We've gone from ... physical distribution ... to a record store, to buying something over the Internet or stealing over the Internet. You know, it's very well-documented that the decline in physical sales has not even remotely been matched by the rise of digital distribution.... It's a challenge ... because it's all about being fairly compensated for your work. I mean that is what we are supposed to be doing and when people are stealing your work, you know, you don't make as much money ... and it's killing the major labels. They didn't react to the rise of technology with the kind of swift transition that might have kept the money flowing.... So, the Internet, the upside of the Internet is that it is much easier to promote yourself.... I wrote my own press for years because I could never afford to hire a press agent, you know? ... I mean the things we had to do to promote ourselves.... I've kept some of my little promo packages from years gone by and they are so primitive and horrible. And now it's like, man, everybody has a digital camera.

In this era of self-promotion, the union instructs the individual artist in the art of negotiating a fair deal for a job under a union contract. As Bill put it:

> You have got to stand up for yourself. And at a certain point, you've got to start trying to promote doing the right thing ... we [union members] are the salespeople. Somebody calls up and says, hey, we got a session next Saturday 10 o'clock. Where is it? So-and-so. Okay, cool. Who is playing?

Oh, okay cool.... And if you are not in the union, you just go, what's it pay? And you can try to have a negotiation, but you are going to get what everybody else is getting, most likely. But you can say, is it on the [union] card? ... We have all had to learn how to do that.... We have to learn how to be the union salesperson, yet, the union never taught us how to do that. We had to learn for ourselves.

Vision of an Arts Union

An arts union, for Bill, is a platform and instrument of artist self-promotion. It is an age-diverse, occupational community that serves emerging and established, enterprising artists by providing a foundation of health insurance and a pension and by instructing the artist to individually negotiate work under a union contract. Bill delighted in the union's new group health insurance arrangement:

People come in [to the union] and go, man, this new healthcare thing is great, I'm saving $800 a month. We had a guy ... come in ... a couple of weeks ago, he was a prostate cancer survivor that was paying $1,200 a month, $5,000 deductible and was for lousy coverage. Now, he's got $400 a month and $1,200 deductible, so like man that gets me through a lot. And so, it's just like, it's really about the sense of community.

The arts union also informs its members of benefits. Bill explained how touring musicians often are unaware of their pension benefits when they negotiate with their employers:

These poor guys who were out on the road for twenty-five years never got any pension. There was a pension plan available. Nobody sold it to them. Nobody helped them sell it to their boss.... It saves them money. If everybody in a band defers 10 percent of their wages to put in a pension fund, then the employer doesn't have to pay payroll taxes on that 10 percent. So, they are actually going to save money by mailing one check to the pension fund on the behalf of all their musicians. But somebody has to teach those people that. It's like passing it down, the passing of the torch.

Member awareness of benefits is important for recruiting young artists into the union, and for strengthening the pension fund for older union members. Bill explained: "The music business has changed so drastically that we have to adapt and we have to be flexible. And if we don't get young members, our pension is going to run out. Or at some point. I think at this point I think they have it amortized out to 2041. So we've got forty-one years. I'll be eighty-four. It'll be a real drag to have my pension run out at eighty-four. The arts union also empowers young enterprising artists by instructing them in the art of individual union-contract negotiation. Bill illustrated this point with the hypothetical case of an artist negotiating a limited-press, union session agreement:

You need to know how to talk to people and say, it is a series of questions, you know, where we working? Okay. What time? Two sessions or one? Uh, so is this a record? Well, what kind of record? Okay, so, are we on the card? Silence. What's that mean? Well, is this a union session? I don't know man, I've never done that before. Well whose on the date? Okay, so-and-so. So have you talked to anyone about being a band leader on this thing? I don't know, no. Well, like, if we do it as a union thing and if you were for example to make me your band leader. I'll write the charts. Oh, you haven't called the players yet? I'll help you call the players. We'll get together and talk about guys you want. Guys, if you can't get the guy you want, I can get somebody else who does that same sort of thing. You know. I'll be there at the studio to make sure everything gets done. I'll take care of all the paperwork. All you've got to do is sign these couple of pieces of paper. Doesn't cost anything to have a limited pressing agreement. And that way, until you sell 10 thousand copies of this record, you know? We are all good. If you get to 10 thousand, everybody gets a little bump. But you know, you'll be happy at 10 thousand, right? ... I've learned how to do these for 20 years.... But some young kid, it's just, who has just moved to town—he doesn't know how to say that. We have to teach him how to say that. And you know, it's like how to get something on the card.

The union also helps the touring indie artist to enforce the contract. Bill illustrated how the union contract protected the touring artist from intellectual property theft and from last-minute broken deals:

I think we have to help these people [touring indie artists] protect themselves. We are going to help them look out for their intellectual property, because there is always going to be big ... entertainment companies, you know, who are eventually going to be the gatekeepers for all this, you know, individual music. So, ... you do your little record with your friends and you pay everybody and you are just paying cash and there is no contract. And then you go out and you are on the road and you are booking yourself, you know. One scenario is you get to Vail, Colorado to do that ski lodge that you booked and the guy goes, no man, slow week, sorry man, can't pay you. It's like, I know we said two weeks, but we can only do one week. You get fired. If you don't have a contract, you just did a verbal handshake, you are screwed, and you've got to go home.... Or, you get there to the gig and the gig goes fine. And you are selling CDs at your gig in the ski lodge and [famous Hollywood movie director]'s assistant buys your CD and really likes that one song that you wrote about your grandma and then goes back to California and she is playing the CD in her office and [famous director] walks by and goes, man, that is a cool song about grandma. That'd be pretty for that thing we are about to do. Oh great. You know and they put it in the movie and you go to the movie theater one day and there is your song. And maybe they got a hold of you, maybe they didn't. But it's you against [major film production company] or you've got a paper trail because you did the record with your buddies and the same amount of money changed hands, but it is on paper. And we've got a contract and we can enforce.

Although the arts union does not line up work for individual members, the union should, Bill maintained, facilitate job seeking by helping the artist to network and negotiate with other artists and employers: "What we [the union] can't do is make a value judgment and say guitar player X.... It's like, here is a list of people who are available.... We're not going to get you work. It's like, okay, but we can teach people how to network. We can help people network. We can help people understand how these contracts work."

Strategic Orientation

Having financial success is only secondary to the meaning Bill derives from being creative. His own satisfaction with being creative derives from his passionate pursuit of a music career and is reinforced by recognition from his peers, his many music awards, and from his association with award-winning recordings:

> Financial security probably means more to a lot of people than it means to me.... I try not to be oblivious to it, but I've never let money rule my life or make my decisions for me. I've probably made some mistakes in that area, but to me creative and personal satisfaction is much more important than how much money I've got in the bank. As long as I can pay my bills, I'm pretty happy ... if you think about it ... I can make a living doing what I love to do and would do for free. What could be better than that? I'm not rich but ... I have had a very rich life and very varied experiences. And a lot of it is because I went out and ... took the initiative. I didn't wait for it to come to me.... I went and found it, it happened to be here. If you had told me when I was 16 that by the time I was 21 I'd be living in Nashville, I'd have thought you were out of your mind.

The satisfaction Bill gains from earning a living by doing what he loves to do is reinforced by the peer recognition he receives for his contributions and achievements:

> So those kinds of things [music awards] and ... playing on records that got Grammy nominations or Grammy awards. That is nice. I think I've been on six records that won Grammys over the years ... but honestly,

I think the recognition of my peers with or without awards is more meaningful and to me the satisfaction of a job well done is still the single most rewarding thing and that kind of just applies all across the board. Just knowing that I did the best I could do and it helped other people do the best they can do. Those are all, those are all good feelings.

Pathway

Bill was swept away by the Beatles and rock 'n' roll of his youth and adolescence in Eastern City. He was also swept away by the movement of loud, playing-by-ear, self-contained bands. The son of a career military officer and homemaker, Bill took a movement-inspired career path to becoming a union activist, as he transitioned from playing the notes on acoustic instruments to playing by ear on electric instruments:

I fell in love with music … and at that time, the Beatles were taking off, the Rolling Stones were coming along and there were, they were on TV constantly … I loved it … I mean I was still messing around with it, but somebody had showed me the riff to "Sunshine of Your Love" and I just sort of played that over and over again. This is cool. I'm not having to read this. This is just like I know where to put my fingers. It was all very incremental and then I remember I mowed yards for a summer and I earned $42 for the whole summer and I bought this really cheap electric [instrument] and I started playing it because my parents had kind of pooh-poohed the other thing. But then when they saw how serious I was they said okay, well, you aren't playing this other thing. So, I traded my [acoustic instrument] from 5th and 6th grade for an electric [instrument] … I would have been 13. And, from that point, everything really changed. You know, I just wanted to rock. I just wanted to rock 'n' roll … I guess I had enough rudimentary skills. I knew all the names of the notes and I knew a few things about major and minor and that was about it. And a lot of it was you just tried to get with guys who knew more about it than you did … that is what my heroes were doing. That's what the Beatles were doing … I loved popular music. I loved all that stuff. I loved Motown. Because you know back then, the radio was very eclectic and you heard a lot of different things on the same radio. I didn't hear a lot of country growing up, but it would be The Electric Prunes and then it would be Tom Jones and then it would be The Mike Curb Congregation and then—it was just, I just remember liking almost everything I heard…. Because for me, all I really wanted from the time I was 13 was to get into a successful band or just a band that was doing something…. So that was kind of how the fire got started and then it was just a question of learning and just, and you know it was all trial and error and you know, reading music is very empirical and playing by ear is very subjective. And I was just drawn to that and you know, I was always better at coming up with my own version of a song rather than sitting down and perfecting it note for note. I was always like, I think we are close enough, let's do it.... And I was just into rock 'n' roll, I was into guitars, I was into volume. I liked loud, drove my mom crazy. I blew up amps left and right, you know? That was just ... what we were doing.

For Bill, the self-contained band would become not only a vehicle for artistic professional development and self-expression but also a tight, human learning community. The compassionate and award-winning country artist led the band with an inclusive, democratic ethos during the decade Bill served as a band member under his tutelage. As the band came to enjoy market success, the band leader co-wrote with Bill, encouraged Bill's own professional development, and instilled in Bill the value of maintaining one's own artistic integrity. Although the band leader never discussed trade unionism with Bill, Bill partly attributed his formation as a trade union activist to his band leader as mentor.

The band leader took the young Bill under his wing:

I'm coming from this high energy, oh man, I just want to impress everybody and man. And all of a sudden I'm in some kind of slow motion movie ... but, I sensed right away, even with ... some ignorance of the subtleties of country music, ... that [band leader] was ... a nice guy even though he didn't say much. And so, we do the first job and it's 5 or 6 thousand people and I had never played to people who didn't make noise before and who would shut up and listen and it freaked me out.

Bill's band leader became his late-night mentor on the road:

And so, ... the rest of my career was like ... almost all because of [band leader]. He really taught me a whole lot about everything.... He saw some things in me. He saw potential in me that I was completely oblivious to and nurtured it and pulled it out in a way that most artists and stars would not do. So I was very fortunate in that respect.... He always treated me kind of like an equal even though, you know, when I joined his band, he was probably in his, I guess, mid-40s and I was 20 years old, you know, I was half his age. And yet, ... when we were all on one bus, [band leader] was the relief driver. And I've always been kind of an insomniac anyways and so I stay up pretty late, most of the time. And everybody else would go to bed and [band leader] would be the relief driver. He'd crash out for a few hours after the show and then the driver would pull over and [band leader] would be the relief driver and I'd just sit up and talk to him. We'd just drive all night and just talk about all kinds of stuff.

Bill's band leader led the band with a selfless, paternal, and democratic ethos, including at large shows:

They'd want to put [band leader] way out front and put us like way in the back. And [band leader] would go, no, we are a band, I'm just the singer. I gotta have my guys. And we'd get up there and because I was up close and in proximity and in pretty good camera shape on the sideline and singing, I would get extra money because ... I would get money to sing, as well as to play. And [band leader] would always just take care of us, he treated us good. But it was never from a unionism point of view.

Bill recalled one especially momentous evening of his band leader's selfless support of the band at a large stage show:

There was one night we were on stage.... I'll never forget this, I don't think any of us will. [band leader] would introduce the band in the middle of the show.... He would stop and introduce and say some nice things about everybody, not a lot ... he would say and now these guys are going to play a couple of songs for you. And he just walked off the stage and we are like, what? What did you just do? He's giving us his audience in the middle of a show, which no one would ever do. And so, we did like two songs and everybody liked it and then [band leader] came out and ... the show was back on and we are all looking at each other like, wow, what just happened ... and [band leader] was just amazingly generous that way.

As his own career unfolded and ramified, Bill became known as a musician advocate among his peers. As he developed his advocacy skills and interest in arts unionism, he became increasingly involved in the union:

And so I sort of became the source for useful information for people who are working. And it got to the point where people ... called, hey [Bill], I've got a union question.... I was getting that all the time. Hey, can I do this? How do you do such? And I just started, well if I didn't know, I'd find out. And I just started getting more knowledgeable about some of these things.... You know, so I just started to realize, I've got some kind of affinity for this ... I just started to be a little more assertive and I began to take on the powers ... a little more.... And ... all I'm trying to do is look out for the guys and look out for what is right and I'm coming from a ... a pretty pure place.

Bill carries his original torch every day:

I'm still a fan ... I still get excited. I don't ever want to lose that. I really really don't want to lose that. And I think that that maybe has helped me sustain ... doing a lot of different things and willingly putting myself in crazy situations.... Not very well organized, but a helluva lot of fun. So to me the excitement that I had as a kid just starting to play, that still colors everything I do.

Marty

An enterprising artist, Marty is a recording and performing artist, musician and singer, a self-published songwriter, a board member of an international music professional association, a music teacher at two area schools, the owner-operator of an instrument repair business, and an owner-manager of a few residential rental properties, as well as a trade union activist. He embarked on his music career in the 1980s shortly before the advent of the entrepreneurial era of music production. His activism in an arts union is part and parcel of the increasingly diverse ensemble of professional and entrepreneurial activities that he has developed to support his artistic career and generate multiple income streams:

> The business has certainly changed drastically since I've moved here. And I think the people that survive in the creative arts in general in any career involving intellectual property are the ones that are able to bob and weave and reinvent themselves. So that's why now I'm doing a little more work in my [repair] shop, ... [d]oing a little more teaching, concentrating also on my own individual solo career as a singer and [musician], and trying to develop ideas for clinician work, the [music] education community. Just trying to stay viable and active.

If the union provides him and his fellow artists with an economic foundation, Marty's repair business affords him a measure of economic self-determination:

> Most of the areas of my professional life I have no control over. Certainly if I work in a recording studio, or if I work on a television show or something like that, there are negotiated rates and I get paid fairly. But for live work and for teaching, it's take it or leave it kind of a situation.... The only area of my professional life that I have control of is my workshop.... I can charge what I think is fair, I can work when I want to, and not work when I don't want to. I have total control of that. Oddly enough I can make better money per hour out there. And I have a lot of respect for what I do out there. It's validating in a whole other area. I always say it's one of the few areas of work, apart from the music business, that the business will sort of forgive you for. It's sort of considered an extension of who I am as a player.

Vision of an Arts Union

Marty envisions an arts union that addresses both general, enduring employment issues and contemporary compensation issues in live music among emerging and established artists and musicians. His general vision of arts unionism rests on a deeply held belief in fairness:

In the arts without a union you're just out there. Once you do what you do, it's in the ether. If you haven't been paid for it, there's nothing tangible to show. Particularly live music. In the recording sense, without a union you may do a recording session for a songwriter demo that ends up being part of a commercial, or part of a movie or whatever. And so without the union you have no protection, and it just seemed to be as a person pursuing a career, that the only way to make the career viable was to put a few locks on the doors when you left the office at night. So I still believe that. Again, I'm annoyed that we have to do it, in a perfect world everybody would treat everyone fairly, we would all make a reasonable percentage of the revenue streams. But it just doesn't ever happen.

Marty explained that a chief contemporary challenge for arts unions is compensation for live artists and musicians:

There's two definitions of non-union. There's non-union that hires people who aren't members of the union, and then there's non-union work, what we call dark dates, done by union musicians that don't go on a union card. The [union] here has never been effective at policing live work.... For one thing it's a huge issue of man hours. There are a lot of places to play. How do you get around to all of them and make sure that everybody's paid up members and that they're being treated right? The other issue is that in order to accommodate those on the low end of pay scales, the clubs, the coffee houses and places that have lower margins of profitability, the scales are so low that most of us don't work for scale. I can't even tell you what scale for a live two- or three-hour date in a club would be because I don't work for that, it's too low. It would be like maybe for a side man maybe $60 for a four-hour gig or $70 maybe, but I'm not going to play for four hours for $70 unless it's so enjoyable I couldn't stand it. Most of the time it's enjoyable, but not that enjoyable.

Marty noted that much of the live non-union work is performed by aspiring artists and musicians who are attempting to gain audience and market exposure and by non-professional music aficionados:

They're sort of fringe guys who have come here to try to get in the music business, or the Lower Broadway type guys, or Opryland guys, or the kids that come out of [music school] who have two or three years singing those tunes under their belt at school, ... so they're trying to get whatever gig they can get to get started. So they're going to do whatever they do, they'll play a coffeehouse for $15 or $20, whatever they can do just to say they're up there on stage performing for a live audience. And that's where they should be, frankly. But then you have the other side of the coin, you have well-meaning folks who have made their monies in other industries and may even have a nice pension built up, health insurance and all that, and find themselves in love with this music so they'll go out and play for free and pay their band, and give the club owner a quintet what I would give them a trio for. So that's an issue. And I think it's an issue country-wide, I really do. My friends in New York tell me that you used to work a week or two weeks in a venue for a set fee, and now it's a night or two for the door at the ... clubs. So it's just what it is.... The music business is not for the faint of heart. It's a business that there are always more people wanting to be in it than there's room for. So consequently it's always difficult to keep any sort of a reasonable scale. The recording industry for musicians is, I always tell people when they ask me why should I fool with the union, I say well you know if it wasn't for union scale, even non-scale work would not be as high as it is. It lifts all boats, as they say. If it wasn't for organized labor we'd all be in a musical sweatshop in essence. In some ways we still are.

Arts unions, according to Marty, are developing new mechanisms for compensating indie and major-labor live work under a union contract by enabling

independent artists and artists on labels to sign union contracts, and for touring artists to have their employers, the main artist, contribute to the health and retirement plan based on their salaries in live music. And for recording artists to contribute into the health and retirement plan based on sales of product on the road. Not just royalties earned through the record companies, which is always hard to trace. So I mean there's some very innovative things to try to continue to add value to the card for a union member. There are things happening.

Strategic Orientation

For Marty, individual artistic expression, professionalism, artistic community, and family well-being cohere as a meaningful whole. He conceives of success and professionalism as peer recognition of his own lifelong legacy of artistic expression:

I think for my individual work, my solo performances and my recording work, feedback from other musicians probably means more to me than anything else. I've always gotten very strong feedback from other per-formers, so that makes it worth doing. And then I've got some recogni-tion from national publications and international publications.

The successful professional, as Marty sees it, is an artist who can financially sustain his peer-recognized artistic legacy:

Having enough preparation to be able to carve out your niche of work areas and hopefully be able to secure a steady enough list of engagements to sustain yourself financially. And then I guess the other aspect of being professional would be to try to turn out a body of work over the course of your musical life that would demonstrate that you have contributed to the music.

The music consumer, Marty acknowledged, helps to sustain artist morale and to generate the financial support of what is otherwise the artist's peer-recognized legacy. Regarding fan recognition of his artistry, Marty noted: "That's important too because it's sustaining. You can't continue to do your work if you have no support, and I think support from a fan base is important psychologically as well as financially."

Pathway

Marty's family-inspired career pathway, coupled with his passive entry into union membership, the encouragement of his fellow union members, and his own pragmatic and religious idealism, led him to run for elected union office. The son of a graduate-school-educated, Southern Baptist music minister father and a mother who worked in a bank and served as a church-based, child music educator, Marty's parents encouraged him and his two sisters to play music and to study music in school. He studied with professionals through college, when he also began performing in live venues in Southern City and considers his fellow Southern City professional musicians to be among his early mentors:

> I was singing in the choir at four years old. I was just by osmosis getting a certain amount of music education in the choir programs and taking piano lessons with the church organist. And so by the time I was in high school I was singing solos in the church choir. Easter and Christmas productions, things like that. My junior year of high school I started studying with a college level ... teacher at the [university].... For me I was already out performing two or three times a week and supporting myself through college, and I realized I was much more interested in a more active performing career, and this music gave me that opportunity. The other thing, little by little as I got to Nashville I realized that as an improvising musician I could perform a whole lot more diverse selection of music, so I loved to be involved with all kinds of things, folk to country to bluegrass to jazz to pop music, whatever.

Having joined the Southern City local union, Marty transferred his union membership to the Nashville local upon his entry into the Nashville music scene. His fellow union members admired his organizational skills and commitment and subsequently successfully recruited him to run for union office.

If Marty's father inspired him to pursue a music career, he did not encourage him to become an arts union activist: "Not my dad certainly. He was an Eisenhower Republican, born in 1912, so he came up under the Red scare and all that business. Unions to him were more socialism. So it didn't come from him." Marty attributed his pro-union beliefs to personal need and pragmatic and religious idealism. He attributed his pragmatic idealism to his personal need to stabilize the musician's volatile income:

> Well the one really radical idea that I have is that when a performing artist works they should be paid, and they should also have access to health insurance and a pension plan ... it comes from a personal need. Unfortunately we use the expression "play music." A lot of people think we're just playing, we're just goofing around, and getting paid for it. The music business is a hard business. Sure when I go out and work I may make $50 or $100 or $200 an hour for whatever I can do or get. But I may not work but three or four times that month. And the rest of the time I'm scuffling, I'm on the phone, I'm writing, I'm organizing and trying to make things happen. And it's an almost impossible business to really be in part-time.

Underlying Marty's pragmatic idealism is a populist religious idealism that is linked to his strong identification with the Democratic Party. Comparing his Democratic Party identification with his union activism, Marty explained:

> It's deeper than just my union affiliation. I look at the Scripture and I see the things that Jesus said about go and sell what you have and take care of the poor and those in need. Those are the kind of things that I think the Democratic Party at least tries to do. Are there abuses? Certainly there are. The democratic system, as my father used to love to say, is not perfect. It's a terrible way of governing. But it's the best we have.

ARTIST ADVOCATES IN AN ENTREPRENEURIAL ERA: TOWARD A NEW ARTS TRADE UNIONISM

Artist advocates are forging a new arts trade unionism for the emerging community of enterprising artists in Nashville. The arts trade unionism of the earlier corporate era addressed the interests of recording musicians through collective bargaining with the major labels, which were signatories to a master union contract. The new arts trade unionism of the contemporary entrepreneurial era addresses the interests of self-promoting enterprising artists who "own their own stuff" by supporting the artist's individual bargaining with employers.

The shift from collective bargaining toward individual bargaining is being driven by transformative and contemporary generations of enterprising artists and artist activists. Arts union activists today hail from the transformative generation of enterprising artists who have taken the union leadership baton from the earlier, corporate-era generation of arts union activists. The transformative generation of enterprising artists is the same generation that initially forged the emerging community of enterprising artists in the 1980s and 1990s; mentored subsequent generations of contemporary enterprising artists; and, along with younger generations of artistic social entrepreneurs, created social spaces—artistic social enterprises—for the professional development of the emerging community of enterprising artists.

The work of artist advocates—i.e., reinventing arts trade unionism—complements and reinforces the efforts of enterprising artists and artistic social entrepreneurs by addressing the economic livelihood of the whole, emerging peer community of diverse enterprising artists. Artist advocates encounter resistance from employers and age-generational differences in interests among the union members that challenge the development of the new unionism and, consequently, the emerging peer community of enterprising artists.

In Nashville, all three types of artist activists—enterprising artists, artistic social entrepreneurs, and artist advocates—theorized in chapter 2 have arisen with the musician migration to forge an emerging and loosely coupled community of diverse enterprising artists as Nashville transitions into an entrepreneurial era of multi-genre music production. The resulting occupational self-determination of enterprising artists is a place-based model of artist peer community whose sustainability in Nashville remains uncertain. Future research should be directed at examining its applicability to other cities, and to other occupations and economic sectors, in this competitive era of precarious employment, identity politics, and entrepreneurial economic production.

CHAPTER 7

Community, Agency, and Artistic Expression

Artist activists are envisioning and building an inclusive, expressive occupational community of musicians in Nashville. They are doing so in an enterprising era of precarious employment relations, identity politics, and risk individualization. By building an inclusive artist community that encourages individual artistic expression and well-being of diverse, independent Nashville musicians, artist activists are also sustaining Nashville's vibrant music scene that produces a widening array of musical genres.

It takes much "entrepreneurial agency" to usher in a risky, post-bureaucratic artistic scene or generate a "competitive field,"[1] and artist activists engage in the requisite act of occupational self-determination for socializing and minimizing risk. In this current phase of "competition and creativity"[2] in the "concentration-competition cycle"[3] of popular-music production, artistic peer communities are especially responsive to the interests and needs of diverse enterprising artists who, as self-promoting occupational generalists, operate with wide portfolios of artistic and art-support activities. In the earlier, corporate and culturally homogeneous cyclical phase, risk was assumed and minimized by large bureaucratic organizations such as production companies, trade unions, and performance rights organizations that engaged mass consumer markets. In this emerging post-bureaucratic cyclical phase, individual self-promoting artists increasingly assume the risk as they engage dynamic niche markets. Artist activists build inclusive, occupational peer communities for re-socializing and minimizing risk, and thereby widen the range of social identities and genres expressed by the musicians.

This book addresses the unfolding repertoire of individual and collective actions taken by artist activists who are recreating musician community in Nashville. Throughout the post-1980 musician migration to Nashville, three types of artist activists—"enterprising artists," "artistic social entrepreneurs," and "artist advocates"—emerged in rough chronological sequence, respectively, as their careers unfolded with the Nashville music scene's transition toward a new entrepreneurial era of music production. Their local organizational initiatives also constituted a cumulating repertoire of increasingly collective, community-building actions, beginning with the most individualistic enterprising artists and culminating in the most collective initiatives in the new arts trade unionism of the artist advocates.

150

During Nashville's transition, artist activists have forged an emerging musician community of enterprising artists. The community consists of a spatial ecology and "loosely coupled"[4] set of local initiatives undertaken by artist activists on behalf of artist and occupational well-being in an urban art scene populated by socially and artistically diverse, self-promoting entrepreneurial artists. A community in formation, this place-based peer community of musicians has yet to fully cohere within an overarching organizational framework.

In this book, I develop a new sociological theory of artist activism in recreating a peer community. The purpose of the theory, presented in chapter 2, is to explain how artist activists fashion their community-building roles as enterprising artists, artistic social entrepreneurs, and artist advocates. Derived from my interviews with seventy-five Nashville music professionals, the theory attributes artist activists' creation, assumption, and enactment of any or all of the three artist activist roles to their subjective orientations toward success, audience, risk, and career inspiration.

Artist activists in Nashville also are reconstituting artist community in an era of identity politics.[5] The contemporary post-bureaucratic cyclical phase of popular-culture production is contextualized by the egalitarian, identity-based social movements and increasing immigration to the United States of the late twentieth and early twenty-first centuries. Post-bureaucratic indie art-making coincides with the civil rights, women's, and LGBT movements, and with the large post-1990 wave of immigration, the largest immigration wave since that of the 1880–1924 era.[6] In his seventy-city study of cultural conflict about public art displays during the 1990s in the United States, Steven Tepper shows that the most conflictual cities were those with the highest rates of immigration, and that Nashville was a "relatively contentious city."[7] Tepper interprets cultural conflict as a "democratic outcome of citizens negotiating the consequences of social change within their communities."[8] Genre diversification, then, is linked not only to the contemporary, competitive phase of the concentration-competition cycle of popular-music production, but also to increasing diversification of social identities that are expressed artistically.[9]

In this concluding chapter, I first link the emergence of a genre-diverse, dual music scene in Nashville to shifts in the organization of music production and distribution, a cumulating sequence of identity-based egalitarian social movements, and increasing global immigration to Nashville. Next, I present a new, collective research agenda in the new sociology of work derived from the sociological theory of artist activism. The research agenda addresses the generalizability of the Nashville model of artist activists, the development of artist activists from, by, and for a peer community, and the effectiveness of multiple models of occupational communities in advancing the livelihoods of individuals and the occupation as a whole. I conclude with policy implications for building and strengthening inclusive and expressive, urban occupational communities in an era of risk individualization.

AN EMERGING ARTIST COMMUNITY IN A DUAL SCENE

In Music City, musicians have been writing, performing, and recording in an expanding range of musical genres at an accelerating pace over the last half-century. In 1963, Tennessee governor Frank G. Clement wrote in *Billboard* magazine that

> country music is an authentic part of Tennessee heritage ... and the musicians and the singers who make country music a Tennessee institution ... bring to the city of Nashville alone in a year's time the staggering total of forty million dollars in income.... Country music also brings to Nashville and to Tennessee a steady stream of recording artists, music industry leaders and out-of-State visitors who have made the "Grand Ole Opry" the worldwide tourist attraction it is.[10]

In 2011, *Rolling Stone* magazine declared Nashville the nation's "Best Music Scene," highlighting that the genre-diverse group of mega-stars "Jack White, Kings of Leon, The Black Keys, Ke\$ha and Taylor Swift have all moved here."[11] *Billboard* reported that Nashville mayor Karl Dean, having recently founded the music-promoting Music City Music Council, stated that "Nashville's best days are still ahead of it, and that is very clear when you look at this music industry.... It's taking off here; it's getting increasingly interesting and increasingly complex."[12] *Billboard* elaborated, noting that although "country music remains the big dog in town," Nashville also supports "vibrant Christian and gospel, punk, pop, folk and roots music scenes."[13]

Decades of genre diversification in Music City coincided with decades of social change in Nashville. A contemporary generation of enterprising artists, profiled in chapter 4, not only make music in diverse genres, they express a wide range of social identities or "roots" that differ by ethnicity-race, gender, sexual orientation, immigrant status, and religion for their fans in niche markets.[14] Just three years before Governor Clement wrote his Tennessee cultural heritage article in *Billboard*, African American college students sat down at Nashville's downtown lunch counters, assuming a leadership role in the civil rights movement that culminated in the demise of Jim Crow in the South in the mid-1960s. With the momentum of the civil rights movement, a cumulating series of social movements—for women's, LGBT, immigrant, and human rights—subsequently unfolded in Nashville, accompanying the growth and globalization of Nashville's robust service economy and labor force, increasing immigration, and the resettlement of residents from the U.S. coasts in Nashville.[15]

Indeed, an earlier transformative generation of enterprising artists, profiled in chapter 3, not only forged the new community of enterprising artists during the 1980s. The transformative generation, inspired by the cultural and political movements of their adolescence—the socially critical movements of the 1960s and 1970s—broke from the corporate music-production system that supported the older cultural heritage described by Governor Clement, and have continued to serve as mentors of successive generations of contemporary enterprising artists.

Genre diversification also coincided with a shift in the systems of production and distribution of popular music in Music City. This shift is a transformation from an oligopolistic, corporate system of major labels and mass distribution through radio airplay toward a competitive, entrepreneurial system of indie labels and self-contained indie bands and artists who self-promote and -distribute their music in live venues and over the Internet. The consolidation of the major labels especially during the 2000s, coupled with the advent of indie music production in a wide range of musical genres consumed in socially differentiated, niche markets, has generated a "dual" Nashville music scene with two interlinked, major-label and indie spheres of music production and distribution.[16]

What is the fate of musician community in this dual music scene, and in our era of identity politics, free agency, and risk individualization?[17] In the Nashville Sound art world of the early 1960s, the community of artists consisted of a complex, occupational division of labor of songwriters, pluggers, producers, an "A-team" of unionized session musicians, and top-charting artists, situated geographically in the Music Row area and organized around one musical genre, major labels, large publishers, big studios, performance rights organizations, and genre-wide industry associations. Music historian Robert K. Oermann described the Nashville Sound art world of the 1960s as "a community [in which] ... country-music people 'circled the wagons' and banded together."[18] Oermann quoted award-winning singer Lynn Anderson as likening that community to a "small town" in which "everybody knows who's dating whom, who's broken up with whom, what kind of car you drive, everything else," and music publisher Bill Denny as asserting that "in Nashville, country music grew on the basis of cooperation.... The music publishers and the artists and the agencies here all kind of work together."[19]

In Nashville's contemporary dual music scene, artist activists are establishing an entrepreneurial, indie artist community alongside of the major-label artist community.[20] These initiatives encourage and facilitate individual artistic expression and professional development, career mobility opportunities, and the economic well-being of the whole occupation. As Jack White recently put it:

> It's definitely very encouraging and supportive because the environment that any artist is in starts to dictate the creativity of the artist and the output of the artist. So if the environment is supportive it can be very helpful to ... creativity.... Obviously in this town you can see from the mayor's office on down that they're very supportive and interested in the idea of Nashville's musical culture.[21]

This community comprises a simple occupational division of labor of generalists who, as self-promoting enterprising artists, perform artistic and support functions and often do not belong to a union.[22] Sociologically, artist activists, as community-builders, are re-socializing risk in an increasingly individualistic, precarious, enterprising, and expressive artistic scene.

TOWARD A SOCIOLOGY OF ARTIST ACTIVISM: AN AGENDA FOR A POST-BUREAUCRATIC SOCIOLOGY OF WORK

Artist activists create expressive occupational communities in our enterprising but precarious era of identity politics and risk individualization.[23] The advent of a diverse, entrepreneurial, and indie artist community in Nashville is microcosmic of changes in expressive occupations in the United States. Increasingly, employment in expressive occupations in the arts, entertainment, and new media sectors is acquiring an independent (freelance) character.[24] The U.S. Bureau of Labor Statistics projects that employment as "*independent* artists, writers, and performers" will increase by 12.4 percent between 2012 and 2022, roughly two to four times the projected growth rate of all—independent as well as wage and salaried—actors, artists, dancers, musicians, photographers, producers and directors, and writers.[25]

The sociological theory of artist activism presented in chapter 2 argues for a new research agenda on the role of artist activists, and of agency more generally, in the formation of expressive occupational peer communities and in occupational self-determination. Specifically, the theory addresses how an artist activist's subjective orientation toward success, audience, risk, and career inspiration shapes one's assumption and enactment of different artist activist roles. As a set of community-building actions, the three artist activist roles, typologized in chapter 2, constitute a repertoire of individual and collective actions undertaken by peers in the formation of an expressive occupational peer community. Based on the empirical case of the emerging indie music scene in Nashville, the theory is intended to generalize within our enterprising era of increasing risk individualization and employment precarity, identity politics, and heightened income inequality associated with the advent of a two-tier service economy.[26]

The sociological theory of artist activism consists of three elements that argue for a new research agenda on the role of artist activists in the formation of expressive occupational communities. The first is a typology of artist activist roles. The second element comprises four typologies of artist activists' subjective orientations pertaining to success, audience, risk, and career inspiration, respectively. The third element of the theory consists of three propositions that together constitute a thesis on how individual variations in an artist activist's subjective orientations toward success, audience, risk, and career inspiration account for variations in a peer's assumption and enactment of any or all of the artist activist roles.

GENERALIZING BEYOND NASHVILLE: URBAN CONTEXT AND THE CONFIGURATION OF ARTIST ACTIVISTS IN AN ART SCENE

Turning to the research agenda, the first research question pertains to the empirical generalizability of the typology of artist activists in social space. The threefold typology of enterprising artists, artistic social entrepreneurs, and artist advocates is derived from the urban context of Nashville that supports them. The specific configuration of artist activists that exist in an urban art scene is likely to vary across cities that differ in terms of artist population size and growth rate, local economy and economic development policy, degree of local cultural inclusivity and diversity, and a history of arts trade unionism.[27] Nashville "scores high" on each of these dimensions of urban context. As a major, U.S. music-recording center, a cradle of the U.S. civil rights movement, and an important "new destination city" for global immigrants, Nashville has one of the largest and fastest-growing and -diversifying musician populations; a robust service economy and local economic development policy that encourage artistic entrepreneurship and expression; a relatively tolerant and inclusive orientation toward cultural diversity; and a history of active arts trade unionism.[28]

Cities whose urban contexts differ from the Nashville context are likely to support configurations of artist activists that differ from the Nashville typology. Cities differ by their levels of art consumption versus art production. The population of artists in art-production cities, such as Nashville, is likely to exceed that in art-consumption cities. Therefore, "enterprising artists" are most likely to thrive in an art-production city that is home to a diverse, critical mass of artist activists. In contrast, "artistic social entrepreneurs" who serve consumers as they support artists are most likely to predominate in art-consumption cities that are on a national and international itinerary of traveling art performances and exhibits whose artists are based primarily in other cities.

Cities also differ in their local labor histories. Lowell Turner distinguishes between "union towns" that have long histories of trade unionism and maintain established local labor unions and "frontier cities" that lack a local history of trade unionism and are often the greenfield sites of new labor organizing.[29] Arts trade unionism in the United States is at least one century old,[30] but it is not a foregone conclusion that "artist advocates" are most likely to predominate in arts "union towns" or "frontier cities." On the one hand, the resource mobilization theory of social movements suggests that new social movement mobilizations are facilitated by pre-existing movement organizations which provide new movements with organizational, human, and financial resources through strategic alliances and coalitions. This implies that arts-union towns would be fertile ground for the spawning of "artist advocates." On the other hand, union-democracy studies stemming from Michels's "iron law of oligarchy" suggest that labor unions ossify and lose their militancy as they age, grow, and bureaucratize. This would suggest that innovative "artist advocates" are more likely to thrive in the open environment of an arts-frontier city than in an arts-union town.[31]

The recent case of insurgency and leadership change in Nashville AFM Local 257, discussed in chapter 6, suggests the urban-contextual conditions that are conducive to the emergence of "artist advocates" in arts-union towns. Consistent with the "status-conflict theory of union leadership change,"[32] the election of insurgent Local 257 officers in a century-old labor union occurred at a moment of union membership decline in an effort to revitalize the union by functionally aligning it with the interests and needs of a growing and younger generation of enterprising artists.

In sum, the Nashville typology of artist activists is most likely to generalize to cities that are at once arts-production and arts-consumption cities. The urban context of these cities provides the diverse critical mass of artists, robust local economy, and organizational and political resources necessary to sustain enterprising artists, artistic social entrepreneurs, and artist advocates. Indeed, the Future of Music Coalition's 2013 Artist Revenue Streams survey of more than 5,000 U.S. musicians indicates that these "music industry cities," such as Los Angeles, Nashville, and New York, afford musicians the greatest professional development and networking opportunities and highest incomes compared to other cities.[33] This is the urban context, then, that is likely to sustain the strongest independent, expressive occupational communities—those that support the individual expression, professional development, and economic well-being of the occupation and its individual members.

ASSUMING AND ENACTING AN ARTIST ACTIVIST ROLE IN AN INDIVIDUALISTIC AGE

The three propositions of the theory argue for a research agenda on becoming an artist activist in an individualistic age. The first proposition states that *members of an artist peer community whose strategic orientations conceive of success as artistic freedom, and audience as their peers, are most likely to become artist activists in their peer community.* Those peers, then, who simultaneously value highly artistic freedom and identify strongly with their occupational community are those who are most likely to engage in actions that advance the individual and group interests of their occupation.

In order to extend the theory, future sociological research should address the biographical pathways of expressive occupational community peers who become artist activists. This research agenda entails examining the biographical pathways of occupational peers who simultaneously value artistic freedom and identify strongly with their occupational community.

Mentoring relationships are an important, research-worthy element of a biographical pathway for discerning how occupational socialization may shape an artist activist's strategic orientation. Intergenerational mentoring relationships are an important source of occupational socialization for the predominantly self-trained Nashville music professionals I interviewed. Almost all of my interviewees indicated that they stood on the shoulders of mentors when I asked "who do you consider to be your instructors and mentors?" Interviewees mentioned a wide range of music professionals, who were often about ten years older than they were and served as their mentors in their early career stages, including band leaders, producers, established artists, music shop owners, custom-guitar builders and luthiers, voice instructors, and music teachers. Interviewees' conversations and interactions with their mentors covered a wide range of topics, including finding their voice, etiquette and ethics, entrepreneurship, professionalism, trade unionism, artist-audience relationships, and the status and meaning of art and artists in society. Sociological examinations of the social context, content, and process of messaging through intergenerational mentoring would further illuminate how occupational socialization shapes strategic orientations and the formation of artist activists in an expressive occupational community.

The second proposition pertains to how a risk orientation shapes the type of artist activist role—enterprising artist, artistic social entrepreneur, and artist advocate—an individual assumes. *Artist activists of a peer community who harbor*

1. *personal risk orientations are most likely to become enterprising artists;*
2. *interpersonal risk orientations are most likely to become artistic social entrepreneurs; and,*
3. *impersonal risk orientations are most likely to become artist advocates.*

The artist activist roles differ in the mix of individual and collective action they entail, with enterprising artists and artist advocates entailing the most individual and collective action, respectively. The second proposition, then, suggests that the more an artist activist attributes the risk of joblessness to systemic rather than personal or characterological causes, the more collective rather than individual will be the initiative she envisions, and the artist activist role she assumes, for minimizing and managing risk.

In order to discern individual variations in types of artist activist roles occupational peers assumed, sociological research should be directed at examining the factors that influence risk orientation. Risk orientations are not unlike general beliefs about the causes of poverty. Histories of the U.S. welfare state, for example, show a progression of individualistic, communitarian, and systemic theories of poverty that attribute poverty to personal, community, and systemic failure and that underlie the evolution of philanthropy and the welfare state through the twentieth century.[34] How one acquires a risk orientation—whether through early childhood socialization of moral, religious, and political values, or from experiencing or witnessing widespread unemployment in epochs such as the Great Depression of the 1930s or the Great Recession of the 2000s—suggests that individual risk-orientation acquisition is linked to the pre-professional and professional stages and social context of one's biographical pathway toward becoming an artist activist.

The third proposition pertains to the enactment of one's artist activist role. In the twofold typology of role enactment, change agents whose role enactment emphasizes artistic functions over support functions engage in *artistic enactment*; and those whose enactment emphasizes support functions over artistic functions engage in *supportive enactment*. The third proposition links type of role enactment to the individual's pathway to becoming an artist activist and, especially, the social meaning of music internalized on the pathway: *those on family-inspired career pathways develop a communal meaning of music that informs a supportive enactment of their artist activist roles; those on movement-inspired pathways develop a culturally expressive meaning of music that informs an artistic enactment of their artist activist roles.*

The third proposition argues for a new research agenda that extends a family-embeddedness theoretical perspective on individual variations in type of role enactment. This perspective suggests that the depth and direction of one's embeddedness in a family, as well as subsequent, extra-familial influences one encounters along one's pathway, may shape how an artist comes to enact his artist activist role. The depth of embeddedness in an individual's childhood family—the closeness and mutual respect among family members—may influence his susceptibility to family versus extra-familial influences on the type of social meaning of music an artist internalizes during his youth. Parenting philosophy and practices and the content of parental messages may influence the social meaning an artist internalizes in his youth. A family-embeddedness perspective, then, suggests that artists who are raised deeply embedded in their families, and whose parents and other senior family members encourage a collective consumption or production of music as an act of family togetherness, are most likely to develop a communal social meaning of music, to be impervious to extra-familial and subsequent influences, and to engage in supportive enactment of their artist activist roles. It also indicates that artists who are least embedded in their childhood families, and whose parents and senior family members discourage or disregard music in the household, are most likely to be susceptible to extra-familial and subsequent influences, to develop a culturally expressive social meaning of music, and to engage in artistic enactment of their artist activist roles.

OCCUPATIONAL COMMUNITIES IN AN ERA OF EMPLOYMENT PRECARITY

In our risky era of declining unionization, employment precarity, and sharpening income inequality,[35] strong occupational communities socialize risk and secure livelihoods for free agents. Guild-like freelancers' advocacy organizations, contrary to Elliott Krause's observation of the death of guilds,[36] are emerging and vary by the range of occupations in their membership jurisdictions, strength of their occupational identity and labor ideology, the array of membership services they offer, the extent of their geographical jurisdiction, and whether or not they engage in collective bargaining.

Freelancers Union founder Sara Horowitz refers to an economy of freelancers as a "gig economy" and maintains that "[i]n today's economy, there's a huge chunk of the middle class that's being pushed down into the working class and working poor, ... and freelancers are the first group that's happening to."[37] The 200,000-member Freelancers Union provides health insurance to its membership of "lawyers, software developers, graphic artists, accountants, consultants, nannies, writers, editors, Web site designers or sellers on Etsy."[38] The Freelancers Union practices a "new mutualism" by providing a wide array of social welfare benefits, discounts on business resources such as co-working space, online contract creators, and reviews of client employers.[39] Unlike conventional labor unions, the Freelancers Union does not conduct collective bargaining with employers, and, unlike arts trade unions, comprises a wide range of occupations.[40] Horowitz characterizes "the standard workweek as a prison of the past," and maintains that freelancers are "establishing a new way to work—and in the process, they're cultivating a new way of life."[41]

In contrast, the occupationally homogeneous Writers Guild of America engages in collective bargaining with employers. In 2007–08, the Guild, for example, conducted a 100-day strike against the Alliance of Motion Picture and Television Producers over the formula for compensating writers for their digitally distributed artistic work that involved some 12,000 TV and movie writers.[42] The Guild also performs a wide range of professional development services and provides health and pension coverage and protection of financial and creative rights for its members.[43]

In the arts, unions are adjusting their functions and membership jurisdictions to a new occupational generalism. Traditionally, freelance artists have invoked a risk-management strategy of occupational generalism based on performance competency in multiple genres and instruments.[44] The new occupational generalism, in contrast, entails artist competency in both artistic and art-support functions and artistic role consolidation that accompany self-promoting, independent, entrepreneurial art-making.[45] The new occupational generalism accompanies occupational blurring brought about by changes in production and distribution technology and indie art-making, as well as corporate multi-media production.[46] As Kristin Thomson, co-director of the Future of Music Coalition's Artist Revenue Streams (ARS) research project, put it:

> Being a working musician in the United States in the 21st century presents both opportunities and challenges. Technology has ushered in meteoric changes in the music landscape. Digital music stores, streaming services, and webcasting stations have greatly reduced the cost barriers to the distribution and sale of music, giving musicians the ability to promote and sell their own music—globally—without having to sign away their copyrights. Social media, websites, blogs, and videos help musicians

connect directly with fans, who will then, in theory, support their creative output by donating to projects, buying merchandise or recordings, or attending concerts.[47]

The 2011 ARS survey results indicate that roughly two-thirds of more than 5,000 musician respondents played three to seven income-generating roles, including performer, teacher, session player, composer, recording artist, salaried player, and administrator.[48]

The Writers Guild of America conceives of occupational generalism as hyphenated occupational roles, such as "writer-producer," known in the vernacular as the "hyphenate world"[49] or the "artistic hyphenate."[50] According to Guild rules, for hyphenate members, "[d]ues are payable on income from 'writing services' only, not the usually larger sums paid for producing."[51] The Guild advises its members who become hyphenates that "[t]heoretically, being named a writer-producer provides the opportunity to prove you're more than just a pencil, to demonstrate leadership skills in the writers' room, editorial skills on rewrites, and production skills in such areas as casting and post-production. As a hyphenate, you must start thinking about the show more globally as your responsibilities grow."[52]

In the case of the 2012 merger of the Screen Actors Guild (SAG) and the American Federation of Television and Radio Artists (AFTRA), the merger was partly motivated by the effective consolidation of their membership jurisdictions by their common, multi-media corporate employers. As AFTRA stated prior to the merger, "the employers with whom AFTRA and SAG have contracts have increasingly consolidated into large, multinational corporations that span all industries in which our members work."[53] Consequently, both unions recognized that they "jointly and separately represent performers, broadcasters and other media artists employed in the entertainment, broadcast, journalism and electronic communications industries" and that "SAG and AFTRA believe that increased collective bargaining and organizing strength can be attained by uniting their organizations."[54]

In light of the growth of traveling musicians in this era of self-promotion through live-venue performance, in 1993 a group of union folksingers founded the North American Traveling Musicians Union, Local 1000 of the American Federation of Musicians (AFM). The 500-member local, according to its mission statement posted on its "virtual union hall," "represent[s] acoustic musicians who perform most of their gigs away from the AFM jurisdiction where they live. Unlike a traditional geographical local, we draw members from all over the U.S. and Canada, and we represent our members wherever they work."[55] In recounting the pragmatic rationale for the founding of Local 1000, the local explains that

[l]ocal 1000 was started ... by a small group of folk musicians who believed in the power of collective action. They and their peers had the privilege of traveling throughout North America doing the work they

loved; but the price they paid was isolation and constant risk—risk of illness, of instrument theft, of employers backing out on contracts, and especially risk of poverty, if age or disability stopped them from working. Now we work together to make things better for all traveling folk, bluegrass, blues and acoustic musicians. Our members also include performance poets and sign language interpreters.[56]

The local provides a wide array of membership services, including AFM recording and other union contracts, contract support, instrument insurance, health and disability insurance and pension coverage, and an emergency relief fund.

Local 1000 adheres to a general pro-labor philosophy and strong solidarity with the broader labor movement. Its Joe Hill Scholarship Fund is intended to support individual member attendance at local and national labor organization events, and the local has held its annual retreats at the legendary Highlander Center in New Market, Tennessee. In celebrating the life of the late Pete Seeger, Local 1000 President Emeritus John McCutcheon stated that "Pete Seeger was not only a proud, charter member of Local 1000, he was the person that introduced so many of us to unionism. It was not with speeches, but with songs. It was not with agitation, but with action. There he was, whenever he was needed, lending a hand and a voice to workers' struggles."[57]

In Nashville, artist advocates are the most collectively engaged of the three artist activists, based as they are in lobbying and bargaining on behalf of the collective economic interests of arts occupations. Nashville advocates are long-standing, multi-level (local and national) organizations that are effectively transforming themselves into multi-purpose guilds. As such, songwriters' associations and arts unions are broadening the range of social welfare, professional development, economic, legal, intellectual property, and policy functions they perform. The Nashville Songwriters Association International (NSAI), for example, recently expanded its professional development and social welfare functions by acquiring the iconic Bluebird Café, where Nashville songwriters perform their work in the round on writers' night, and established a health insurance program for NSAI members. Similarly, Nashville Local 257 of the American Federation of Musicians recently established a health insurance program for its members, practice space in the union hall, and several specialized wage scales for performing and recording enterprising artists.

The movement toward occupational guilds among freelancers is a research-worthy development for a post-bureaucratic sociology of work. Artist activists envision and institute guild-like advocacy organizations for re-socializing risk in an era of risk individualization. A sociological research agenda should address their effectiveness in enhancing the economic livelihoods of occupational peers who work in a range of organizational, social, and geographical contexts, and their generalizability across a range of artistic and non-artistic, freelance occupations. Their effectiveness may originate in how their diverse organizational models optimize among strength of occupational identity and labor ideology, occupational and geographical breadth, array of membership services, and blend of mutualism and adversarial bargaining in their organizational logic.

ARTISTIC EXPRESSION IN A PRECARIOUS AND INDIVIDUALISTIC AGE

In an era of precarious employment in a polarizing service economy, and of risk individualization, occupational self-determination is essential for sustaining artists and artistic expression.[58] More generally, occupational self-determination is essential for sustaining the livelihoods and career-mobility pathways for workers who are struggling to maintain their standing in or gain access to the middle class. Risk individualization, as in a declining societal commitment to socially protective institutions such as social insurance programs and labor unions, compels workers themselves to assume the risk of joblessness. Occupational self-determination—that is, initiatives undertaken by occupational peers on behalf of themselves and their occupation—is a strategy that "resocializes" and minimizes a risk that is decreasingly assumed by large public and private bureaucratic organizations.

Furthermore, in an era of identity politics[59] and "omnivorish"[60] consumption of diverse artistic genres, *socially inclusive* occupational self-determination sustains artistic expression of multiple social identities and artistic genres by a widening array of socially diverse artists. The polarizing service economy itself is embedded in societal group relations in that people of color and immigrants are disproportionately represented in the most precarious and lowest-wage employment sectors. Acts of self-determination by socially inclusive occupations allow for the artistic expression and upward mobility of a diversifying labor force.[61]

Presently, occupational self-determination serves the socially integrative mission of encouraging the expression and sustaining the career mobility of multiple social identity groups.[62] These groups differ by ethnicity, race, nativity, gender, sexual orientation, age, religion, and other social characteristics. In the United States, where 80 percent of the national labor force is employed in services rather than good-producing industries,[63] occupational self-determination as a socially integrative organizing strategy is unfolding in three ways. The first, and the most established, are the professional associations and labor unions of *human services professionals*. The predominantly female human services professions—such as nurses, teachers, social workers, and librarians—are occupationally committed to a humanistic mission. Organized into large, national professional associations and labor unions, these professions are dedicated to professionalism in the universalistic delivery of social services. A countervailing political force to the neoliberal drift toward risk individualization, their political and legislative lobbying agendas are directed at expanding the welfare state.[64]

The second socially integrative organizing effort consists of union organizing campaigns among socially diverse *low-wage service workers* employed in large customer-service bureaucracies and small businesses. These target employment sectors include healthcare, retail, hospitality, higher education, cleaning services, personal services, local transportation, construction, and government. Multiple unions have made organizing gains by conducting large-scale, urban, grassroots and corporate campaigns in diverse and cross-class, community coalitions with civil rights, human rights, faith-based, and consumer groups. These citywide labor-community coalitions often develop out of the worker-consumer interdependence that exists in a local urban service economy with co-extensive labor and product markets.[65] Unions of low-wage service workers serve as a countervailing political force similar to that of organized human services professionals.[66]

Third is the formation of inclusive, place-based occupational communities among *free agents in expressive occupations*. The emergent, indie musician community in Nashville, a community ushered in by the artist activists who are the subject of this book, illustrates this third socially integrative organizing effort. The target economic sectors of these community-building efforts include arts and entertainment, communications, information, and the blogosphere. Inclusive, place-based occupational communities play a meaningful, guild-like role in the daily lives of their members. They endeavor to set prices and wage scales, provide networking opportunities and referrals for professional development and employment, and mentor a socially diverse group of early-career occupation members in an urban art scene. To the extent its individual free agents are unionized or affiliated with national advocacy organizations, this local place-based occupational community may support and be linked to extra-local, countervailing political forces—such as national arts trade unions, arts advocates, and elected public officials—that advocate for favorable intellectual-property and artist-compensation policies for expressive occupations.

Inclusive, place-based expressive occupational communities are the most loosely coupled and decentralized organizational arrangements of the three types of occupational self-determination. The organizations of human services professionals and low-wage service workers are powerful, vertically integrated, nationally coordinated, bureaucratic organizations that operate simultaneously in the halls of Congress, state legislatures, city councils, and among the grassroots. In contrast, place-based occupational communities are ushered in gradually, unevenly, and episodically by local artist activists.[67] As trusted Alinsky-like, complete "native" leaders[68] who hail from the emergent community, artist activists create meaningful social spaces for advancing artistic, professional, and economic interests that resonate with their occupational peers. As small organizations in a competitive field, however, these meaningful social spaces suffer the liabilities of newness and small size. These organizational liabilities generate high organizational turnover rates that can destabilize a place-based, entrepreneurially activated occupational community.[69]

In order to manage risk in this precarious and polarized age, artist activists must stabilize, solidify, and diversify membership in place-based, expressive occupational communities. The sociological theory of artist activists presented here argues for a dual strategy of horizontal integration. Horizontal integration, as distinguished from the vertical integration of organizations of human services professions and low-wage service workers, refers to extending the initiatives of artist activists across a wider range of peers and genres in an urban art scene. Implementing this dual strategy, in turn, rests on a foundation of *shared strategic orientations and risk orientations.*[70]

The first component of the dual strategy is developing enduring, cooperative, resource-sharing arrangements among the three types of artist activists in a local urban art scene. The objective of this component is to stabilize and increase the operating capacity of artist activists and their enterprises and add to membership in the peer community. Cooperative arrangements among enterprising artists, artistic social entrepreneurs, and artist advocates include mutual aid in social welfare benefits, co-sponsoring artistic events, discounted membership reciprocity, co-working studio space agreements, buyers' cooperatives for supplies, and joint promotion initiatives. Instituting cooperative arrangements rests on an *artist-consumer strategic orientation* that is shared by artist activists. In light of the growing importance of direct, artist-consumer engagements, sharing an artist-consumer strategic orientation focused on the interests of both the artist and the consumer facilitates collaboration among artist activists. Furthermore, in this era of risk individualization, the simple division of labor based in occupational generalism exposes self-promoting artists to a wider range of risk factors than the risk exposure occupational specialists face in the large corporate sector of art production. Sharing an *integrated risk orientation* that is focused on all three types of risk factors—personal, interpersonal, and impersonal—facilitates collaboration among the three types of artist activists.

The second component of the dual strategy of horizontal integration is developing enduring, citywide "strategic alliances"[71] between artist activists and the leaders of underrepresented and marginalized minority groups in the metropolitan location of the art scene. In this era of identity politics and "omnivorish" art-consumption preferences, genre diversification is linked to the diversification of artist social identities in an urban art scene, and to the diversification of consumer preferences. The objective of this component is to diversify the community of artistic occupational peers by generating trust and mutual respect among socially diverse and genre-diverse artists in a local urban art scene. Developing strategic alliances, then, rests on an *inclusive strategic orientation* shared by artist activists. An inclusive strategic orientation is one in which an artist activist envisions the development of an integrated, socially diverse, and genre-diverse group of peers. The civil society sector of a metropolitan area comprises leaders in local government, the arts, social justice and human rights, community-based social work, the clergy, business, and academia who broker the formation of strategic alliances between artist activists and minority artists. Nashville, for example, has capitalized on its pioneering place in the histories of civil rights and popular music by sustaining an inclusive and expressive, contemporary civil society sector of diverse artists and "business, labor, religious, civil liberties, civil rights and social services groups"[72] who broker relationships among diverse Nashvillians.

Artist activists perform the vital role of sustaining the expression of mainstream and minority voices in the United States. Their enterprising initiatives are especially vital in this post-bureaucratic era of identity politics, free agency, and employment precarity, conditions that at once support and stymie the establishment of inclusive, expressive occupational communities. By assuming and managing the risk of joblessness that is decreasingly assumed by large bureaucratic organizations, artist activists create inclusive, place-based, expressive occupational communities for artistic expression in urban art scenes. As acts of occupational self-determination in an era of risk individualization, the initiatives taken by artist activists advance the artistic, professional development, and economic interests of diverse artists who express themselves in a widening array of genres and constitute initiatives worthy of emulation by other community builders. The sociological theory and research agenda presented here address how artist activists envision, assume, and enact their roles as artist activists, and offer a pathway toward building an inclusive and expressive society.

APPENDIX

Interview Schedule

Musician Careers Project, Daniel B. Cornfield, PI

Again, thank you for agreeing to participate in this interview. IF INTER-VIEWEE HAS AGREED TO BE AUDIOTAPED: I'm turning on the tape recorder. Let's begin.

1. First, let's discuss the type of work you do, and how you got there [prompt start and end years of each position or situation respondent has had throughout this first section of questions].

   a. What is your current line of work?—prompts: musician (perform, record; voice, instrument), songwriter, engineer, producer, publisher, manager, DJ, teacher, labor union officer—any or all of these? Which, if any, is your primary line of work?
   b. Who and what inspired you to pursue a music career?
   c. When and how did you start your career in music?
   d. Who do you consider to be your instructors and mentors?
   e. How were you trained?
   f. What positions have you held that led you to your current position?
   g. Looking back, which of the following have helped you to advance your career?—prompts: the union, professional association, individuals in your line of work, plugger, club promoter, booking agent, managers, producers, music executives, bankers, family members, friends, clergy, any others? How so?
   h. What obstacles, if any, have you had to overcome to advance your music career?
   i. Which opportunities came along to help advance your career?
   j. How have you been recognized for your work, and whose recognition means the most to you?

2. Now I'd like to turn to how you synchronize your music-related work with other activities in your life.

   a. How important to who you are, is your work in music?
   b. Are you in lines of work other than music?
   c. Are you involved in activities other than music and work that you consider to be an important part of who you are?
   d. In a typical week, how many hours do you devote to your work in music? Practice, rehearsals, performance, session work, composing?

166

e. In creating music, how often do you work

   (1) in Nashville, other parts of the United States, and other nations?
   (2) in the same type of music?
   (3) in the same studio?
   (4) with the same producer, songwriters, engineers, and musicians?
   (5) with the same label and publisher?
   (6) in the same clubs?
   (7) on the same travel circuit?
   (8) for the same employers and audiences?

f. How often do you make music—volunteer or paid—for

   (1) political causes?
   (2) religious groups?
   (3) schools?
   (4) organization fund-raisers and benefit events?
   (5) local communities and neighborhoods?

g. How important is it to you that the music you make pleases

   (1) other music professionals?
   (2) the fans?
   (3) the listening public? Who listens to your music?
   (4) music executives and management?
   (5) your family and friends?
   (6) people who share your political or religious orientation?
   (7) others?

h. Have you ever owned a music-related business, such as a studio, label, production or publishing company, or club? Why or why not? If yes, what percentage of your annual income is or was from this business?

i. Have you ever belonged to a union? Why/why not? If yes, which, and have you served as an officer in the union? How often have you attended union meetings?

j. Have you ever belonged to any professional associations? Why/why not? If yes, which ones, and why?

k. Do you ever represent your profession in a political forum?

3. Next I'd like to discuss your views about being a music professional.

a. What does it mean to you to be a "professional"?

b. How often

   (1) do you achieve the highest quality of artistic expression in your work? What do you consider to be "high-quality artistic expression"?
   (2) do you satisfy the expectations of the producers, labels, music publishers, and music executives?
     • How would you characterize their expectations?
     • How do you know about their expectations?

- How similar or different are their expectations and those of your listeners and fellow music professionals?

(3) are you called upon to make musical choices contrary to your own creative tastes?

(4) do you give creative advice and suggestions to other music professionals?

(5) do you mentor aspiring music professionals?

(6) do you have the opportunity to be creative in your work?

(7) do you work with others whose work you respect?

(8) do you feel obliged to offer creative input in a project?

c. What percentage of your fellow music professionals do you not get along with?

d. How do you and your fellow music professionals control overly competitive colleagues?

4. Now I'd like to turn to your concept of the "Nashville music scene."

a. Do you live in Nashville? If no, where do you live? If yes, how and why did you come to settle in Nashville? [prompt: what does "Nashville" mean to you and your audience?]

b. How much of your work takes place in Nashville? Why?

c. Do you know of others in your line of work who

(1) do not live in Nashville and who work in Nashville? If yes, where do they live, and how frequently do they typically work in Nashville?

(2) live in Nashville and who work in other places in the United States and world? If yes, how frequently do they typically work outside of Nashville and in what other parts of the United States and world do they work?

d. What comes to mind when you think of the expression "Nashville music scene"? Is it a scene in which

(1) you participate professionally? What percentage of your work is associated with the Nashville music scene?

(2) music is written, produced, recorded, and/or performed?

(3) new music is debuted before critical audiences?

(4) specific types of music originate?

(5) music for specific audiences is produced or performed?

(6) music is made by specific labels, publishing companies, and songwriters?

(7) music is produced by specific artists, producers, and musicians?

(8) an aspiring music professional can launch a career?

(9) a music professional can have a successful life-time career?

(10) an aspiring owner of a studio, label, or publishing or production company can launch an enterprise?

(11) an owner of a music-related business can be successful?

(12) a music professional can get union benefits, like job referrals, health insurance, retirement pension, decent wages and royalties, and professional development opportunities?

(13) a music professional can keep up professionally by learning from his or her fellow music professionals?

e. Is the "Nashville music scene" a place where

(1) you live all or part of the year?

(2) one can find an affordable and comfortable living situation? How so?

f. How, if at all, has the Internet influenced how you do business?

g. What would you say are the geographical boundaries of the "Nashville music scene"?

h. Do you sense an unwritten code of ethics regarding job competition in Nashville?

i. Have you ever heard of Nashville music professionals who have left the Nashville music scene to pursue their careers elsewhere and in other ways? If yes, when and why did they leave the Nashville music scene?

j. Have you ever considered leaving the Nashville music scene and pursuing your career elsewhere and in other ways?

k. How competitive is your business?

l. Are there any other social or cultural characteristics of the "Nashville music scene"?

5. Now I'd like to hear your views about the meaning of "success."

a. What does it mean to be "successful" in your line of work? To you?

b. What, if anything, does "achieving the American Dream" mean to someone in your line of work? To you?

c. How important to you is it to be known outside of Nashville? In the United States, internationally? In your profession generally?

d. How do you gauge your own success?

e. What kind of advice would you give to others about how to succeed in your line of work?

6. Let's discuss trends in the availability of work Recently, in a typical year,

a. how easy or difficult has it been for you to find work?

b. how steady is the work?

7. Now I'd like to hear your attitudes about working conditions.

a. Over the last twelve months, how satisfied or dissatisfied were you with each of the following aspects of work and employment?

- pay
- health insurance

- retirement pension
- hours
- ease of finding work
- frequency of work
- how team members get along with one another
- the quality of the music you participated in making
- opportunity to be creative
- career advancement opportunities
- recognition from your profession

b. Over the last few years, how, if at all, has the introduction of new, more advanced music technology in Nashville influenced

(1) music careers?
(2) opportunities for starting a music company?
(3) opportunities for individual musician creativity?
(4) opportunities for long-distance networking and collaboration?
(5) your songwriting?

c. Over the last few years, how, if at all, has the changing number of major and independent labels in Nashville influenced

(1) music careers?
(2) opportunities for starting a music company?
(3) opportunities for individual musician creativity?

8. Finally, I'd like to ask you some questions about your background.

a. What is the highest level of education your parents attained and what are their main occupations?
b. Have your parents been involved in music?
c. How would you describe your

(1) ethnic background?
(2) religious beliefs?
(3) political attitudes?
(4) educational background?

d. Where and in what year were you born? Where did you grow up?
e. Are you married? Do you have children?
f. Would you mind telling me which letter corresponds to your individual annual income from all sources last year?

A—Less than $30k
B—$30k–$64k
C—$65k–$99k
D—$100k–$134k
E—$135k–$169k
F—$170k–$199k
G—$200k or more

9. Anything else you'd like to discuss?
10. Please refer me to five other music professionals of the "Nashville music scene" with whom you have worked over the last two years and who I might contact to interview. They need not live in Nashville. How well, for how long, and in what ways do you know each of these people? May I mention that you referred me to them?
11. Thanks a million!!!!

Notes

CHAPTER 1. CREATING COMMUNITY IN AN INDIVIDUALISTIC AGE

1. Ulrich Beck, *The Brave New World of Work* (Malden: Polity Press, 2000).
2. "Third Man Records," March 22, 2014, http://thirdmanrecords.com/about/.
3. Josh Eels, "Jack Outside the Box," *New York Times*, April 5, 2012, http://www.nytimes.com/2012/04/08/magazine/jack-white-is-the-savviest-rock-star-of-our-time.html?pagewanted=all&_r=2&.
4. Eels, "Jack Outside the Box"; "United Records Pressing," March 22, 2014, http://www.urpressing.com/history.php; Knight Stivender, "Wedgewood-Houston Builds New Generation of Artists," *Tennessean*, August 12, 2013, http://www.tennessean.com/article/20130812/NEWS01/308120037/Wedgewood-Houston-builds-new-generation-artists.
5. "Douglas Corner Café," October 8, 2011, http://www.douglascorner.com/overtheyears.php.
6. Brantley Hargrove, "A Power Shift within Nashville's Musicians Union Signals Changing Times on Music Row," *Nashville Scene*, March 19, 2009, http://www.nashvillescene.com/nashville/a-power-shift-within-nashvilles-musicians-union-signals-changing-times-on-music-row/Content?oid=1200399.
7. Office of Labor-Management Standards, LM2 Reports, American Federation of Musicians Local 257, March 4, 2014, http://kcerds.dol-esa.gov/query/orgReport.do.
8. "Best Music Scene, 2011: Nashville, Tennessee," *Rolling Stone*, April 28, 2011, http://www.rollingstone.com/music/pictures/best-music-scene-2011-nashville-tennessee-20110502. On the increasing concentration of musicians in Nashville, see these three articles by Richard Florida: "The Changing Geography of Pop Music," *Atlantic*, February 17, 2011, http://www.theatlantic.com/entertainment/archive/2011/02/the-changing-geography-of-pop-music/71341/; "The Nashville Effect," *Atlantic*, May 21, 2009, http://www.theatlantic.com/national/archive/2009/05/the-nashville-effect/17288/; and "The Nashville Effect, cont'd," *Atlantic*, July 6, 2009, http://www.theatlantic.com/national/archive/2009/07/the-nashville-effect-contd/20385/.
9. Robert Oermann, *A Century of Country: An Illustrated History of Country Music* (New York: TV Books), 176.
10. Richard Peterson and David Berger, "Cycles in Symbol Production: The Case of Popular Music," *American Sociological Review* 40, no. 2 (1975): 158.
11. John Van Maanen and Stephen Barley, "Occupational Communities: Culture and Control in Organizations," in *Research in Organizational Behavior* 6, eds. Barry Staw and L. L. Cummings (Greenwich: JAI Press, 1984), 287–365.
12. Ibid., 289–94.
13. Richard Peterson and N. Anand, "How Chaotic Careers Create Orderly Fields," in *Career Creativity: Explorations in the Remaking of Work*, eds. Maury Peiperl, Michael Arthur, and N. Anand (Oxford: Oxford University Press, 2002), 272.
14. Paul Berliner, *Thinking in Jazz: The Infinite Art of Improvisation* (Chicago: University of Chicago Press, 1994), especially chs. 1 and 2; Howard Becker, "Art as Collective Action," *American Sociological Review* 39, no. 6 (1974): 767–76; Beth Bechky, "Gaffers, Gofers, and Grips: Role-Based Coordination in Temporary Organizations," *Organization Science*, 17, no. 1 (2006): 3–21; Robert Faulkner and Howard Becker, *"Do You Know …?" The Jazz Repertoire in Action* (Chicago: University of Chicago Press, 2009).

173

15. Peterson and Berger, "Cycles in Symbol Production." Also see Timothy J. Dowd, "Concentration and Diversity Revisited: Production Logics and the U.S. Mainstream Recording Market, 1940–1990," *Social Forces* 82, no. 4 (2004):1411–55, and Paul Hirsch, "Processing Fads and Fashions: An Organization-Set Analysis of Cultural Industry Systems," *American Journal of Sociology* 77, no. 4 (1972): 639–59.

16. Sherry Ortner, *Not Hollywood: Independent Film at the Twilight of the American Dream* (Durham: Duke University Press, 2013); Elizabeth Long Lingo and Steven Tepper, "Looking Back, Looking Forward: Arts-Based Careers and Creative Work," *Work and Occupations* 40, no. 4 (2013): 337–63; Kristin Thomson, "Roles, Revenue, and Responsibilities: The Changing Nature of Being a Working Musician," *Work and Occupations* 40, no. 4 (2013): 514–25; Maria-Rosario Jackson et al., *Investing in Creativity: A Study of the Support Structure for U.S. Artists* (Washington, DC: Urban Institute, Culture, Creativity & Communities Program, 2003), http://www.urban.org/UploadedPDF/411311_investing_in_creativity.pdf.

17. Emile Durkheim, *Division of Labor in Society* (New York: Free Press, 1964 [orig. 1893]).

18. Personal interview with Ken Paulson at the Sunset Grille in Nashville, August 1, 2013. Paulson is dean of the College of Mass Communication at Middle Tennessee State University, president of the First Amendment Center, a member of Nashville mayor Karl Dean's Music City Music Council, and an officer in Leadership Music and the Nashville Songwriters Hall of Fame.

19. Durkheim, *Division of Labor.*

20. Richard Peterson, *Creating Country Music: Fabricating Authenticity* (Chicago: University of Chicago Press, 1997), 230.

21. Beck, *Brave New World of Work*; Gina Neff, *Venture Labor* (Cambridge: MIT Press, 2012).

22. Steven Tepper, *Not Here, Not Now, Not That! Protest over Art and Culture in America* (Chicago: University of Chicago Press, 2011).

23. Daniel Cornfield, "Integrative Organizing in Polarized Times: Toward Dynamic Trade Unionism in the Global North," in *Mobilizing against Inequality: Unions, Immigrant Workers, and the Crisis of Capitalism*, eds. Lee Adler et al. (Ithaca: Cornell University Press, 2014), 151–68.

24. Vicki Smith, *Crossing the Great Divide* (Ithaca: Cornell University Press, 2001), 157.

25. Ibid. Also see Daniel Cornfield, Karen Campbell, and Holly McCammon, eds., *Working in Restructured Workplaces: Challenges and New Directions for the Sociology of Work* (Thousand Oaks: Sage Publications, 2001).

26. Arne Kalleberg, *Good Jobs, Bad Jobs: The Rise of Polarized and Precarious Employment Systems in the United States, 1970s to 2000s* (New York: Russell Sage Foundation, 2011).

27. Timothy J. Dowd, "Structural Power and the Construction of Markets: The Case of Rhythm and Blues," *Comparative Social Research* 21 (Bingley: Emerald, 2003), 147–201; Tepper, *Not Here, Not Now, Not That!*

28. Daniel Cornfield, "Immigrant Labor Organizing in a 'New Destination City': Approaches to the Unionization of African, Asian, Latino, and Middle Eastern Workers in Nashville," in *Global Connections and Local Receptions: New Latino Migration to the Southeastern United States*, eds. Fran Ansley and Jon Shefner (Knoxville: University of Tennessee Press, 2009), 279–97; Jamie Winders, *Nashville in the New Millennium* (New York: Russell Sage Foundation, 2013).

29. Tepper, *Not Here, Not Now, Not That!*, 18.

30. Jennifer Lena and Daniel Cornfield, "Immigrant Arts Participation: A Pilot Study of Nashville Artists," in *Engaging Art: The Next Great Transformation of America's Cultural Life*, eds. Steven J. Tepper and Bill Ivey (New York: Routledge, 2008), 147–69; Daniel Cornfield and Steering Committee of Nashville for All of Us, "Partnering for an Equitable and Inclusive Nashville: Background Report on Equity and Inclusion," submitted to the Steering Committee of NashvilleNext, Nashville's 2040 General Plan, January 2013, http://www.nashville.gov/Portals/0/SiteContent/Planning/docs/NashvilleNext/next-report-Equity-and-Inclusion.pdf.

31. Richard Peterson and Roger Kern, "Changing Highbrow Taste: From Snob to Omnivore," *American Sociological Review* 61, no. 5 (1996): 900–907; Tony Bennett and Elizabeth Silva, "Introduction: Cultural Capital—Histories, Limits, Prospects," *Poetics* 39, no. 6 (2011): 427–43.

32. Jewly Hight, "Strange Bedfellows: Some Gay Artists in Nashville Are Making Unapologeti-cally Christian Music," *Nashville Scene*, June 15, 2006, http://www.nashvillescene.com/nashville/strange-bedfellows/Content?oid=1193263; Beverly Keel, "Rebel With a Cause: Lari White Be-comes the First Female to Produce a Major Male Country Star, *Nashville Scene*, June 1, 2006, http://www.nashvillescene.com/nashville/rebel-with-a-cause/Content?oid=1193199; Sean L. Maloney, "Local Urban-Music Promoters Lovenoise Make Hip-Hop, Soul and R&B Accessi-ble to Nashville's Masses," *Nashville Scene*, October 27, 2011, http://www.nashvillescene.com/nashville/local-urban-music-promoters-lovenoise-make-hip-hop-soul-and-randb-accessible-to-nashvilles-masses/Content?oid=2661308; Jewly Hight, "Americana Acts Are Getting on the Mainstream Radar," *Nashville Scene*, October 13, 2011, http://www.nashvillescene.com/nashville/americana-acts-are-getting-on-the-mainstream-radar/Content?oid=2650847; Edd Hurt, "For Nashville Indie Musicians Like Lambchop and Cortney Tidwell, It Was the Post-Post-Rock Decade," *Nashville Scene*, December 24, 2009, http://www.nashvillescene.com/nashville/for-nashville-indie-musicians-like-lambchop-and-cortney-tidwell-it-was-the-post-post-rock-decade/Content?oid=1204257; Steve Haruch, "Paramore Broke the Nashville Curse and Never Looked Back," *Nashville Scene*, October 29, 2009, http://www.nashvillescene.com/nashville/paramore-broke-the-nashville-curse-and-never-looked-back/Content?oid=1203328; Jewly Hight, "On Its Tenth Anniversary, the Americana Music Association Has Reason to Look Both Back-ward and Forward," *Nashville Scene*, September 17, 2009, http://www.nashvillescene.com/nashville/on-its-tenth-anniversary-the-americana-music-association-has-reason-to-look-both-backward-and-forward/Content?oid=1202672.

33. Randy Hodson, *Dignity at Work* (New York: Cambridge University Press, 2001), 16; Holly McCammon, *The U.S. Women's Jury Movements and Strategic Adaptation: A More Just Verdict* (New York: Cambridge University Press, 2012); Arne Kalleberg, "Precarious Work, Insecure Workers: Employment Relations in Transition," *American Sociological Review* 74, no. 1 (2009): 1–22; Ida Harper Simpson, "The Sociology of Work: Where Have the Workers Gone?," *Social Forces* 67, no. 3 (March 1989): 563–81.

34. Kalleberg, *Good Jobs, Bad Jobs*; Beck, *Brave New World of Work*.

35. Susan Silbey, "Taming Prometheus: Talk About Safety and Culture," *Annual Review of Sociol-ogy* 35 (2009), 341–69. Also see Martin Ruef, *The Entrepreneurial Group: Social Identities, Rela-tions, and Collective Action* (Princeton: Princeton University Press, 2010); Lowell Turner and Daniel Cornfield, eds., *Labor in the New Urban Battleground: Local Solidarity in a Global Econ-omy* (Ithaca: Cornell University Press, 2007); Charles Heckscher, Sara Horowitz, and Althea Erickson, "Civil Society and the Provision of Services: The Freelancers Union Experience," in *Transforming the U.S. Workforce Development System: Lessons from Research and Practice*, eds. David Finegold et al. (Champaign: Labor and Employment Relations Association, 2010), 237–59.

36. Jennifer Lena, *Banding Together: How Communities Create Genres in Popular Music* (Princeton: Princeton University Press, 2012).

37. Dowd, "Concentration and Diversity Revisited"; Peterson and Berger, "Cycles of Symbol Production."

38. Howard Becker, *Art Worlds* (Berkeley: University of California Press, 1982).

39. Ibid., 233–46, 301–10.

40. Robert Faulkner, *Music on Demand: Composers and Careers in the Hollywood Film Industry* (New Brunswick: Transaction Publishers, 1983), and *Hollywood Studio Musicians: Their Work and Careers in the Recording Industry* (Lanham: University Press of America, 1985); Robert Faulkner and Andy Anderson, "Short-Term Projects and Emergent Careers: Evidence from Hollywood," *American Journal of Sociology* 92, no. 4 (1987): 879–909.

41. Faulkner and Becker, *"Do You Know …?."*

42. See, for example, Timothy J. Dowd, Susanne Janssen, and Marc Verboord, "Introduction: Fields in Transition—Fields in Action," editorial introduction to a special issue of *Poetics* 37, no. 5 (2009): 399–401; Matthew Oware, "(Un)conscious (Popular) Underground: Restricted Cultural Production and Underground Rap Music," *Poetics* 42, no. 1 (2014): 60–81.

43. Andy Bennett, "'Heritage Rock': Rock Music, Representation and Heritage Discourse," *Poetics* 37, no. 5 (2009): 474–89.

44. Richard Lloyd, *Neo-Bohemia: Art and Commerce in the Postindustrial City*, 2^d ed. (New York: Routledge, 2010).

45. Larry Isaac, "Movements, Aesthetics, and Markets in Literary Change: Making the American Labor Problem Novel," *American Sociological Review* 74, no. 6 (2009): 938–65; Paul Dimaggio, "Cultural Entrepreneurship in Nineteenth-Century Boston: The Creation of an Organizational Base for High Culture in America," *Media, Culture and Society* 4 (1982): 33–50.

46. William Roy, *Reds, Whites, and Blues: Social Movements, Folk Music, and Race in the United States* (Princeton: Princeton University Press, 2010), 103.

47. Dowd et al., "Fields in Transition."

48. Everett Hughes, *Men and Their Work* (Glencoe: Free Press, 1958); Steven Vallas, "Rediscovering the Color Line within Work Organizations: The 'Knitting of Racial Groups' Revisited," *Work and Occupations* 30, no. 4 (2003): 379–400; Stephen Barley, "Careers, Identities, and Institutions: The Legacy of the Chicago School of Sociology," in *Handbook of Career Theory*, eds. Michael Arthur, Douglas Hall, and Barbara Lawrence (New York: Cambridge University Press, 1989), 41–65.

49. Dowd, "Concentration and Diversity Revisited"; Peterson and Berger, "Cycles of Symbol Production."

50. Kalleberg, *Good Jobs, Bad Jobs.*

51. Pierre-Michel Menger, "Artistic Labor Markets and Careers," *Annual Review of Sociology* 25 (Palo Alto: Annual Reviews, 1999): 541–74 and "Artists as Workers: Theoretical and Methodological Challenges," *Poetics* 28, no. 4 (2001): 241–54.

52. Pierre Bourdieu, *The Field of Cultural Production* (New York: Columbia University Press, 1993), 61–62.

53. Hodson, *Dignity at Work*, 16.

54. Stephen Barley, "Coalface Institutionalism," in *Handbook of Organizational Institutionalism*, eds. R. Greenwood et al. (Thousand Oaks: Sage, 2008), 490–515.

55. Stephen Barley and Gideon Kunda, *Gurus, Hired Guns, and Warm Bodies: Itinerant Experts in a Knowledge Economy* (Princeton: Princeton University Press, 2004); Vicki Smith, *Crossing the Great Divide: Worker Risk and Opportunity in the New Economy* (Ithaca: Cornell University Press, 2001); Debra Osnowitz, *Freelancing Expertise: Contract Professionals in the New Economy* (Ithaca: Cornell University Press, 2010); Gina Neff, "The Lure of Risk: Surviving and Welcoming Uncertainty in the New Economy," in *Surviving the New Economy*, eds. John Amman, Tris Carpenter, and Gina Neff (Boulder: Paradigm Publishers, 2007), 33–46; Gina Neff, Elizabeth Wissinger, and Sharon Zukin, "Entrepreneurial Labor Among Cultural Producers: 'Cool' Jobs in 'Hot' Industries," *Social Semiotics* 15, no. 3 (2005): 307–34; Neff, *Venture Labor*.

56. Kalleberg, *Good Jobs, Bad Jobs.*

57. Neff, "The Lure of Risk"; Jackson et al., *Investing in Creativity*; Lois Gray and Ronald Seeber, eds., *Under the Stars: Essays on Labor Relations in Arts and Entertainment* (Ithaca: ILR Press/Cornell University Press, 1996); Lois Gray and Maria Figueroa, *Empire State's Cultural Capital at Risk? Assessing Challenges to the Workforce and Educational Infrastructure of Arts and Entertainment in New York*, Report to New York Empire State Development Corporation by Cornell University ILR School, June 2009; Roland Kushner and Randy Cohen, *National Arts Index 2010: An Annual Measure of the Vitality of Arts and Culture in the United States: 1998–2009* (Washington, DC and New York: Americans for the Arts, 2011); Bill Ivey, *Arts, Inc.: How Greed and Neglect Have Destroyed Our Cultural Rights* (Berkeley: University of California Press, 2008).

58. Barry Hirsch and David MacPherson, *Union Membership and Coverage Database*, January 24, 2015, http://www.unionstats.com/.

59. U.S. Bureau of Labor Statistics, Employment Projections, tables 1.2 and 2.7, December 31, 2014, http://www.bls.gov/emp/ep_table_102.htm and http://www.bls.gov/emp/ep_table_207.htm. The industry label "*independent* artists, writers, and performers" [my italics] refers to a wide range of freelance expressive occupations classified under code 7115 of the 2007 North American Industry Classification System.

60. Keith Negus, *Musical Genres and Corporate Cultures* (New York: Routledge, 1999); Peterson and Anand, "Chaotic Careers"; Patrick Raines and LaTanya Brown, "The Economic Impact of the Music Industry in the Nashville-Davidson-Murfreesboro MSA," Report sponsored by Belmont University and the Nashville Area Chamber of Commerce, Nashville, Tennessee, January 2006.

61. Florida, "Nashville Effect"; Florida, "Changing Geography of Pop Music"; D. Patrick Rodgers, "The Black Keys Have Moved to Nashville. What Does That Say about Them—And What Does That Say about Us?" *Nashville Scene*, March 31, 2011, http://www.nashvillescene.com/nashville/the-black-keys-have-moved-to-nashville-what-does-that-say-about-them-and-what-does-that-say-about-us/Content?oid=2345298; Sean L. Maloney, "Local Urban-Music Promoters Lovenoise"; Jewly Hight, "Americana Acts"; Edd Hurt, "Nashville Indie Musicians"; Steve Haruch, "Paramore Broke the Nashville Curse"; Jewly Hight, "Americana Music Association"; "Nashville Invasion: Nashville represents at SXSW 2008," *Nashville Scene*, March 6, 2008, http://www.nashvillescene.com/nashville-invasion/Content?oid=1196166; Chris Talbott, "Black Keys Find New Home in Nashville," *Billboard*, December 13, 2010, http://www.billboard.com/news/black-keys-find-new-home-in-nashville-1004134569.story#/news/black-keys-find-new-home-in-nashville-1004134569.story; Michael McCall, "The Bold and the Beautiful: Country Radio's Female Voices Just Got Younger and Gutsier," *Nashville Scene*, August 30, 2007, http://www.nashvillescene.com/nashville/the-bold-and-the-beautiful/Content?oid=1195132; Michael McCall, "A Little Bit Country, a Lot Rock 'n' Roll: Three New Country Bands Point to A Trend on Music Row," *Nashville Scene*, July 19, 2007, http://www.nashvillescene.com/nashville/a-little-bit-country-a-lot-rock-andrsquonandrsquo-roll/Content?oid=1194954; "Hangin' Tough: David Olney's Latest is Dressed for the Vaudeville Circuit," *Nashville Scene*, June 14, 2007, http://www.nashvillescene.com/nashville/hanginandrsquo-tough/Content?oid=1194814; Jason Moon Wilkins, "No Doubt: Why are Industry Insiders Picking a Franklin Band to Break Out Big in 2007?" *Nashville Scene*, February 8, 2007, http://www.nashvillescene.com/nashville/no-doubt/Content?oid=1194277; Lee Stabert, "Boom! Bang Bang Bang Might Just be the Quintessential Nashville Rock Band," *Nashville Scene*, January 11, 2007, http://www.nashvillescene.com/nashville/boom/Content?oid=1194175; Chris Neal, "Ain't That Americana? The Americana Music Conference Casts an Ever-Widening Net—Musically and Politically," *Nashville Scene*, September 14, 2006, http://www.nashvillescene.com/nashville/ainandrsquot-that-americana/Content?oid=1193659; Chris Neal, "The City That Lost Its Country: LA's Last Country Radio Station Goes Pop," *Nashville Scene*, August 31, 2006, http://www.nashvillescene.com/nashville/the-city-that-lost-its-country/Content?oid=1193597; Grayson Currin, "Vanity Fair: Musicians with Labels Are Just People Who Like Music Too," *Nashville Scene*, June 15, 2006, http://www.nashvillescene.com/nashville/vanity-fair/Content?oid=1193248; Hight, "Strange Bedfellows"; Keel, "Rebel with a Cause"; Lee Stabert, "The Next Big Thing? ASCAP's Next Big Nashville Music Festival Makes a Case for Local Rock and Pop," *Nashville Scene*, May 25, 2006, downloaded June 24, 2012 from: http://www.nashvillescene.com/nashville/the-next-big-thing/Content?oid=1193169; Tracy Moore, "Let the Sun Shine In: Why Nashville Could Stand to Be a Little—Just a Little—Like L.A.," *Nashville Scene*, May 18, 2006, http://www.nashvillescene.com/nashville/let-the-sun-shine-in/Content?oid=1193135; Lee Stabert, "Friends With Benefits: Local Rock Collective Movement Nashville Doesn't Care about Indie Cred—They Just Wanna Draw a Crowd," *Nashville Scene*, May 11, 2006, http://www.nashvillescene.com/nashville/friends-with-benefits/Content?oid=1193117; Chris Neal, "The Beat Goes On: Billy Block's Western Beat Celebrates 10 years of Alt-Country Bliss," *Nashville Scene*, February 2, 2006, http://www.nashvillescene.com/nashville/the-beat-goes-on/Content?oid=1192771; Jon Caramanica, "Nashville Inches, Ever So Grudgingly, Into the Future," *New York Times*, December 31, 2009, http://www.nytimes.com/2010/01/03/arts/music/03nashville.htm; Michael McCall, "Crowd Control: Local Musicians on Nashville Audiences, *Nashville Scene*, February 15, 1996, http://www.nashvillescene.com/nashville/crowd-control/Content?oid=1180248; Michael McCall, "A Sellout Performance: Business as Usual at Extravaganza '96," *Nashville Scene*, February 22, 1996, http://www.nashvillescene.com/nashville/a-sellout-performance/Content?oid=1180263; Michael McCall, Joel Moses and Jim Ridley, "Woolgathering: Lambchop's Brush with British

Critics," *Nashville Scene*, February 22, 1996, http://www.nashvillescene.com/nashville/wool gathering/Content?oid=1180272; Bill Friskics-Warren, "On the Beat: Nashville's Ekemode Launches Studio," *Nashville Scene*, February 22, 1996, http://www.nashvillescene.com/nashville/ on-the-beat/Content?oid=1180267; Daniel Cooper, "Music City Gets Stoned: Dylan's Impact on Nashville's Music," *Nashville Scene*, March 7, 1996, http://www.nashvillescene.com/nashville/ music-city-gets-stoned/Content?oid=1180296; Michael McCall, "Bass Master: Local Talent Finally Comes into His Own," *Nashville Scene*, April 4, 1996, http://www.nashvillescene.com/ nashville/bass-master/Content?oid=1180368; David D. Duncan and Jim Ridley, "It Came From Nashville! The Saga of Music City's First Family of Film," *Nashville Scene*, April 18, 1996, http:// www.nashvillescene.com/nashville/it-came-from-nashville/Content?oid=1180396; Jim Ridley, "Cut and Print: An Indie Film Sets Down in Music City," *Nashville Scene*, May 9, 1996, http:// www.nashvillescene.com/nashville/cut-and-print/Content?oid=1180438; Edward Morris, "Pure (and Simple): Back to Basics in the Music Industry," *Nashville Scene*, May 23, 1996, http://www .nashvillescene.com/nashville/pure-and-simple/Content?oid=1180487; Bill Friskics-Warren, "Homegrown: A Couple of Locals," *Nashville Scene*, June 13, 1996, http://www.nashvillescene .com/nashville/homegrown/Content?oid=1180538; Edward Morris, "Poor No More: Country Roots? Not Likely," *Nashville Scene*, June 20, 1996, http://www.nashvillescene.com/nashville/ poor-no-more/Content?oid=1180558; Peter Loesch, "Dialing for Dollars: Old vs. New Again in Nashville," *Nashville Scene*, September 12, 1996, http://www.nashvillescene.com/nashville/ dialing-for-dollars/Content?oid=1180739; Michael McCall, "Ready to Rock: Anderson does a Tightrope Act," *Nashville Scene*, October 3, 1996, http://www.nashvillescene.com/nashville/ ready-to-rock/Content?oid=1180791; Jim Ridley, "Banding Together: All in One Accord," *Nashville Scene*, October 24, 1996, http://www.nashvillescene.com/nashville/banding-together/ Content?oid=1180827; Michael McCall, "Keepin' It Country: Alan Jackson Follows the True Path," *Nashville Scene*, October 31, 1996, http://www.nashvillescene.com/nashville/keepin-it -country/Content?oid=1180854.

62. Ron Wynn, "Rahsaan Barber Serves as Jazz Player and Advocate with His Label, Jazz Music City Records: Barber of the 'Ville," *Nashville Scene*, August 23, 2012, http://www.nashvillescene .com/nashville/rahsaan-barber-serves-as-jazz-player-and-advocate-with-his-label-jazz-music -city-records/Content?oid=2989024.

63. Florida, "The Nashville Effect"; Florida, "The Changing Geography of Pop Music"; Richard Florida and Scott Jackson, "Sonic City: The Evolving Economic Geography of the Music Industry," *Journal of Planning Education and Research* 29, no. 3 (2010): 310–21; Richard Florida, Charlotta Mellander, and Kevin Stolarick, "Music Scenes to Music Clusters: The Economic Geography of Music in the US, 1970–2000," *Environment and Planning A* 42, no. 4 (2010): 785–804.

64. On Nashville's growing concentration of musicians, see Michael Kosser, *How Nashville Became Music City, U.S.A.: 50 Years of Music Row* (Milwaukee: Hal Leonard Corporation, 2006); "Labels Look South for Signings Pop/Rock Offices Sprout in Nashville," *Billboard*, August 08, 1991, http://www.billboard.biz/bbbiz/others/labels-look-south-for-signings-pop-rock-765755 .story; "NASHVILLE SCENE," *Billboard*, May 28, 1994, http://www.billboard.biz/bbbiz/others/ nashville-scene-740055.story; "NASHVILLE SCENE—Country Music's Growth Tapers Off, But Labels Are Continuing to Emerge, Change," *Billboard*, December 23, 1995, http://www .billboard.biz/bbbiz/others/nashville-scene-country-music-s-growth-tapers-736464.story; Florida, "The Nashville Effect"; Florida, "The Changing Geography of Pop Music"; Florida and Jackson, "Sonic City"; Florida, Mellander, and Stolarick, "Music Scenes to Music Clusters"; Adam Gold, "Kings of Leon's Serpents and Snakes Records Signs Turbo Fruits and the Weeks," *Nashville Scene*, April 5, 2012, http://www.nashvillescene.com/nashville/kings-of-leons -serpents-and-snakes-records-signs-turbo-fruits-and-the-weeks/Content?oid=2830588; Colleen Creamer, "Feeling Nashville's Pull," *Nashville Ledger*, November 04, 2011, http://www.nashville ledger.com/editorial/Article.aspx?id=55680; Center for Regional Economic Competitiveness, "Leveraging the Labor Force for Economic Growth: Assessing the Nashville Economic Market Area's Readiness for Work after the Recession," August 2010, pp. 7 and 49–53, http://www .nashvillechamber.com/Homepage/WorkNashville/WorkforceStudy.aspx; Larry Knechtel Fam-

ily Estate, "Larry Knechtel's Prolific and Varied Music Career Spanned over 50 Years," http://www.larryknechtel.com/LarryKnechtel/larry-knechtel-biography.htm; Jayne Moore, "Dennis Matkosky Co-Writes Top Hits for LeAnn Rimes, Keith Urban, Clay Aiken and Other Artists," http://www.songwriteruniverse.com/matkosky.htm; Jim Ridley and Michael McCall, "Goodbye Larry: Exiting Nashville on Both Feet," Nashville Scene, May 23, 1996, http://www.nashvillescene.com/nashville/goodbye-larry/Content?oid=1180481; Jim Ridley, "Out of Commission: Meeley Leaves the NFC," Nashville Scene, May 30, 1996, http://www.nashvillescene.com/nashville/out-of-commission/Content?oid=1180509; Edward Morris, "Facing the Music Videos: Producers on the Offensive," Nashville Scene, June 6, 1996, http://www.nashvillescene.com/nashville/facing-the-music-videos/Content?oid=1180519; Morris, "More than Music: A Foray into Clickable Country, Nashville Scene, June 13, 1996, http://www.nashvillescene.com/nashville/more-than-music/Content?oid=1180539; Morris, "Getting Lyrical: Avoiding Mealymouthed Music," Nashville Scene, August 1, 1996, http://www.nashvillescene.com/nashville/getting-lyrical/Content?oid=1180643; Michael McCall, "Stock and Trade: Economic Thinking Down on the Row," http://www.nashvillescene.com/nashville/stock-and-trade/Content?oid=1180665; Edward Morris, "Close Shave: A Scare for Carter," Nashville Scene, August 15, 1996, http://www.nashvillescene.com/nashville/close-shave/Content?oid=1180669.

65. Center for Regional Economic Competitiveness, "Leveraging the Labor Force for Economic Growth: Assessing the Nashville Economic Market Area's Readiness for Work after the Recession," August 2010, pp. 7 and 49–53, http://www.nashvillechamber.com/Homepage/WorkNashville/WorkforceStudy.aspx.

66. David Halberstam, The Children (New York: Random House, 1998); Larry W. Isaac et al., "'Movement Schools' and Dialogical Diffusion of Nonviolent Praxis: Nashville Workshops in the Southern Civil Rights Movement" in Nonviolent Resistance, eds. Sharon Erickson Nepstad and Lester Kurtz, Research in Social Movements, Conflicts, and Change 34 (Bingley: Emerald Group Publishing Limited, 2012), 155–84.

67. Daniel Cornfield et al., Final Report of the Immigrant Community Assessment of Nashville, Tennessee, August, 2003, Commissioned by Mayor Bill Purcell and prepared under contract #14830 for Metropolitan Government of Nashville and Davidson County, Tennessee; Lena and Cornfield, "Immigrant Arts Participation."

68. Joey Garrison, "Metro Council's Black Caucus becomes Minority Caucus," City Paper, January 4, 2012, http://nashvillecitypaper.com/content/city-news/metro-councils-black-caucus-becomes-minority-caucus.

69. Nate Rau, "Council Passes Update to Nondiscrimination Ordinance," City Paper, September 15, 2009, http://nashvillecitypaper.com/content/city-news/council-passes-update-non discrimination-ordinance.

70. I am grateful to John Rumble, Senior Historian at the Country Music Hall of Fame and Museum in Nashville, who gave me access to the museum's collection of Billboard magazines and shared with me his encyclopedic knowledge about the Nashville music industry, including the history and ownership characteristics of music labels.

71. U.S. Census Bureau, County Business Patterns, http://www.census.gov/econ/cbp/index.html.

72. Kathleen Blee, Democracy in the Making: How Activist Groups Form (New York: Oxford University Press, 2012), 32; italics in original.

CHAPTER 2. ARTIST ACTIVISM

1. Chris Talbott, "Nashville Rock Scene Moves Out of the Shadows," Huffington Post, September 4, 2012, http://www.huffingtonpost.com/2012/09/04/nashville-rock-scene-move_0_n_1853928.html.

2. Maloney, "Local Urban-Music Promoters Lovenoise Make Hip-Hop, Soul and R&B Accessible to Nashville's Masses," Nashville Scene, October 27, 2011, http://www.nashvillescene.com/nashville/local-urban-music-promoters-lovenoise-make-hip-hop-soul-and-randb-accessible-to-nashvilles-masses/Content?oid=2661308.

3. Ulrich Beck, The Brave New World of Work (Malden: Polity Press, 2000).

4. Everett Hughes, Men and Their Work (Glencoe: Free Press, 1958), 44–45, 53.

5. Ibid., 63.

6. Catherine Corrigall-Brown, *Patterns of Protest: Trajectories of Participation in Social Movements* (Stanford: Stanford University Press, 2011); Doug McAdam, "Recruitment to High-Risk Activism: The Case of Freedom Summer," *American Journal of Sociology* 92, no. 1 (1986): 64–90.

7. James Truslow Adams, *The Epic of America* (Boston: Little, Brown, 1931), 404–5. Also, for a survey-based depiction of the American Dream, see Jennifer Hochschild, *Facing Up to the American Dream: Race, Class, and the Soul of the Nation* (Princeton: Princeton University Press, 1995).

8. Ely Chinoy, *Automobile Workers and the American Dream* (Garden City: Doubleday, 1955); William Whyte, *The Organization Man* (New York: Simon & Schuster, 1956); Diogo L. Pinheiro and Timothy J. Dowd, "All that Jazz: The Success of Jazz Musicians in Three Metropolitan Areas," *Poetics* 37, no. 5 (2009) 490–506; Studs Terkel, *American Dreams: Lost and Found* (New York: The New Press, 1980); Katherine Newman, *Declining Fortunes: The Withering of the American Dream* (New York: Basic Books, 1993); Thomas Kochan, *Restoring the American Dream: A Working Families'Agenda for America* (Cambridge: MIT Press, 2005); Timothy Dowd and Maureen Blyer, "Charting Race: The Success of Black Performers in the Mainstream Recording Market, 1940–1990," *Poetics* 30, nos. 1–2 (2002): 87–110; Timothy Dowd, Kathleen Liddle, and Maureen Blyer, "Charting Gender: The Success of Female Acts in the U.S. Mainstream Recording Market, 1940–1990," *Research in the Sociology of Organizations* 23 (Bingley: Emerald, 2005): 81–123; Lois Gray and Ronald Seeber, eds., *Under the Stars: Essays on Labor Relations in Arts and Entertainment* (Ithaca: ILR Press/Cornell University Press, 1996); David Hesmondhalgh and Sarah Baker, "'A Very Complicated Version of Freedom': Conditions and Experiences of Creative Labour in Three Cultural Industries," *Poetics* 38, no. 1 (2010) 4–20.

9. Gabriel Rossman, *Climbing the Charts: What Radio Airplay Tells Us about the Diffusion of Innovation* (Princeton: Princeton University Press, 2012); Jennifer Lena, *Banding Together: How Communities Create Genres in Popular Music* (Princeton: Princeton University Press, 2012); Pierre-Michel Menger, "Artistic Labor Markets and Careers," *Annual Review of Sociology* 25 (1999), 541–74 and "Artists as Workers: Theoretical and Methodological Challenges," *Poetics* 2001, 28, no. 4 (2001): 241–54.

10. Howard S. Becker, *Outsiders: Studies in the Sociology of Deviance* (New York: Free Press, 1963), 85 and 95.

11. Steven Tepper and Bill Ivey, eds., *Engaging Art: The Next Great Transformation of America's Cultural Life* (New York: Routledge, 2008); David Grazian, *Blue Chicago: The Search for Authenticity in Urban Blues Clubs* (Chicago: University of Chicago Press, 2003); Richard lloyd, *Neo-Bohemia: Art and Commerce in the Postindustrial City*, 2ᵈ ed. (New York: Routledge, 2010).

12. Howard Becker, *Art Worlds* (Berkeley: University of California Press, 1982), 348–49.

13. Paul Hirsch, "Processing Fads and Fashions: An Organization-Set Analysis of Cultural Industry Systems," *American Journal of Sociology* 77, no. 4 (1972): 639–59; Victoria Alexander, *Sociology of the Arts: Exploring Fine and Popular Forms* (Malden: Blackwell, 2003); Richard Peterson and Roger Kern, "Changing Highbrow Taste: From Snob to Omnivore," *American Sociological Review* 61 no. 5 (1996): 900–907; Tepper and Ivey, *Engaging Art*.

14. Pierre Bourdieu, *The Field of Cultural Production* (New York: Columbia University Press, 1993), 49.

15. Jennifer Lena and Daniel Cornfield, "Immigrant Arts Participation: A Pilot Study of Nashville Artists" in *Engaging Art: The Next Great Transformation of America's Cultural Life*, eds. Steven J. Tepper and Bill Ivey (New York: Routledge, 2008), 147–69.

16. Smith, *Crossing the Great Divide* (Ithaca: Cornell University Press, 2002), 157. Also see Stephen Barley and Gideon Kunda, *Gurus, Hired Guns, and Warm Bodies* (Princeton: Princeton University Press, 2004); Gina Neff, *Venture Labor* (Cambridge: MIT Press, 2012); Martin Ruef, *The Entrepreneurial Group* (Princeton: Princeton University Press, 2010); Debra Osnowitz, *Freelancing Expertise* (Ithaca: Cornell University Press, 2010); Joy Pixley, "Life Course Patterns of Career-Prioritizing Decisions and Occupational Attainment in Dual-Earner Couples," *Work and Occupations* 35, no. 2 (2008): 127–63; Phyllis Moen et al., "Time Work by Overworked Professionals: Strategies in Response to the Stress of Higher Status," *Work and Occupations* 40,

no. 2 (2013): 79–114; Susan Silbey, "Taming Prometheus: Talk About Safety and Culture," *Annual Review of Sociology* 35 (2009), 341–69; Damian Williams, "Grounding the Regime of Precarious Employment: Homeless Day Laborers' Negotiation of the Job Queue," *Work and Occupations* 36, no. 3 (2009): 209–46; Steve Tombs and Dave Whyte, "Work and Risk," in *Beyond the Risk Society: Critical Reflections on Risk and Human Security*, eds. Gabe Mythen and Sandra Walklate (Berkshire: Open University Press, 2006), 169–93; Stephen Lyng, "Edgework, Risk, and Uncertainty," in *Social Theories of Risk and Uncertainty: An Introduction*, ed. Jens Zinn (Malden: Blackwell , 2008), 106–37; Louise Amoore, "Risk, Reward and Discipline at Work," *Economy and Society* 33, no. 2 (2004): 174–96.

17. Smith, *Crossing the Great Divide*.

18. Silbey, "Taming Prometheus."

19. W. Lloyd Warner and J. O. Low, *The Social System of the Modern Factory; The Strike: A Social Analysis* (New Haven: Yale University Press, 1947), 16–17, 89.

20. E. Wight Bakke, *The Unemployed Worker: A Study of the Task of Making a Living without a Job* (New Haven: Yale University Press, 1940), 61–80.

21. Becker, *Art Worlds*, 2–6.

22. Studs Terkel, *And They All Sang: Adventures of an Eclectic Disc Jockey* (New York: New Press, 2005); Paul Berliner, *Thinking in Jazz: The Infinite Art of Improvisation* (Chicago: University of Chicago Press, 1994), especially chs.1 and 2; Menger, "Artistic Labor Markets" and "Artists as Workers."

23. Howard Aldrich and Jennifer Cliff, "The Pervasive Effects of Family on Entrepreneurship: Toward a Family Embeddedness Perspective," *Journal of Business Venturing* 18, no. 5 (2003): 573–96.

24. "Jerome" is a pseudonym.

25. "Barry" is a pseudonym.

26. Aldrich and Cliff, "Pervasive Effects of Family."

27. Berliner, *Thinking in Jazz*.

28. Blee, *Democracy in the Making*, 32; italics in original.

29. Ibid., 31.

CHAPTER 3. SELF-CONTAINED, SELF-EXPRESSION

1. Steve Haruch, "Infinity Cat 'Visitors Center' to 'Never Open' Starting April 27," *Nashville Scene*, April 16, 2013, http://www.nashvillescene.com/nashvillecream/archives/2013/04/16/infinity-cat-visitors-center-to-never-open-starting-april-27.

2. Hann, "Why the Garages of East Nashville Are Now American Rock's Hottest Property," *Guardian*, March 24, 2012, http://www.guardian.co.uk/music/2012/mar/25/east-nashville-garage-rock-scene-feature.

3. Talbott, "Nashville Rock Scene Moves Out of the Shadows," *Huffington Post*, September 4, 2012, http://www.huffingtonpost.com/2012/09/04/nashville-rock-scene-move_0_n_1853928.html#.

4. Richard Florida, "The Nashville Effect," *Atlantic*, May 21, 2009, http://www.theatlantic.com/national/archive/2009/05/the-nashville-effect/17288/; Florida, "The Changing Geography of Pop Music," *Atlantic*, February 17, 2011, http://www.theatlantic.com/entertainment/archive/2011/02/grammys-big-city-winner/71341/; Florida and Scott Jackson, "Sonic City: The Evolving Economic Geography of the Music Industry," *Journal of Planning Education and Research* 29, no. 3 (2010): 310–21; Richard Florida, Charlotta Mellander, and Kevin Stolarick, "Music Scenes to Music Clusters: The Economic Geography of Music in the US, 1970–2000," *Environment and Planning A* 42, no. 4 (2010): 785–80.

5. Quotation is from Michael Kosser, *How Nashville Became Music City, U.S.A.: 50 Years of Music Row* (Milwaukee: Hal Leonard Corporation, 2006), 211. On Nashville's growing concentration of musicians, see Kosser, *How Nashville Became Music City*; "Labels Look South for Signings Pop/Rock Offices Sprout In Nashville," *Billboard*, August 8, 1991, http://www.billboard.biz/bbbiz/others/labels-look-south-for-signings-pop-rock-765755.story; "NASHVILLE SCENE— Country Music's Growth Tapers Off, But Labels Are Continuing to Emerge, Change," *Billboard*,

December 23, 1995, http://www.billboard.biz/bbbiz/others/nashville-scene-country-music-s -growth-tapers-736464.story ; Florida, "Nashville Effect"; Florida, "The Changing Geography of Pop Music"; Florida and Jackson, "Sonic City"; Florida, Mellander, and Stolarick, "Music Scenes to Music Clusters"; Adam Gold, "Kings of Leon's Serpents and Snakes Records signs Turbo Fruits and The Weeks," *Nashville Scene*, April 5, 2012, http://www.nashvillescene.com/ nashville/kings-of-leons-serpents-and-snakes-records-signs-turbo-fruits-and-the-weeks/Con tent?oid=2830588; Colleen Creamer, "Feeling Nashville's Pull," *Nashville Ledger*, November 4, 2011, http://www.nashvilleledger.com/editorial/Article.aspx?id=55680; Center for Regional Economic Competitiveness, "Leveraging the Labor Force for Economic Growth: Assessing the Nashville Economic Market Area's Readiness for Work after the Recession," August 2010, 7 and 49–53, http://www.nashvillechamber.com/Homepage/WorkNashville/WorkforceStudy .aspx; Larry Knechtel Family Estate, 2011, "Larry Knechtel's Prolific and Varied Music Career Spanned over 50 Years," http://www.larryknechtel.com/LarryKnechtel/larry-knechtel-biography .htm; Jim Ridley and Michael McCall," "Goodbye Larry: Exiting Nashville on Both Feet," *Nashville Scene*, May 23, 1996, http://www.nashvillescene.com/nashville/goodbye-larry/Content ?oid=1180481; Jim Ridley, "Out of Commission: Meeley Leaves the NFC," *Nashville Scene*, May 30, 1996, http://www.nashvillescene.com/nashville/out-of-commission/Content?oid=1180509; Edward Morris, "Facing the Music Videos: Producers on the Offensive," *Nashville Scene*, June 6, 1996, http://www.nashvillescene.com/nashville/facing-the-music-videos/Content?oid=1180519; Morris, " More than Music: A Foray into Clickable Country, *Nashville Scene*, June 13, 1996, http://www.nashvillescene.com/nashville/more-than-music/Content?oid=1180539; Morris, "Get- ting Lyrical: Avoiding Mealymouthed Music," *Nashville Scene*, August 1, 1996, http://www .nashvillescene.com/nashville/getting-lyrical/Content?oid=1180643; Michael McCall, "Stock and Trade: Economic Thinking Down on the Row," http://www.nashvillescene.com/nashville/ stock-and-trade/Content?oid=1180665; Morris, "Close Shave: A Scare for Carter," *Nashville Scene*, August 15, 1996, http://www.nashvillescene.com/nashville/close-shave/Content?oid=1180669.

6. All profiled artists' names are pseudonyms.

Chapter 4. Identities in Play

1. Personal interview with Will Kimbrough conducted by Dan Cornfield in the living room of Will Kimbrough's Nashville home on June 5, 2013.
2. Will Kimbrough's website, http://www.willkimbrough.com/bio/.
3. Jon Pareles, "Wary Coronation," *New York Times*, September 10, 2010, http://www.nytimes .com/2010/09/12/arts/music/12pareles.html?pagewanted=all; Adam Gold, "Jack White's Third Man Records Tells the World: Your Music City Is Not Dead: The House that Jack Built," *Nashville Scene*, January 20, 2011, http://www.nashvillescene.com/nashville/jack-whites-third -man-records-tells-the-world-your-music-city-is-not-dead/Content?oid=2171963; Dave Paulson, "Jack White Attaches New Song to Helium Balloons," *Tennessean*, April 2, 2012, http://blogs .tennessean.com/tunein/2012/04/02/jack-white-attaches-new-song-to-helium-balloons/ ?repeat=w3tc; D. Patrick Rodgers, "The Black Keys Have Moved to Nashville: What Does that Say about Them—and What Does that Say about Us?" *Nashville Scene*, March 31, 2011, http:// www.nashvillescene.com/nashville/the-black-keys-have-moved-to-nashville-what-does-that -say-about-them-and-what-does-that-say-about-us/Content?oid=2345298; Ron Wynn, "Rahsaan Barber Serves as Jazz Player and Advocate with his Label, Jazz Music City Records: Barber of the 'Ville," *Nashville Scene*, August 23, 2012, http://www.nashvillescene.com/nashville/rahsaan -barber-serves-as-jazz-player-and-advocate-with-his-label-jazz-music-city-records/Content ?oid=2989024; Sean L. Maloney, "Local Urban-Music Promoters Lovenoise Make Hip-Hop, Soul and R&B Accessible to Nashville's Masses," *Nashville Scene*, October 27, 2011, http://www .nashvillescene.com/nashville/local-urban-music-promoters-lovenoise-make-hip-hop-soul -and-randb-accessible-to-nashvilles-masses/Content?oid=2661308; Jewly Hight, "Americana Acts Are Getting on the Mainstream Radar," *Nashville Scene*, October 13, 2011, http://www.nashville scene.com/nashville/americana-acts-are-getting-on-the-mainstream-radar/Content?oid =2650847; Edd Hurt, "For Nashville Indie Musicians Like Lambchop and Cortney Tidwell,

It Was the Post-Post-Rock Decade," *Nashville Scene*, December 24, 2009, http://www.nashville scene.com/nashville/for-nashville-indie-musicians-like-lambchop-and-cortney-tidwell-it-was -the-post-post-rock-decade/Content?oid=1204257; Steve Haruch, "Paramore Broke the Nashville Curse and Never Looked Back," *Nashville Scene,* October 29, 2009, http://www.nashville scene.com/nashville/paramore-broke-the-nashville-curse-and-never-looked-back/Content ?oid=1203328; Jewly Hight, "On Its Tenth Anniversary, the Americana Music Association Has Reason to Look Both Backward and Forward," *Nashville Scene*, September 17, 2009, http://www .nashvillescene.com/nashville/on-its-tenth-anniversary-the-americana-music-association -has-reason-to-look-both-backward-and-forward/Content?oid=1202672; Chris Talbott, "Black Keys Find New Home in Nashville," *Billboard*, December 13, 2010, http://www.billboard.com/ news/black-keys-find-new-home-in-nashville-1004134569.story#/news/black-keys-find-new -home-in-nashville-1004134569.story; Delgado Guitars website, http://www.delgadoguitars .com/x/; Richard Fausset, "A New Sound in Nashville," *Los Angeles Times*, April 4, 2007, http:// articles.latimes.com/2007/apr/04/nation/na-nashville4; Nashville Jazz Workshop website, http:// www.nashvillejazz.org/MissionHistory.php; Jazz Music City website, http://www.jazzmusic city.com/#!

4. All profiled artists' names are pseudonyms.

5. The historically black university Tennessee A & I was renamed Tennessee State University in 1968.

6. Names of live venues in the text and quotation are pseudonyms.

CHAPTER 5. CREATING SOCIAL SPACES FOR ARTISTS

1. The Bluebird Café website, http://www.bluebirdcafe.com/about/.

2. Toyah L. Miller et al., "Venturing for Others with Heart and Head: How Compassion Encourages Social Entrepreneurship," *Academy of Management Review* 37, no. 4 (2012): 616, 619.

3. Jeremy Short, Todd Moss, and G. Lumpkin, "Research in Social Entrepreneurship: Past Contributions and Future Opportunities," *Strategic Entrepreneurship Journal* 3, no. 2 (2009): 162.

4. Richard Peterson, *Creating Country Music: Fabricating Authenticity* (Chicago: University of Chicago Press, 1997); Richard Peterson and N. Anand, "How Chaotic Careers Create Orderly Fields," in *Career Creativity: Explorations in the Remaking of Work*, eds. Maury Peiperl, Michael Arthur, and N. Anand (Oxford: Oxford University Press, 2002), 257–79.

5. Robert Faulkner and Howard Becker, *"Do You Know …?" The Jazz Repertoire in Action* (Chicago: University of Chicago Press, 2009), especially ch. 8. Also see Richard Lloyd, *Neo-Bohemia: Art and Commerce in the Postindustrial City*, 2^d ed. (New York: Routledge, 2010); David Grazian, *Blue Chicago: The Search for Authenticity in Urban Blues Clubs* (Chicago: University of Chicago Press, 2003), especially ch. 3; Charles Simpson, *Soho: The Artist in the City* (Chicago: University of Chicago Press, 1981); Maria-Rosario Jackson et al., *Investing in Creativity: A Study of the Support Structure for U.S. Artists* (Washington, DC: Urban Institute, Culture, Creativity & Communities Program, 2003), http://www.urban.org/UploadedPDF/411311_investing_in _creativity.pdf.

6. Short, Moss, and Lumpkin, "Research in Social Entrepreneurship."

7. See chapter 2 for definitions of strategic and risk orientations and family-inspired and movement-inspired career pathways.

8. Richard Peterson and Roger Kern, "Changing Highbrow Taste: From Snob to Omnivore," *American Sociological Review* 61, no. 5 (1996): 900–907.

9. Ibid.

CHAPTER 6. ARTIST ADVOCATES

1. Brantley Hargrove, "A Power Shift within Nashville's Musicians Union Signals Changing Times on Music Row," *Nashville Scene,* March 19, 2009, http://www.nashvillescene.com/nash ville/a-power-shift-within-nashvilles-musicians-union-signals-changing-times-on-music-row/ Content?oid=1200399.

2. Mark T. Jordan, Election Committee Member, "Record Vote Sweeps in New 257 Officers," *Nashville Musician*, January–March 2009, p. 2, http://www.nashvillemusicians.org/uploaded/archive/1258009742January-March2009.pdf.

3. National U.S. labor unions often refer to themselves as "international" unions in light of their Canadian memberships.

4. Warren Denney, "Delegates Deal Winning Hand in Vegas," *Nashville Musician*, July–September 2010, pp. 19–22, http://www.nashvillemusicians.org/uploaded/archive/1283226562TheNash villeMusicianJulyAugSept.pdf ; Laura Ross, "Convention Diary," *The Nashville Musician*, July–September 2010, p. 23, http://www.nashvillemusicians.org/uploaded/archive/1283226562The NashvilleMusicianJulyAugSept.pdf.

5. Denney, "Delegates Deal Winning Hand," pp. 21–22.

6. AFL-CIO Department for Professional Employees, "Professional Performers," http://dpeaflcio .org/professionals/professionals-in-the-workplace/professional-performers/. AFM membership statistics are from AFL-CIO, "Membership Report," p. 70, http://www.aflcio.org/content/download/99671/2676111/ECReporttoConv_FINAL.pdf .

7. Office of Labor-Management Standards, LM2 Reports, American Federation of Musicians Local 257, http://kcerds.dol-esa.gov/query/orgReport.do.

8. Harold Bradley, "Committee Reports, Freelance Task Force," *International Musician*, August 2000, http://home.comcast.net/~syoungafm/freelance.htm.

9. The amendments were first introduced in the 1st session of the 101st Congress as H.R. 2025 on April 18, 1989 and last introduced in the 1st session of the 107th Congress as H.R. 1083 on March 15, 2001.

10. John Amman, "The New Media Union: What New Media Professionals Can Learn from Old Media Unions," in *Surviving the New Economy*, eds. John Amman, Tris Carpenter, and Gina Neff (Boulder: Paradigm, 2007), 157–71; Jon Burlingame, *For the Record: The Struggle and Ultimate Political Rise of American Recording Musicians within Their Labor Movement* (Hollywood: Recording Musicians Association, 1997); Lois Gray and Maria Figueroa, *Empire State's Cultural Capital at Risk? Assessing Challenges to the Workforce and Educational Infrastructure of Arts and Entertainment in New York*, Report to New York Empire State Development Corporation by Cornell University ILR School, June 2009; Edmund Heery, "Trade Unions and Contingent Labour: Scale and Method," *Cambridge Journal of Regions, Economy and Society* 2, no. 3 (2009): 429–42; Lois Gray and Ronald Seeber, eds., *Under the Stars: Essays on Labor Relations in Arts and Entertainment* (Ithaca: ILR Press/Cornell University Press, 1996).

11. On Local 257 history, see the Local 257 website: http://www.nashvillemusicians.org/about-us.

12. Daniel B. Cornfield and Randy Hodson, eds., *Worlds of Work: Building an International Sociology of Work* (New York: Kluwer Academic/Plenum, 2002); Daniel B. Cornfield and Holly J. McCammon, eds., *Labor Revitalization: Global Perspectives and New Initiatives* (Amsterdam: Elsevier, 2003); Lowell Turner and Daniel B. Cornfield, eds., *Labor in the New Urban Battlegrounds: Local Solidarity in a Global Economy* (Ithaca: Cornell University Press, 2007). C. Wright Mills's *The New Men of Power* (New York: Harcourt, Brace, 1948) is the classic treatment of intergenerational changes of labor leaders with new visions of trade unionism during the era of the rivalry between the older American Federation of Labor and the new Congress of Industrial Organizations, published seven years before their merger in 1955.

13. For definitions of risk orientations, see chapter 2.

14. Wayne Baker and Robert Faulkner, "Role as Resource in the Hollywood Film Industry," *American Journal of Sociology* 97, no. 2 (1991): 292.

15. For definitions of strategic and risk orientations, career inspiration, and pathways, see chapter 2.

16. I define an arts trade union activist as a music professional who served in an arts union position for at least five years. In order to maintain the anonymity of the four trade union activists, I have given them pseudonyms, not identified the union(s) in which they were active, and not indicated in which level (national or local) and type (elected, appointed, paid, volunteer) of union position(s) they served.

17. Kristin Thomson, "Roles, Revenue, and Responsibilities: The Changing Nature of Being a Working Musician," *Work and Occupations* 40, no. 4 (2013): 514–25.

18. See the AFM Local 257 websites for networking, live performance scales, and single song overdub scales, respectively: http://www.nashvillemusicians.org/?pg=networking, http://www.nashvillemusicians.org/?pg=live_contract; and http://www.nashvillemusicians.org/?pg=scales. Also see Gray and Figueroa, *Empire State's Cultural Capital*, 33–40.

19. "The World of Country Music," *Billboard*, November 2, 1963; Robert K. Oermann, *America's Music: The Roots of Country* (Atlanta: Turner Publishing, 1996), 115–34; Oermann, *A Century of Country: An Illustrated History of Country Music* (New York: TV Books, 1999), 152–173; Richard A. Peterson, *Creating Country Music: Fabricating Authenticity* (Chicago: University of Chicago Press, 1997), 221–33.

CHAPTER 7. COMMUNITY, AGENCY, AND ARTISTIC EXPRESSION

1. Richard Peterson and N. Anand, "How Chaotic Careers Create Orderly Fields," in *Career Creativity: Explorations in the Remaking of Work*, eds. Maury Peiperl, Michael Arthur, and N. Anand (Oxford: Oxford University Press, 2002), 258–64.

2. Richard Peterson and David Berger, "Cycles in Symbol Production: The Case of Popular Music," *American Sociological Review* 40, no. 2 (1975): 159.

3. Ibid., 158.

4. Peterson and Anand, "Chaotic Careers," 272.

5. Steven Tepper, *Not Here, Not Now, Not That! Protest over Art and Culture in America* (Chicago: University of Chicago Press, 2011), 68.

6. U.S. Office of Immigration Statistics, Department of Homeland Security, *Yearbook of Immigration Statistics: 2012*, Table 1: Persons Obtaining Legal Permanent Resident Status: Fiscal Years 1820 to 2012, https://www.dhs.gov/yearbook-immigration-statistics-2012-legal-permanent-residents.

7. Tepper, *Not Here, Not Now, Not That!*, 18.

8. Ibid., 2.

9. Timothy J. Dowd, "Concentration and Diversity Revisited: Production Logics and the U.S. Mainstream Recording Market, 1940–1990," *Social Forces* 82, no. 4 (2004):1411–55; Dowd, "Structural Power and the Construction of Markets: The Case of Rhythm and Blues," *Comparative Social Research* 21 (Bingley: Emerald, 2003), 147–201; Richard Peterson and Roger Kern, "Changing Highbrow Taste: From Snob to Omnivore," *American Sociological Review* 61, no. 5 (1996): 900–907; William Roy, *Reds, Whites, and Blues: Social Movements, Folk Music, and Race in the United States* (Princeton: Princeton University Press, 2010); Jennifer Lena, *Banding Together: How Communities Create Genres in Popular Music* (Princeton: Princeton University Press, 2012).

10. Frank G. Clement, "Country Music a Tennessee Heritage," *Billboard*, November 2, 1963, p. 22.

11. "Best Music Scene, 2011: Nashville, Tennessee," *Rolling Stone*, April 28, 2011, http://www.rollingstone.com/music/pictures/best-music-scene-2011-nashville-tennessee-20110502.

12. Associated Press, "Nashville Music Council Seeks to Leverage City's Vast Music Resources," *billboard.biz*, June 23, 2011, http://www.billboard.com/biz/articles/news/1177360/nashville-music-council-seeks-to-leverage-citys-vast-music-resources.

13. Ibid.

14. Jennifer Lena and Daniel Cornfield, "Immigrant Arts Participation: A Pilot Study of Nashville Artists," in *Engaging Art: The Next Great Transformation of America's Cultural Life*, eds. Steven J. Tepper and Bill Ivey (New York: Routledge, 2008), 147–69; Richard Faussett, "A New Sound in Nashville," *Los Angeles Times*, April 4, 2007, http://articles.latimes.com/2007/apr/04/nation/na-nashville4.

15. David Halberstam, *The Children* (New York: Random House, 1998); Larry W. Isaac et al., "'Movement Schools' and Dialogical Diffusion of Nonviolent Praxis: Nashville Workshops in the Southern Civil Rights Movement." in *Nonviolent Resistance*, eds. Sharon Erickson Nepstad

and Lester Kurtz, *Research in Social Movements, Conflicts, and Change* 34 (Bingley: Emerald Group Publishing Limited, 2012), 155–84; Daniel Cornfield and Steering Committee of Nashville for All of Us, "Partnering for an Equitable and Inclusive Nashville: Background Report on Equity and Inclusion," submitted to the Steering Committee of NashvilleNext, Nashville's 2040 General Plan, January 2013, http://www.nashville.gov/Portals/0/SiteContent/Planning/docs/NashvilleNext/next-report-Equity-and-Inclusion.pdf.

16. Peterson and Anand, "Chaotic Careers," 272.

17. Daniel Cornfield, "Integrative Organizing in Polarized Times: Toward Dynamic Trade Unionism in the Global North," in *Mobilizing against Inequality: Unions, Immigrant Workers, and the Crisis of Capitalism*, eds. Lee Adler, Maite Tapia, and Lowell Turner (Ithaca: Cornell University Press, 2014), 151–68.

18. Oermann, *A Century of Country*, 175.

19. Ibid., 176. Also, see Richard Lloyd, "Differentiating Music City: Legacy, Industry and Scene in Nashville," in *Music City: Musical Approaches to the "Creative City*," eds. A. Barber-Kersovan, V. Kirchberg, and R. Kuchar (Bielefeld: Transcript Verlag, 2014), 139–68.

20. Peterson and Anand, "Chaotic Careers."

21. Associated Press, "Nashville Music Council."

22. Howard Becker, "Art as Collective Action," *American Sociological Review* 39, no. 6 (1974): 767–76.

23. Peterson and Kern, "Changing Highbrow Taste"; Peterson and Anand, "Chaotic Careers."

24. Sherry Ortner, *Not Hollywood: Independent Film at the Twilight of the American Dream* (Durham: Duke University Press, 2013); Kristin Thomson, "Roles, Revenue, and Responsibilities: The Changing Nature of Being a Working Musician," *Work and Occupations* 40, no. 4 (2013): 514–25.

25. U.S. Bureau of Labor Statistics, Employment Projections, tables 1.2 and 2.7, http://www.bls.gov/emp/ep_table_102.htm and http://www.bls.gov/emp/ep_table_207.htm. The industry label "*independent* artists, writers, and performers" [my italics] refers to a wide range of freelance expressive occupations classified under code 7115 of the 2007 North American Industry Classification System.

26. Arne Kalleberg, *Good Jobs, Bad Jobs: The Rise of Polarized and Precarious Employment Systems in the United States, 1970s to 2000s* (New York: Russell Sage Foundation, 2011); Cornfield, "Integrative Organizing."

27. Richard Lloyd, *Neo-Bohemia: Art and Commerce in the Postindustrial City*, 2^d ed. (New York: Routledge, 2010); Richard Florida, "The Nashville Effect," *Atlantic*, May 21, 2009, http://www.theatlantic.com/national/archive/2009/05/the-nashville-effect/17288/; Florida, "The Changing Geography of Pop Music," *Atlantic*, February 17, 2011, http://www.theatlantic.com/entertainment/archive/2011/02/grammys-big-city-winner/71341/; Daniel Cornfield, "Conclusion: Seeking Solidarity ... Why and With Whom?," in *Labor in the New Urban Battlegrounds: Local Solidarity in a Global Economy*, eds. Lowell Turner and Daniel B. Cornfield (Ithaca: Cornell University Press, 2007), 235–51; Samuel Shaw, *Off-Center: Art Careers in Peripheral Places*, Doctoral Dissertation (Nashville: Department of Sociology, Vanderbilt University, May 2014).

28. Nashville Public Television, "Next Door Neighbors," television documentary series, http://ndn.wnpt.org/about/; Damian Williams, "Grounding the Regime of Precarious Employment: Homeless Day Laborers' Negotiation of the Job Queue," *Work and Occupations* 38, no. 3 (2009): 209–46; Daniel Cornfield, "Immigrant Labor Organizing in a 'New Destination City': Approaches to the Unionization of African, Asian, Latino, and Middle Eastern Workers in Nashville," in *Global Connections and Local Receptions: New Latino Migration to the Southeastern United States*, eds. Fran Ansley and Jon Shefner (Knoxville: University of Tennessee Press, 2009), 279–97; Daniel B. Cornfield and William Canak, "Immigrants and Labor in a Globalizing City: Prospects for Coalition Building in Nashville," in *Labor in the New Urban Battlegrounds: Local Solidarity in a Global Economy*, eds. Lowell Turner and Daniel B. Cornfield (Ithaca: Cornell University Press, 2007), 163–77; Center for Regional Economic Competitiveness, "Leveraging the Labor Force for Economic Growth: Assessing the Nashville Economic

Market Area's Readiness for Work after the Recession," August 2010, pp. 7 and 49–53, http://www.nashvillechamber.com/Homepage/WorkNashville/WorkforceStudy.aspx; Patrick Raines and LaTanya Brown, "The Economic Impact of the Music Industry in the Nashville-Davidson-Murfreesboro MSA," Report sponsored by Belmont University and the Nashville Area Chamber of Commerce, Nashville, January 2006; Isaac et al., "Movement Schools"; Cornfield and Steering Committee of Nashville for All of Us, "Partnering for an Equitable and Inclusive Nashville"; Shaw, *Off-Center.*

29. Lowell Turner, "Introduction: An Urban Resurgence of Social Unionism," in *Labor in the New Urban Battlegrounds: Local Solidarity in a Global Economy*, eds. Lowell Turner and Daniel B. Cornfield (Ithaca: Cornell University Press, 2007), 1–18; Cornfield, "Seeking Solidarity."

30. Lois Gray and Ronald Seeber, eds., *Under the Stars: Essays on Labor Relations in Arts and Entertainment* (Ithaca: ILR Press/Cornell University Press, 1996); Lois Gray and Maria Figueroa, *Empire State's Cultural Capital at Risk? Assessing Challenges to the Workforce and Educational Infrastructure of Arts and Entertainment in New York*, Report to New York Empire State Development Corporation by Cornell University ILR School, June 2009.

31. Turner, "Urban Resurgence"; Daniel Cornfield, *Becoming a Mighty Voice Conflict and Change in the United Furniture Workers of America* (New York: Russell Sage Foundation, 1989).

32. Cornfield, *Becoming a Mighty Voice.*

33. Future of Music Coalition, Artist Revenue Streams, "Money from Music: Where We Live," http://money.futureofmusic.org/location/; also see Florida, "Nashville Effect" and Florida, "Changing Geography of Pop Music."

34. Harold L. Wilensky and Charles N. Lebeaux, *Industrial Society and Social Welfare* (New York: Free Press, 1965); John Garraty, *Unemployment in History* (New York: Harper & Row, 1978).

35. Kalleberg, *Good Jobs, Bad Jobs*; Ulrich Beck, *The Brave New World of Work* (Malden: Polity Press, 2000).

36. Elliott Krause, *Death of the Guilds: Professions, States, and the Advance of Capitalism, 1930 to the Present* (New Haven: Yale University Press, 1996).

37. Steven Greenhouse, "Tackling Concerns of Independent Workers," *New York Times*, March 23, 2013, http://www.nytimes.com/2013/03/24/business/freelancers-union-tackles-concerns-of-independent-workers.html?_r=0.

38. Ibid.

39. "Freelancers Union," February 7, 2014, http://www.freelancersunion.org/; Charles Heckscher, Sara Horowitz, and Althea Erickson, "Civil Society and the Provision of Services: The Freelancers Union Experience," in *Transforming the U.S. Workforce Development System: Lessons from Research and Practice*, eds. David Finegold et al. (Champaign: Labor and Employment Relations Association, 2010), 237–59.

40. Greenhouse, "Tackling Concerns."

41. Rachel Swarns, "Freelancers in the 'Gig Economy' Find a Mix of Freedom and Uncertainty," *New York Times*, February 10, 2014, http://www.nytimes.com/2014/02/10/nyregion/for-freelancers-in-the-gig-economy-a-mix-of-freedom-and-uncertainty.html?ref=todayspaper.

42. Writers Guild of America, West, "Writers Guild Members Vote to End Strike," February 12, 2008, http://www.wga.org/subpage_newsevents.aspx?id=2775; Writers Guild of America, West, "Writers Guild Members Overwhelmingly Ratify New Contract," February 26, 2008, http://www.wga.org/subpage_newsevents.aspx?id=2780; Lacey Rose, "Strike Strategy," *Forbes*, January 10, 2008, http://www.forbes.com/2008/01/10/labor-hollywood-wga-biz-media-cx_lr_0110strike.html; Brooks Barnes and Michael Cieply, "In Strike, Separate Deals Draw Ire of Big Producers," *New York Times*, January 7, 2008, http://www.nytimes.com/2008/01/07/business/media/07strike.html?_r=0.

43. Writers Guild of America, West, "Guide to the Guild," http://www.wga.org/uploadedFiles/who_we_are/fyi09.pdf.

44. Timothy Dowd and Diogo Pinheiro, "The Ties among the Notes: The Social Capital of Jazz Musicians in three Metro Areas," *Work and Occupations* 40, no. 4 (2013): 431–64; Ezra Zuckerman, "Typecasting and Generalism in Firm and Market: Genre-based Career Concentration

in the Feature film industry, 1933–1995," in *Transformation in Cultural Industries*, eds. Candace Jones and Patricia Thornton, *Research in the Sociology of Organizations* 23 (Amsterdam: Elsevier, 2005), 171–214.

45. Wayne Baker and Robert Faulkner, "Role as Resource in the Hollywood Film Industry," *American Journal of Sociology* 97, no. 2 (1991): 279–309.

46. Elizabeth Long Lingo and Steven Tepper, "Looking Back, Looking Forward: Arts-Based Careers and Creative Work," *Work and Occupations* 40, no. 4 (2013): 337–63.

47. Kristin Thomson, "Roles, Revenue, and Responsibilities: The Changing Nature of Being a Working Musician," *Work and Occupations* 40, no. 4 (2013): 515.

48. Ibid., 518.

49. Writers Guild of America, West, "Chapter 3: Writer-Producers," http://www.wga.org/uploaded Files/writers_resources/ep3.pdf

50. Baker and Faulkner, "Role as Resource," 292.

51. Writers Guild of America, West, "Chapter 3: Writer-Producers."

52. Ibid., 31.

53. "AFTRA National Board Approves New Union Committee and Mission Statement," AFTRA press release of May 14, 2011, http://www.sagaftra.org/press-releases/may-14-2011/aftra-national -board-approves-new-union-committee-and-mission-statement .

54. Merger Agreement Between Screen Actors Guild and the American Federation of Television and Radio Artists http://www.sagaftra.org/files/sag/documents/Merger%20Agreement%20 Final%20Approved%20120131a.pdf

55. AFM Local 1000, "About Us," February 10, 2014, http://local1000.org/about-us/.

56. Ibid.

57. AFM Local 1000, "Local 1000 Remembers Pete Seeger," January 28, 2014, February 10, 2014, http://local1000.org/2014/01/local-1000-remembers-pete-seeger/#.UvkE5fsvI40.

58. Bruce Barry, *Speechless: The Erosion of Free Expression in the American Workplace* (San Francisco: Berrett-Koehler, 2007).

59. Tepper, *Not Here, Not Now, Not That!*, 68.

60. Peterson and Kern, "Changing Highbrow Taste."

61. Kevin Stainback and Donald Tomaskovic-Devey, *Documenting Desegregation: Racial and Gender Segregation in Private-Sector Employment since the Civil Rights Act* (New York: Russell Sage Foundation, 2012); Lena and Cornfield, "Immigrant Arts Participation"; Cornfield, "Integrative Organizing."

62. Cornfield, "Integrative Organizing."

63. Ibid.

64. Dan Cornfield, "High-Wage Service Workers Would Have to Unite with Low-Wage Service Workers," September 11, 2013, http://www.zocalopublicsquare.org/2013/09/11/there-is-power -in-a-union-potentially-we-hope/ideas/up-for-discussion/#Dan+Cornfield; Daniel B. Cornfield and Holly J. McCammon, "Approaching Merger: The Converging Public Policy Agendas of the AFL and CIO, 1938–1955," in *Strategic Alliances: New Studies of Social Movement Coalitions*, eds. Nella Van Dyke and Holly J. McCammon (Minneapolis: University of Minnesota Press, 2010), 79–98.

65. Cornfield, "Seeking Solidarity"; Ruth Milkman, *L.A. Story: Immigrant Workers and the Future of the U.S. Labor Movement* (New York: Russell Sage Foundation, 2006).

66. Cornfield, "High-Wage Service Workers"; Cornfield and McCammon, "Approaching Merger."

67. Lloyd, *Neo-Bohemia*.

68. Saul Alinsky, *Reveille for Radicals* (New York: Vintage, 1946), ch. 5.

69. Peterson and Anand, "Chaotic Careers"; Lloyd, *Neo-Bohemia*; Daniel Cornfield, "Plant Shutdowns and Union Decline: The United Furniture Workers of America, 1963–1981," *Work and Occupations* 14, no. 3 (1987): 434–451.

70. For a definitions of "strategic and risk orientations," see chapter 2.

71. Nella Van Dyke and Holly J. McCammon, eds., *Strategic Alliances: New Studies of Social Movement Coalitions* (Minneapolis: University of Minnesota Press, 2010).

72. Hedy Weinberg, "English-Only Opposition," *New York Times*, January 15, 2009, http://www
.nytimes.com/2009/01/16/opinion/l16nashville.html?partner=rss&emc=rss. Also see Cornfield
and Steering Committee of Nashville for All of Us, "Partnering for an Equitable and Inclusive Nashville"; Lena and Cornfield, "Immigrant Arts Participation"; Cornfield and Canak,
"Immigrants and Labor in a Globalizing City."

Bibliography

Scholarly Works Cited

Adams, James Truslow. *The Epic of America*. Boston: Little, Brown, 1931.

AFL-CIO. *Executive Council Report to the AFL-CIO 2013 Convention*. 2013. http://www.aflcio.org/content/download/99671/2676111/ECReporttoConv_FINAL.pdf.

AFL-CIO Department for Professional Employees. "Professional Performers." August 2013. http://dpeaflcio.org/professionals/professionals-in-the-workplace/professional-performers/.

AFM Local 1000. "About Us." February 10, 2014. http://local1000.org/about-us/.

AFM Local 1000. "Local 1000 Remembers Pete Seeger." January 28, 2014. http://local1000.org/2014/01/local-1000-remembers-pete-seeger/#.UvkE5fsvI40.

"AFTRA National Board Approves New Union Committee and Mission Statement." AFTRA press release May 14, 2011. http://www.sagaftra.org/press-releases/may-14-2011/aftra-national-board-approves-new-union-committee-and-mission-statement.

Aldrich, Howard, and Jennifer Cliff. "The Pervasive Effects of Family on Entrepreneurship: Toward a Family Embeddedness Perspective." *Journal of Business Venturing* 18, no. 5 (2003): 573–96.

Alexander, Victoria. *Sociology of the Arts: Exploring Fine and Popular Forms*. Malden, MA: Blackwell, 2003.

Alinsky, Saul. *Reveille for Radicals*. New York: Vintage, 1946.

Amman, John. "The New Media Union: What New Media Professionals Can Learn from Old Media Unions." In *Surviving the New Economy*, edited by John Amman, Tris Carpenter, and Gina Neff, 157–71. Boulder, CO: Paradigm, 2007.

Amoore, Louise. "Risk, Reward and Discipline at Work." *Economy and Society* 33, no. 2 (2004): 174–96.

Baker, Wayne, and Robert Faulkner. "Role as Resource in the Hollywood Film Industry." *American Journal of Sociology* 97, no. 2 (1991): 279–309.

Bakke, E. Wight. *The Unemployed Worker: A Study of the Task of Making a Living without a Job*. New Haven, CT: Yale University Press, 1940.

Barley, Stephen. "Careers, Identities, and Institutions: The Legacy of the Chicago School of Sociology." In *Handbook of Career Theory*, edited by Michael Arthur, Douglas Hall, and Barbara Lawrence, 41–65. New York: Cambridge University Press, 1989.

———. "Coalface Institutionalism." In *Handbook of Organizational Institutionalism*, edited by R. Greenwood, C. Oliver, R. Suddaby, and K. Sahlin-Anderson, 490–515. Thousand Oaks, CA: Sage, 2008.

Barley, Stephen, and Gideon Kunda. *Gurus, Hired Guns, and Warm Bodies: Itinerant Experts in a Knowledge Economy*. Princeton: Princeton University Press, 2004.

Barnes, Brooks, and Michael Cieply. "In Strike, Separate Deals Draw Ire of Big Producers." *New York Times*, January 7, 2008. http://www.nytimes.com/2008/01/07/business/media/07strike.html?_r=0.

Barry, Bruce. *Speechless: The Erosion of Free Expression in the American Workplace*. San Francisco: Berrett-Koehler, 2007.

Bechky, Beth. "Gaffers, Gofers, and Grips: Role-Based Coordination in Temporary Organizations." *Organization Science* 17, no. 1 (2006): 3–21.

Beck, Ulrich. *The Brave New World of Work*. Malden, MA: Polity Press, 2000.

191

Becker, Howard. "Art as Collective Action." *American Sociological Review* 39, no. 6 (1974): 767–76.
———. *Art Worlds.* Berkeley: University of California Press, 1982.
Becker, Howard S. *Outsiders: Studies in the Sociology of Deviance.* New York: Free Press, 1963.
Bennett, Andy. "'Heritage Rock': Rock Music, Representation and Heritage Discourse." *Poetics* 37, no. 5 (2009): 474–89.
Bennett, Tony, and Elizabeth Silva. "Introduction: Cultural Capital—Histories, Limits, Prospects." *Poetics* 39, no. 6 (2011): 427–43.
Berliner, Paul. *Thinking in Jazz: The Infinite Art of Improvisation.* Chicago: University of Chicago Press, 1994.
Blee, Kathleen. *Democracy in the Making: How Activist Groups Form.* New York: Oxford University Press, 2012.
Bourdieu, Pierre. *The Field of Cultural Production.* New York: Columbia University Press, 1993.
Bradley, Harold. "Committee Reports, Freelance Task Force." *International Musician*, August 2000. http://home.comcast.net/~syoungafm/freelance.htm.
Burlingame, Jon. *For the Record: The Struggle and Ultimate Political Rise of American Recording Musicians within Their Labor Movement.* Hollywood: Recording Musicians Association, 1997.
Center for Regional Economic Competitiveness. "Leveraging the Labor Force for Economic Growth: Assessing the Nashville Economic Market Area's Readiness for Work after the Recession." August 2010. http://www.nashvillechamber.com/Homepage/WorkNashville/Workforce Study.aspx.
Chinoy, Ely. *Automobile Workers and the American Dream.* Garden City, NY: Doubleday, 1955.
Cornfield, Dan. "High-Wage Service Workers Would Have to Unite with Low-Wage Service Workers." September 11, 2013. http://www.zocalopublicsquare.org/2013/09/11/there-is-power-in-a -union-potentially-we-hope/ideas/up-for-discussion/#Dan+Cornfield.
Cornfield, Daniel. "Plant Shutdowns and Union Decline: The United Furniture Workers of America, 1963–1981." *Work and Occupations* 14, no. 3 (1987): 434–51.
———. *Becoming a Mighty Voice Conflict and Change in the United Furniture Workers of America.* New York: Russell Sage Foundation, 1989.
———. "Immigrant Labor Organizing in a 'New Destination City': Approaches to the Unionization of African, Asian, Latino, and Middle Eastern Workers in Nashville." In *Global Connections and Local Receptions: New Latino Migration to the Southeastern United States*, edited by Fran Ansley and Jon Shefner, 279–97. Knoxville: University of Tennessee Press, 2009.
———. "Integrative Organizing in Polarized Times: Toward Dynamic Trade Unionism in the Global North." In *Mobilizing against Inequality: Unions, Immigrant Workers, and the Crisis of Capitalism*, edited by Lee Adler, Maite Tapia, and Lowell Turner, 151–68. Ithaca, NY: Cornell University Press, 2014.
Cornfield, Daniel, Angela Arzubiaga, Rhonda BeLue, Susan Brooks, Tony Brown, Oscar Miller, Douglas Perkins, Peggy Thoits, and Lynn Walker. Final Report of the Immigrant Community Assessment of Nashville, Tennessee, August 2003. Commissioned by Mayor Bill Purcell and prepared under contract #14830 for Metropolitan Government of Nashville and Davidson County, Tennessee.
Cornfield, Daniel, Karen Campbell, and Holly McCammon, eds. *Working in Restructured Workplaces: Challenges and New Directions for the Sociology of Work.* Thousand Oaks, CA: Sage Publications, 2001.
Cornfield, Daniel, and William Canak. "Immigrants and Labor in a Globalizing City: Prospects for Coalition Building in Nashville." In *Labor in the New Urban Battlegrounds: Local Solidarity in a Global Economy*, edited by Lowell Turner and Daniel B. Cornfield, 163–77. Ithaca, NY: Cornell University Press, 2007.
Cornfield, Daniel, and Randy Hodson, eds. *Worlds of Work: Building an International Sociology of Work.* New York: Kluwer Academic/Plenum, 2002.
Cornfield, Daniel, and Holly J. McCammon. "Approaching Merger: The Converging Public Policy Agendas of the AFL and CIO, 1938–1955." In *Strategic Alliances: New Studies of Social Movement Coalitions*, edited by Nella Van Dyke and Holly J. McCammon, 79–98. Minneapolis: University of Minnesota Press, 2010.

Cornfield, Daniel, and Holly J. McCammon, eds. *Labor Revitalization: Global Perspectives and New Initiatives.* Amsterdam: Elsevier, 2003.

Cornfield, Daniel, and Steering Committee of Nashville for All of Us. "Partnering for an Equitable and Inclusive Nashville: Background Report on Equity and Inclusion." Submitted to the Steering Committee of NashvilleNext, Nashville's 2040 General Plan, January 2013. http://www.nashville.gov/Portals/0/SiteContent/Planning/docs/NashvilleNext/next-report-Equity-and-Inclusion.pdf.

Corrigall-Brown, Catherine. *Patterns of Protest: Trajectories of Participation in Social Movements.* Stanford, CA: Stanford University Press, 2011.

Dimaggio, Paul. "Cultural Entrepreneurship in Nineteenth-Century Boston: The Creation of an Organizational Base for High Culture in America." *Media, Culture and Society* 4 (1982): 33–50.

Dowd, Timothy J. "Structural Power and the Construction of Markets: The Case of Rhythm and Blues." *Comparative Social Research* 21 (2003): 147–201.

———. "Concentration and Diversity Revisited: Production Logics and the U.S. Mainstream Recording Market, 1940–1990." *Social Forces* 82, no. 4 (2004):1411–55.

Dowd, Timothy, and Maureen Blyer. "Charting Race: The Success of Black Performers in the Mainstream Recording Market, 1940–1990." *Poetics* 30, nos. 1–2 (2002): 87–110.

Dowd, Timothy J., Susanne Janssen, and Marc Verboord. "Introduction: Fields in Transition—Fields in Action." *Poetics* 37, no. 5 (2009): 399–401.

Dowd, Timothy, Kathleen Liddle, and Maureen Blyer. "Charting Gender: The Success of Female Acts in the U.S. Mainstream Recording Market, 1940–1990." *Research in the Sociology of Organizations* 23 (Bingley: Emerald, 2005): 81–123.

Dowd, Timothy, and Diogo Pinheiro. "The Ties among the Notes: The Social Capital of Jazz Musicians in Three Metro Areas." *Work and Occupations* 40, no. 4 (2013): 431–64.

Durkheim, Emile. *Division of Labor in Society.* New York: Free Press, 1964 [originally published 1893].

Faulkner, Robert. *Music on Demand: Composers and Careers in the Hollywood Film Industry.* New Brunswick, NJ: Transaction Publishers, 1983.

———. *Hollywood Studio Musicians: Their Work and Careers in the Recording Industry.* Lanham, MD: University Press of America, 1985.

Faulkner, Robert, and Andy Anderson. "Short-Term Projects and Emergent Careers: Evidence from Hollywood." *American Journal of Sociology* 92, no. 4 (1987): 879–909.

Faulkner, Robert, and Howard Becker. *"Do You Know ...?" The Jazz Repertoire in Action.* Chicago: University of Chicago Press, 2009.

Florida, Richard. "The Nashville Effect." *Atlantic,* May 21, 2009. http://www.theatlantic.com/national/archive/2009/05/the-nashville-effect/17288/.

———. "The Nashville Effect, Cont'd." *Atlantic,* July 6, 2009. http://www.theatlantic.com/national/archive/2009/07/the-nashville-effect-contd/20385/.

———. "The Changing Geography of Pop Music." *Atlantic,* February 17, 2011. http://www.theatlantic.com/entertainment/archive/2011/02/the-changing-geography-of-pop-music/71341/.

Florida, Richard, and Scott Jackson. "Sonic City: The Evolving Economic Geography of the Music Industry." *Journal of Planning Education and Research* 29, no. 3 (2010): 310–32.

Florida, Richard, Charlotta Mellander, and Kevin Stolarick. "Music Scenes to Music Clusters: The Economic Geography of Music in the US, 1970–2000." *Environment and Planning A* 42, no. 4 (2010): 785–804.

"Freelancers Union." February 7, 2014. http://www.freelancersunion.org/.

Future of Music Coalition. Artist Revenue Streams, "Money from Music: Where We Live." September 11, 2013. http://money.futureofmusic.org/location/.

Garraty, John. *Unemployment in History.* New York: Harper & Row, 1978.

Gray, Lois, and Maria Figueroa. *Empire State's Cultural Capital at Risk? Assessing Challenges to the Workforce and Educational Infrastructure of Arts and Entertainment in New York.* Report to New York Empire State Development Corporation by Cornell University ILR School, June 2009.

Gray, Lois, and Ronald Seeber, eds. *Under the Stars: Essays on Labor Relations in Arts and Entertainment.* Ithaca, NY: ILR Press/Cornell University Press, 1996.

Grazian, David. *Blue Chicago: The Search for Authenticity in Urban Blues Clubs.* Chicago: University of Chicago Press, 2003.

Greenhouse, Steven. "Tackling Concerns of Independent Workers." *New York Times.* March 23, 2013. http://www.nytimes.com/2013/03/24/business/freelancers-union-tackles-concerns-of-independent-workers.html?_r=0.

Halberstam, David. *The Children.* New York: Random House, 1998.

Heckscher, Charles, Sara Horowitz, and Althea Erickson. "Civil Society and the Provision of Services: The Freelancers Union Experience." In *Transforming the U.S. Workforce Development System: Lessons from Research and Practice,* edited by David Finegold, Mary Gatta, Hal Saltzman, and Susan Schurman, 237–59. Champaign, IL: Labor and Employment Relations Association, 2010.

Heery, Edmund. "Trade Unions and Contingent Labour: Scale and Method." *Cambridge Journal of Regions, Economy and Society* 2, no. 3 (2009): 429–42.

Hesmondhalgh, David, and Sarah Baker. "'A Very Complicated Version of Freedom': Conditions and Experiences of Creative Labour in Three Cultural Industries." *Poetics* 38, no. 1 (2010): 4–20.

Hirsch, Barry, and David MacPherson. *Union Membership and Coverage Database,* January 24, 2015. http://www.unionstats.com/.

Hirsch, Paul. "Processing Fads and Fashions: An Organization-Set Analysis of Cultural Industry Systems." *American Journal of Sociology* 77, no. 4 (1972): 639–59.

Hochschild, Jennifer. *Facing Up to the American Dream: Race, Class, and the Soul of the Nation.* Princeton: Princeton University Press, 1995.

Hodson, Randy. *Dignity at Work.* New York: Cambridge University Press, 2001.

Hughes, Everett. *Men and Their Work.* Glencoe, IL: Free Press, 1958.

Isaac, Larry. "Movements, Aesthetics, and Markets in Literary Change: Making the American Labor Problem Novel." *American Sociological Review* 74, no. 6 (2009): 938–65.

Isaac, Larry W., Daniel B. Cornfield, Dennis C. Dickerson, James M. Lawson, Jr., and Jonathan S. Coley. "'Movement Schools' and Dialogical Diffusion of Nonviolent Praxis: Nashville Workshops in the Southern Civil Rights Movement." In *Nonviolent Resistance,* edited by Sharon Erickson Nepstad and Lester Kurtz, 155–84. *Research in Social Movements, Conflicts, and Change* 34. Bingley: Emerald Group Publishing Limited, 2012.

Ivey, Bill. *Arts, Inc.: How Greed and Neglect Have Destroyed Our Cultural Rights.* Berkeley: University of California Press, 2008.

Jackson, Maria-Rosario, Florence Kabwasa-Green, Daniel Swenson, Joaquin Herranz, Kadija Ferryman, Caron Atlas, Eric Wallner, and Carole Rosenstein. *Investing in Creativity: A Study of the Support Structure for U.S. Artists.* Washington, DC: Urban Institute, Culture, Creativity & Communities Program, 2003. http://www.urban.org/UploadedPDF/411311_investing_in_creativity.pdf.

Kalleberg, Arne. "Precarious Work, Insecure Workers: Employment Relations in Transition." *American Sociological Review* 74, no. 1 (2009): 1–22.

———. *Good Jobs, Bad Jobs: The Rise of Polarized and Precarious Employment Systems in the United States, 1970s to 2000s.* New York: Russell Sage Foundation, 2011.

Kochan, Thomas. *Restoring the American Dream: A Working Families' Agenda for America.* Cambridge, MA: MIT Press, 2005.

Kosser, Michael. *How Nashville Became Music City, U.S.A.: 50 Years of Music Row.* Milwaukee, WI: Hal Leonard Corporation, 2006.

Krause, Elliott. *Death of the Guilds: Professions, States, and the Advance of Capitalism, 1930 to the Present.* New Haven, CT: Yale University Press, 1996.

Kushner, Roland, and Randy Cohen. *National Arts Index 2010: An Annual Measure of the Vitality of Arts and Culture in the United States: 1998–2009.* Washington, DC and New York: Americans for the Arts, 2011.

Lena, Jennifer. *Banding Together: How Communities Create Genres in Popular Music.* Princeton: Princeton University Press, 2012.

Lena, Jennifer, and Daniel Cornfield. "Immigrant Arts Participation: A Pilot Study of Nashville Artists." In *Engaging Art: The Next Great Transformation of America's Cultural Life*, edited by Steven J. Tepper and Bill Ivey, 147–69. New York: Routledge, 2008.

Lloyd, Richard. *Neo-Bohemia: Art and Commerce in the Postindustrial City*, 2d ed. New York: Routledge, 2010.

———. "Differentiating Music City: Legacy, Industry and Scene in Nashville." In *Music City: Musical Approaches to the "Creative City,"* edited by A. Barber-Kersovan, V. Kirchberg, and R. Kuchar, 139–68. Bielefeld: Transcript Verlag, 2014.

Long Lingo, Elizabeth, and Steven Tepper. "Looking Back, Looking Forward: Arts-Based Careers and Creative Work." *Work and Occupations* 40, no. 4 (2013): 337–63.

Lyng, Stephen. "Edgework, Risk, and Uncertainty." In *Social Theories of Risk and Uncertainty: An Introduction*, edited by Jens Zinn, 106–37. Malden, MA: Blackwell, 2008.

McAdam, Doug. "Recruitment to High-Risk Activism: The Case of Freedom Summer." *American Journal of Sociology* 92, no. 1 (1986): 64–90.

McCammon, Holly. *The U.S. Women's Jury Movements and Strategic Adaptation: A More Just Verdict.* New York: Cambridge University Press, 2012.

Menger, Pierre-Michel. "Artistic Labor Markets and Careers." *Annual Review of Sociology* 25 (1999): 541–74.

———. "Artists as Workers: Theoretical and Methodological Challenges." *Poetics* 28, no. 4 (2001): 241–54.

Milkman, Ruth. *L.A. Story: Immigrant Workers and the Future of the U.S. Labor Movement.* New York: Russell Sage Foundation, 2006.

Miller, Toyah L., Matthew G. Grimes, Jeffery S. Mcmullen, and Timothy I. Vogus. "Venturing for Others with Heart and Head: How Compassion Encourages Social Entrepreneurship." *Academy of Management Review* 37, no. 4 (2012): 616–40.

Mills, C. Wright. *The New Men of Power.* New York: Harcourt, Brace, 1948.

Moen, Phyllis, Jack Lam, Samantha Ammons, and Erin Kelly. "Time Work by Overworked Professionals: Strategies in Response to the Stress of Higher Status." *Work and Occupations* 40, no. 2 (2013): 79–114.

Nashville Public Television. "Next Door Neighbors," television documentary series on immigrant communities in Nashville. 2014. http://ndn.wnpt.org/about/.

Neff, Gina. "The Lure of Risk: Surviving and Welcoming Uncertainty in the New Economy." In *Surviving the New Economy*, edited by John Amman, Tris Carpenter, and Gina Neff, 33–46. Boulder, CO: Paradigm, 2007.

———. *Venture Labor.* Cambridge, MA: MIT Press, 2012.

Neff, Gina, Elizabeth Wissinger, and Sharon Zukin. "Entrepreneurial Labor Among Cultural Producers: 'Cool' Jobs in 'Hot' Industries." *Social Semiotics* 15, no. 3 (2005): 307–34.

Negus, Keith. *Musical Genres and Corporate Cultures.* New York: Routledge, 1999.

Newman, Katherine. *Declining Fortunes: The Withering of the American Dream.* New York: Basic Books, 1993.

Oermann, Robert. *America's Music: The Roots of Country.* Atlanta, GA: Turner Publishing, 1996.

———. *A Century of Country: An Illustrated History of Country Music.* New York: TV Books, 1999.

Ortner, Sherry. *Not Hollywood: Independent Film at the Twilight of the American Dream.* Durham, NC: Duke University Press, 2013.

Osnowitz, Debra. *Freelancing Expertise: Contract Professionals in the New Economy.* Ithaca, NY: Cornell University Press, 2010.

Oware, Matthew. "(Un)conscious (Popular) Underground: Restricted Cultural Production and Underground Rap Music." *Poetics* 42, no. 1 (2014): 60–81.

Peterson, Richard. *Creating Country Music: Fabricating Authenticity.* Chicago: University of Chicago Press, 1997.

Peterson, Richard, and N. Anand. "How Chaotic Careers Create Orderly Fields." In *Career Creativity: Explorations in the Remaking of Work*, edited by Maury Peiperl, Michael Arthur, and N. Anand, 257–79. Oxford: Oxford University Press, 2002.

Peterson, Richard, and David Berger. "Cycles in Symbol Production: The Case of Popular Music." *American Sociological Review* 40, no. 2 (1975): 158–73.

Peterson, Richard, and Roger Kern. "Changing Highbrow Taste: From Snob to Omnivore." *American Sociological Review* 61, no. 5 (1996): 900–907.

Pinheiro, Diogo, and Timothy J. Dowd. "All that Jazz: The Success of Jazz Musicians in Three Metropolitan Areas." *Poetics* 37, no. 5 (2009) 490–506.

Pixley, Joy. "Life Course Patterns of Career-Prioritizing Decisions and Occupational Attainment in Dual-Earner Couples." *Work and Occupations* 35, no. 2 (2008): 127–63.

Raines, Patrick, and LaTanya Brown. "The Economic Impact of the Music Industry in the Nashville-Davidson-Murfreesboro MSA." Report sponsored by Belmont University and the Nashville Area Chamber of Commerce, Nashville, TN, January 2006.

Rose, Lacey. "Strike Strategy," *Forbes*, January 10, 2008. http://www.forbes.com/2008/01/10/labor-hollywood-wga-biz-media-cx_lr_0110strike.html.

Rossman, Gabriel. *Climbing the Charts: What Radio Airplay Tells Us about the Diffusion of Innovation.* Princeton: Princeton University Press, 2012.

Roy, William. *Reds, Whites, and Blues: Social Movements, Folk Music, and Race in the United States.* Princeton: Princeton University Press, 2010.

Ruef, Martin. *The Entrepreneurial Group: Social Identities, Relations, and Collective Action.* Princeton: Princeton University Press, 2010.

SAG-AFTRA. "Merger Agreement Between Screen Actors Guild and the American Federation of Television and Radio Artists." January 28, 2012. http://www.sagaftra.org/files/sag/documents/Merger%20Agreement%20Final%20Approved%20120131a.pdf.

Shaw, Samuel. *Off-Center: Art Careers in Peripheral Places.* Doctoral Dissertation. Nashville: Department of Sociology, Vanderbilt University, 2014.

Short, Jeremy, Todd Moss, and G. Lumpkin. "Research in Social Entrepreneurship: Past Contributions and Future Opportunities." *Strategic Entrepreneurship Journal* 3, no. 2 (2009): 161–94.

Silbey, Susan. "Taming Prometheus: Talk About Safety and Culture." *Annual Review of Sociology* 35 (2009): 341–69.

Simpson, Charles. *Soho: The Artist in the City.* Chicago: University of Chicago Press, 1981.

Simpson, Ida Harper. "The Sociology of Work: Where Have the Workers Gone?" *Social Forces* 67, no. 3 (1989): 563–81.

Smith, Vicki. *Crossing the Great Divide.* Ithaca, NY: Cornell University Press, 2001.

Stainback, Kevin, and Donald Tomaskovic-Devey. *Documenting Desegregation: Racial and Gender Segregation in Private-Sector Employment since the Civil Rights Act.* New York: Russell Sage Foundation, 2012.

Swarns, Rachel. "Freelancers in the 'Gig Economy' Find a Mix of Freedom and Uncertainty." *New York Times*, February 10, 2014. http://www.nytimes.com/2014/02/10/nyregion/for-freelancers-in-the-gig-economy-a-mix-of-freedom-and-uncertainty.html?ref=todayspaper.

Tepper, Steven. *Not Here, Not Now, Not That! Protest over Art and Culture in America.* Chicago: University of Chicago Press, 2011.

Tepper, Steven, and Bill Ivey, eds. *Engaging Art: The Next Great Transformation of America's Cultural Life.* New York: Routledge, 2008.

Terkel, Studs. *American Dreams: Lost and Found.* New York: New Press, 1980.

———. *And They All Sang: Adventures of an Eclectic Disc Jockey.* New York: New Press, 2005.

Thomson, Kristin. "Roles, Revenue, and Responsibilities: The Changing Nature of Being a Working Musician." *Work and Occupations* 40, no. 4 (2013): 514–25.

Tombs, Steve, and Dave Whyte. "Work and Risk." In *Beyond the Risk Society: Critical Reflections on Risk and Human Security*, edited by Gabe Mythen and Sandra Walklate, 169–93. Berkshire: Open University Press, 2006.

Turner, Lowell. "Introduction: An Urban Resurgence of Social Unionism." In *Labor in the New Urban Battlegrounds: Local Solidarity in a Global Economy*, edited by Lowell Turner and Daniel B. Cornfield, 1–18. Ithaca, NY: Cornell University Press, 2007.

Turner, Lowell, and Daniel Cornfield, eds. *Labor in the New Urban Battlegrounds: Local Solidarity in a Global Economy.* Ithaca, NY: Cornell University Press, 2007.

U.S. Bureau of Labor Statistics, Employment Projections, tables 1.2 and 2.7. December 31, 2014. http://www.bls.gov/emp/ep_table_102.htm and http://www.bls.gov/emp/ep_table_207.htm.

U.S. Census Bureau. *County Business Patterns*, May 2014. http://www.census.gov/econ/cbp/index .html.

U.S. Office of Immigration Statistics, Department of Homeland Security. *Yearbook of Immigration Statistics: 2012*, Table 1: Persons Obtaining Legal Permanent Resident Status: Fiscal Years 1820 to 2012. https://www.dhs.gov/yearbook-immigration-statistics-2012-legal-permanent-residents.

U.S. Office of Labor-Management Standards, LM2 Reports, American Federation of Musicians Local 257. March 4, 2014. http://kcerds.dol-esa.gov/query/orgReport.do.

Vallas, Steven. "Rediscovering the Color Line within Work Organizations: The 'Knitting of Racial Groups' Revisited." *Work and Occupations* 30, no. 4 (2003): 379–400.

Van Dyke, Nella, and Holly J. McCammon, eds. *Strategic Alliances: New Studies of Social Movement Coalitions.* Minneapolis: University of Minnesota Press, 2010.

Van Maanen, John, and Stephen Barley. "Occupational Communities: Culture and Control in Organizations." In *Research in Organizational Behavior* 6, edited by Barry Staw and L. L. Cummings, 287–365. Greenwich, CT: JAI Press, 1984.

Warner, W. Lloyd, and J. O. Low. *The Social System of the Modern Factory; The Strike: A Social Analysis.* New Haven, CT: Yale University Press, 1947.

Whyte, William. *The Organization Man.* New York: Simon & Schuster, 1956.

Wilensky, Harold, and Charles N. Lebeaux. *Industrial Society and Social Welfare*. New York: Free Press, 1965.

Williams, Damian. "Grounding the Regime of Precarious Employment: Homeless Day Laborers' Negotiation of the Job Queue." *Work and Occupations* 36, no. 3 (2009): 209–46.

Winders, Jamie. *Nashville in the New Millennium*. New York: Russell Sage Foundation, 2013.

Writers Guild of America, West. "Writers Guild Members Vote to End Strike." February 12, 2008. http://www.wga.org/subpage_newsevents.aspx?id=2775.

———. "Writers Guild Members Overwhelmingly Ratify New Contract." February 26, 2008. http://www.wga.org/subpage_newsevents.aspx?id=2780.

———. "Chapter 3: Writer-Producers." December 12, 2014. http://www.wga.org/uploadedFiles/ writers_resources/ep3.pdf.

———. "Guide to the Guild." December 12, 2014. http://www.wga.org/uploadedFiles/who_we_are/ fyi09.pdf.

Zuckerman, Ezra. "Typecasting and Generalism in Firm and Market: Genre-based Career Concentration in the Feature Film Industry, 1933–1995." In *Transformation in Cultural Industries*, edited by Candace Jones and Patricia Thornton, 171–214. *Research in the Sociology of Organizations* 23. Amsterdam: Elsevier, 2005.

CITED SOURCES ON NASHVILLE

In writing *Beyond the Beat*, I consulted documentary and scholarly sources about the changing Nashville music scene, and about Nashville as a city of social movements, immigration, growth, and change. I divide this bibliography of sources on Nashville into two sections. The first is a list of articles from the *Nashville Scene*, an alternative weekly newspaper and important documentary source of trends in the Nashville indie music scene. The second pertains to documentary and scholarly sources on Nashville as Music City and the social context of making music in Nashville.

Articles from the *Nashville Scene*

[no author] "Hangin' Tough: David Olney's Latest is Dressed for the Vaudeville Circuit." June 14, 2007. http://www.nashvillescene.com/nashville/hanginandrsquotough/Content?oid=1194814.

[no author] "Nashville Invasion: Nashville Represents at SXSW 2008." March 6, 2008. http://www.nashvillescene.com/nashville/nashville-invasion/Content?oid=1196166.

Cooper, Daniel. "Music City Gets Stoned: Dylan's Impact on Nashville's Music." March 7, 1996. http://www.nashvillescene.com/nashville/music-city-gets-stoned/Content?oid=1180296.

Currin, Grayson. "Vanity Fair: Musicians with Labels Are Just People Who Like Music Too." June 15, 2006. http://www.nashvillescene.com/nashville/vanity-fair/Content?oid=1193248.

Duncan, David, and Jim Ridley. "It Came From Nashville! The Saga of Music City's First Family of Film." April 18, 1996. http://www.nashvillescene.com/nashville/it-came-from-nashville/Content?oid=1180396.

Friskics-Warren, Bill. "On the Beat: Nashville's Ekemode Launches Studio." February 22, 1996. http://www.nashvillescene.com/nashville/on-the-beat/Content?oid=1180267.

Friskics-Warren, Bill. "Homegrown: A Couple of Locals." June 13, 1996. http://www.nashvillescene.com/nashville/homegrown/Content?oid=1180538.

Gold, Adam. "Jack White's Third Man Records Tells the World: Your Music City Is Not Dead: The House that Jack Built." January 20, 2011. http://www.nashvillescene.com/nashville/jack-whites-third-man-records-tells-the-world-your-music-city-is-not-dead/Content?oid=2171963.

———. "Kings of Leon's Serpents and Snakes Records Signs Turbo Fruits and the Weeks." April 5, 2012. http://www.nashvillescene.com/nashville/kings-of-leons-serpents-and-snakes-records-signs-turbo-fruits-and-the-weeks/Content?oid=2830588.

Hargrove, Brantley. "A Power Shift within Nashville's Musicians Union Signals Changing Times on Music Row." March 19, 2009. http://www.nashvillescene.com/nashville/a-power-shift-within-nashvilles-musicians-union-signals-changing-times-on-music-row/Content?oid=1200399.

Haruch, Steve. "Paramore Broke the Nashville Curse and Never Looked Back." October 29, 2009. http://www.nashvillescene.com/nashville/paramore-broke-the-nashville-curse-and-never-looked-back/Content?oid=1203328.

———. "Infinity Cat 'Visitors Center' to 'Never Open' Starting April 27." April 16, 2013. http://www.nashvillescene.com/nashvillecream/archives/2013/04/16/infinity-cat-visitors-center-to-never-open-starting-april-27.

Hight, Jewly. "Strange Bedfellows: Some Gay Artists in Nashville Are Making Unapologetically Christian Music." June 15, 2006. http://www.nashvillescene.com/nashville/strange-bedfellows/Content?oid=1193263.

———. "On Its Tenth Anniversary, the Americana Music Association Has Reason to Look Both Backward and Forward." September 17, 2009. http://www.nashvillescene.com/nashville/on-its-tenth-anniversary-the-americana-music-association-has-reason-to-look-both-backward-and-forward/Content?oid=1202672.

———. "Americana Acts are Getting on the Mainstream Radar." October 13, 2011. http://www.nashvillescene.com/nashville/americana-acts-are-getting-on-the-mainstream-radar/Content?oid=2650847.

Hurt, Edd. "For Nashville Indie Musicians like Lambchop and Cortney Tidwell, It was the Post-Post-Rock Decade." December 24, 2009. http://www.nashvillescene.com/nashville/for-nashville-indie-musicians-like-lambchop-and-cortney-tidwell-it-was-the-post-post-rock-decade/Content?oid=1204257.

Keel, Beverly. "Rebel With a Cause: Lari White Becomes the First Female to Produce a Major Male Country Star." June 1, 2006. http://www.nashvillescene.com/nashville/rebel-with-a-cause/Content?oid=1193199.

Loesch, Peter. "Dialing for Dollars: Old vs. New Again in Nashville." September 12, 1996. http://www.nashvillescene.com/nashville/dialing-for-dollars/Content?oid=1180739.

Maloney, Sean. "Local Urban-Music Promoters Lovenoise Make Hip-Hop, Soul and R&B Accessible to Nashville's Masses." October 27, 2011. http://www.nashvillescene.com/nashville/local

-urban-music-promoters-lovenoise-make-hip-hop-soul-and-randb-accessible-to-nashvilles
-masses/Content?oid=2661308.

McCall, Michael. "Crowd Control: Local Musicians on Nashville Audiences." February 15, 1996. http://www.nashvillescene.com/nashville/crowd-control/Content?oid=1180248.

———. "A Sellout Performance: Business as Usual at Extravaganza '96." February 22, 1996. http://www.nashvillescene.com/nashville/a-sellout-performance/Content?oid=1180263.

———. "Bass Master: Local Talent Finally Comes into his Own." April 4, 1996. http://www.nashville scene.com/nashville/bass-master/Content?oid=1180368.

———. "Stock and Trade: Economic Thinking Down on the Row." August 8, 1996. http://www.nashvillescene.com/nashville/stock-and-trade/Content?oid=1180665.

———. "Ready to Rock: Anderson Does a Tightrope Act." October 3, 1996. http://www.nashville scene.com/nashville/ready-to-rock/Content?oid=1180791/

———. "Keepin' It Country: Alan Jackson Follows the True Path." October 31, 1996. http://www.nashvillescene.com/nashville/keepin-it-country/Content?oid=1180854.

———. "A Little Bit Country, a Lot Rock 'n' Roll: Three New Country Bands Point to a Trend on Music Row." July 19, 2007. http://www.nashvillescene.com/nashville/a-little-bit-country-a-lot-rock-andrsquonandrsquo-roll/Content?oid=1194954.

———. "The Bold and the Beautiful: Country Radio's Female Voices Just Got Younger and Gutsier." August 30, 2007. http://www.nashvillescene.com/nashville/the-bold-and-the-beautiful/Content?oid=1195132.

McCall, Michael, Joel Moses and Jim Ridley. "Woolgathering: Lambchop's Brush with British Critics." February 22, 1996. http://www.nashvillescene.com/nashville/woolgathering/Content?oid=1180272.

Moore, Tracy. "Let the Sun Shine In: Why Nashville Could Stand to Be a Little—Just a Little— like L.A." May 18, 2006. http://www.nashvillescene.com/nashville/let-the-sun-shine-in/Content?oid=1193135.

Morris, Edward. "Pure (and Simple): Back to Basics in the Music Industry." May 23, 1996. http://www.nashvillescene.com/nashville/pure-and-simple/Content?oid=1180487.

———. "Facing the Music Videos: Producers on the Offensive." June 6, 1996. http://www.nash villescene.com/nashville/facing-the-music-videos/Content?oid=1180519.

———. "More than Music: A Foray into Clickable Country." June 13, 1996. http://www.nashville scene.com/nashville/more-than-music/Content?oid=1180539.

———. "Poor No More: Country Roots? Not Likely." June 20, 1996. http://www.nashvillescene.com/nashville/poor-no-more/Content?oid=1180558.

———. "Getting Lyrical: Avoiding Mealymouthed Music." August 1, 1996. http://www.nashville scene.com/nashville/getting-lyrical/Content?oid=1180643.

———. "Close Shave: A Scare for Carter." August 15, 1996. http://www.nashvillescene.com/nash ville/close-shave/Content?oid=1180669.

Neal, Chris. "The Beat Goes On: Billy Block's Western Beat Celebrates 10 Years of Alt-Country Bliss." February 2, 2006. http://www.nashvillescene.com/nashville/the-beat-goes-on/Content?oid=1192771.

———. "The City That Lost Its Country: LA's Last Country Radio Station Goes Pop." August 31, 2006. http://www.nashvillescene.com/nashville/the-city-that-lost-its-country/Content?oid=1193597.

———. "Ain't That Americana? The Americana Music Conference Casts an Ever-Widening Net— Musically and Politically." September 14, 2006. http://www.nashvillescene.com/nashville/ainandrsquot-that-americana/Content?oid=1193659.

Ridley, Jim. "Cut and Print: An Indie Film Sets Down in Music City." May 9, 1996. http://www.nashvillescene.com/nashville/cut-and-print/Content?oid=1180438.

———. "Out of Commission: Meeley Leaves the NFC." May 30, 1996. http://www.nashvillescene.com/nashville/out-of-commission/Content?oid=1180509.

———. "Banding Together: All in One Accord." October 24, 1996. http://www.nashvillescene.com/nashville/banding-together/Content?oid=1180827.

Ridley, Jim, and Michael McCall. "Goodbye Larry: Exiting Nashville on Both Feet." May 23, 1996. http://www.nashvillescene.com/nashville/goodbye-larry/Content?oid=1180481.

Rodgers, D. Patrick. "The Black Keys Have Moved to Nashville. What Does that Say about Them—and What Does that Say about Us?" March 31, 2011. http://www.nashvillescene.com/nashville/the-black-keys-have-moved-to-nashville-what-does-that-say-about-them-and-what-does-that-say-about-us/Content?oid=2345298.

Stabert, Lee. "Friends With Benefits: Local Rock Collective Movement Nashville Doesn't Care about Indie Cred—They Just Wanna Draw a Crowd." May 11, 2006. http://www.nashvillescene.com/nashville/friends-with-benefits/Content?oid=1193117.

———. "The Next Big Thing? ASCAP's Next Big Nashville Music Festival Makes a Case for Local Rock and Pop." May 25, 2006. http://www.nashvillescene.com/nashville/the-next-big-thing/Content?oid=1193169.

———. "Boom! Bang Bang Bang Might Just be the Quintessential Nashville Rock Band." January 11, 2007. http://www.nashvillescene.com/nashville/boom/Content?oid=1194175.

Wilkins, Jason Moon. "No Doubt: Why Are Industry Insiders Picking a Franklin Band to Break Out Big in 2007?" February 8, 2007. http://www.nashvillescene.com/nashville/no-doubt/Content?oid=1194277.

Wynn, Ron. "Rahsaan Barber Serves as Jazz Player and Advocate with His Label, Jazz Music City Records: Barber of the 'Ville." August 23, 2012. http://www.nashvillescene.com/nashville/rahsaan-barber-serves-as-jazz-player-and-advocate-with-his-label-jazz-music-city-records/Content?oid=2989024.

Sources on Nashville as Music City and as Social Context of the Music Scene

Associated Press. "Nashville Music Council Seeks to Leverage City's Vast Music Resources." *billboard.biz*, June 23, 2011. http://www.billboard.com/biz/articles/news/1177360/nashville-music-council-seeks-to-leverage-citys-vast-music-resources.

"Best Music Scene, 2011: Nashville, Tennessee." *Rolling Stone*, April 28, 2011. http://www.rollingstone.com/music/pictures/best-music-scene-2011-nashville-tennessee-20110502.

Bradley, Harold. "Committee Reports, Freelance Task Force," *International Musician*, August 2000. http://home.comcast.net/~syoungafm/freelance.htm.

Caramanica, Jon. "Nashville Inches, Ever So Grudgingly, into the Future." *New York Times*, December 31, 2009. http://www.nytimes.com/2010/01/03/arts/music/03nashville.htm.

Center for Regional Economic Competitiveness. "Leveraging the Labor Force for Economic Growth: Assessing the Nashville Economic Market Area's Readiness for Work after the Recession." August 2010. http://www.nashvillechamber.com/Homepage/WorkNashville/Workforce Study.aspx.

Clement, Frank G. "Country Music a Tennessee Heritage." *Billboard*, November 2, 1963, 22.

Cornfield, Daniel. "Immigrant Labor Organizing in a 'New Destination City': Approaches to the Unionization of African, Asian, Latino, and Middle Eastern Workers in Nashville." In *Global Connections and Local Receptions: New Latino Migration to the Southeastern United States*, edited by Fran Ansley and Jon Shefner, 279–97. Knoxville: University of Tennessee Press, 2009.

Cornfield, Daniel, Angela Arzubiaga, Rhonda BeLue, Susan Brooks, Tony Brown, Oscar Miller, Douglas Perkins, Peggy Thoits, and Lynn Walker. Final Report of the Immigrant Community Assessment of Nashville, Tennessee, August 2003. Commissioned by Mayor Bill Purcell and prepared under contract #14830 for Metropolitan Government of Nashville and Davidson County, Tennessee.

Cornfield, Daniel, and William Canak. "Immigrants and Labor in a Globalizing City: Prospects for Coalition Building in Nashville." In *Labor in the New Urban Battlegrounds: Local Solidarity in a Global Economy*, edited by Lowell Turner and Daniel B. Cornfield, 163–77. Ithaca, NY: Cornell University Press, 2007.

Cornfield, Daniel, and Steering Committee of Nashville for All of Us. "Partnering for an Equitable and Inclusive Nashville: Background Report on Equity and Inclusion." Submitted to the Steering Committee of NashvilleNext, Nashville's 2040 General Plan, January 2013. http://www.nashville.gov/Portals/0/SiteContent/Planning/docs/NashvilleNext/next-report-Equity-and-Inclusion.pdf.

Denney, Warren. "Delegates Deal Winning Hand in Vegas." *Nashville Musician*, July–September 2010, 19–22. http://www.nashvillemusicians.org/uploaded/archive/1283226562TheNashville MusicianJulyAugSept.pdf.

Eels, Josh. "Jack Outside the Box." *New York Times*, April 5, 2012. http://www.nytimes.com/2012/04/08/magazine/jack-white-is-the-savviest-rock-star-of-our-time.html?pagewanted=all&_r=2&.

Fausset, Richard. "A New Sound in Nashville." *Los Angeles Times*, April 4, 2007. http://articles.latimes.com/2007/apr/04/nation/na-nashville4.

Florida, Richard. "The Nashville Effect." *Atlantic*, May 21, 2009. http://www.theatlantic.com/national/archive/2009/05/the-nashville-effect/17288/.

———. "The Nashville Effect, Cont'd." *Atlantic*, July 6, 2009. http://www.theatlantic.com/national/archive/2009/07/the-nashville-effect-contd/20385/.

———. "The Changing Geography of Pop Music." *Atlantic*, February 17, 2011. http://www.theatlantic.com/entertainment/archive/2011/02/the-changing-geography-of-pop-music/71341/.

Florida, Richard, and Scott Jackson. "Sonic City: The Evolving Economic Geography of the Music Industry." *Journal of Planning Education and Research* 29, no. 3 (2010): 310–32.

Florida, Richard, Charlotta Mellander, and Kevin Stolarick. "Music Scenes to Music Clusters: The Economic Geography of Music in the US, 1970–2000." *Environment and Planning A* 42, no. 4 (2010): 785–804.

Garrison, Joey. "Metro Council's Black Caucus becomes Minority Caucus." *City Paper*, January 4, 2012. http://nashvillecitypaper.com/content/city-news/metro-councils-black-caucus-becomes-minority-caucus.

Halberstam, David. *The Children.* New York: Random House, 1998.

Hann, Michael. "Why the Garages of East Nashville Are Now American Rock's Hottest Property." *Guardian*, March 24, 2012. http://www.guardian.co.uk/music/2012/mar/25/east-nashville-garage-rock-scene-feature.

Isaac, Larry W., Daniel B. Cornfield, Dennis C. Dickerson, James M. Lawson, Jr., and Jonathan S. Coley. "'Movement Schools' and Dialogical Diffusion of Nonviolent Praxis: Nashville Workshops in the Southern Civil Rights Movement." In *Nonviolent Resistance*, edited by Sharon Erickson Nepstad and Lester Kurtz, 155–84. *Research in Social Movements, Conflicts, and Change* 34. Bingley: Emerald Group Publishing Limited, 2012.

Jordan, Mark. "Record Vote Sweeps in New 257 Officers." *Nashville Musician*, January–March 2009, 2. http://www.nashvillemusicians.org/uploaded/archive/1258009742January-March2009.pdf.

Kosser, Michael. *How Nashville Became Music City, U.S.A.: 50 Years of Music Row.* Milwaukee, WI: Hal Leonard Corporation, 2006.

"Labels Look South for Signings Pop/Rock Offices Sprout in Nashville." *Billboard*, August 8, 1991. http://www.billboard.biz/bbbiz/others/labels-look-south-for-signings-pop-rock-765755.story.

Lena, Jennifer, and Daniel Cornfield. "Immigrant Arts Participation: A Pilot Study of Nashville Artists." In *Engaging Art: The Next Great Transformation of America's Cultural Life*, edited by Steven J. Tepper and Bill Ivey, 147–69. New York: Routledge, 2008.

Lloyd, Richard. "Differentiating Music City: Legacy, Industry and Scene in Nashville." In *Music City: Musical Approaches to the "Creative City,"* edited by A. Barber-Kersovan, V. Kirchberg, and R. Kuchar, 139–68. Bielefeld: Transcript Verlag, 2014.

Moore, Jayne. "Dennis Matkosky Co-Writes Top Hits for LeAnn Rimes, Keith Urban, Clay Aiken and Other Artists." December 12, 2014. http://www.songwriteruniverse.com/matkosky.htm.

Nashville Public Television. "Next Door Neighbors." Television documentary series on immigrant communities in Nashville, 2014. http://ndn.wnpt.org/about/.

"NASHVILLE SCENE." *Billboard*, May 28, 1994. http://www.billboard.biz/bbbiz/others/nashville-scene-740055.story.

"NASHVILLE SCENE—Country Music's Growth Tapers Off, But Labels Are Continuing to Emerge, Change." *Billboard*, December 23, 1995. http://www.billboard.biz/bbbiz/others/nashville-scene-country-music-s-growth-tapers-736464.story.

Oermann, Robert. *America's Music: The Roots of Country*. Atlanta: Turner Publishing, 1996.

———. *A Century of Country: An Illustrated History of Country Music*. New York: TV Books, 1999.

Pareles, Jon. "Wary Coronation." *New York Times*, September 10, 2010. http://www.nytimes.com/2010/09/12/arts/music/12pareles.html?pagewanted=all.

Paulson, Dave. "Jack White Attaches New Song to Helium Balloons." *Tennessean*, April 2, 2012. http://blogs.tennessean.com/tunein/2012/04/02/jack-white-attaches-new-song-to-helium-balloons/?repeat=w3tc.

Peterson, Richard. *Creating Country Music: Fabricating Authenticity*. Chicago: University of Chicago Press, 1997.

Peterson, Richard, and N. Anand. "How Chaotic Careers Create Orderly Fields." In *Career Creativity: Explorations in the Remaking of Work*, edited by Maury Peiperl, Michael Arthur, and N. Anand, 257–79. Oxford: Oxford University Press, 2002.

Raines, Patrick, and LaTanya Brown. "The Economic Impact of the Music Industry in the Nashville-Davidson-Murfreesboro MSA." Report sponsored by Belmont University and the Nashville Area Chamber of Commerce, Nashville, Tennessee, January 2006.

Rau, Nate. "Council Passes Update to Nondiscrimation Ordinance." *City Paper*, September 15, 2009. http://nashvillecitypaper.com/content/city-news/council-passes-update-nondiscrimation-ordinance.

Ross, Laura. "Convention Diary." *Nashville Musician*, July–September 2010, 23. http://www.nashvillemusicians.org/uploaded/archive/1283226562TheNashvilleMusicianJulyAugSept.pdf.

Shaw, Samuel. *Off-Center: Art Careers in Peripheral Places*, Doctoral Dissertation. Nashville: Department of Sociology, Vanderbilt University, 2014.

Stivender, Knight. "Wedgewood-Houston Builds New Generation of Artists." *Tennessean*, August 12, 2013. http://www.tennessean.com/article/20130812/NEWS01/308120037/Wedgewood-Houston-builds-new-generation-artists.

Talbott, Chris. "Black Keys Find New Home in Nashville." *Billboard*, December 13, 2010, http://www.billboard.com/news/black-keys-find-new-home-in-nashville-1004134569.story#/news/black-keys-find-new-home-in-nashville-1004134569.story.

———. "Nashville Rock Scene Moves Out of the Shadows." *Huffington Post*, September 4, 2012. http://www.huffingtonpost.com/2012/09/04/nashville-rock-scene-move_0_n_1853928.html.

"The World of Country Music." *Billboard*, November 2, 1963.

U.S. Office of Labor-Management Standards, LM2 Reports, American Federation of Musicians Local 257, March 4, 2014. http://kcerds.dol-esa.gov/query/orgReport.do.

Weinberg, Hedy. "English-Only Opposition." *New York Times*, January 15, 2009. http://www.nytimes.com/2009/01/16/opinion/l16nashville.html?partner=rss&emc=rss.

Williams, Damian. "Grounding the Regime of Precarious Employment: Homeless Day Laborers' Negotiation of the Job Queue." *Work and Occupations* 36, no. 3 (2009): 209–46.

Winders, Jamie. *Nashville in the New Millennium*. New York: Russell Sage Foundation, 2013.

Index